The Gentle Art of Horseback Riding

Gincy Self Bucklin

Human Kinetics

4863734

Library of Congress Cataloging-in-Publication Data

Bucklin, Gincy Self.
  The gentle art of horseback riding / Gincy Self Bucklin.
    pages cm
  Includes index.
  1. Horsemanship. I. Title.
  SF309.B883 2013
  798.2--dc23

                              2012046054

ISBN-10: 1-4504-1274-2 (print)
ISBN-13: 978-1-4504-1274-2 (print)

This publication is written and published to provide accurate and authoritative information relevant to the subject matter presented. It is published and sold with the understanding that the author and publisher are not engaged in rendering legal, medical, or other professional services by reason of their authorship or publication of this work. If medical or other expert assistance is required, the services of a competent professional person should be sought.

The web addresses cited in this text were current as of January 2013, unless otherwise noted.

Acquisitions Editor: Tom Heine; **Developmental Editor:** Carla Zych; **Assistant Editor:** Claire Marty; **Copyeditor:** Jan Feeney; **Indexer:** Nan N. Badgett; **Graphic Designer:** Nancy Rasmus; **Cover Designer:** Keith Blomberg; **Photographs (cover and interior):** Neil Bernstein; **Visual Production Assistant:** Joyce Brumfield; **Photo Production Manager:** Jason Allen; **Art Manager:** Kelly Hendren; **Associate Art Manager:** Alan L. Wilborn; **Illustrations:** © Human Kinetics; **Printer:** Versa Press

We thank Caryl Richardson of Stone Gate Stables in Putney, Vermont, for assistance in providing the location for the photo shoot for this book.

Human Kinetics books are available at special discounts for bulk purchase. Special editions or book excerpts can also be created to specification. For details, contact the Special Sales Manager at Human Kinetics.

Printed in the United States of America   10 9 8 7 6 5 4 3 2 1

The paper in this book is certified under a sustainable forestry program.

Human Kinetics
Website: www.HumanKinetics.com

United States: Human Kinetics
P.O. Box 5076
Champaign, IL 61825-5076
800-747-4457
e-mail: humank@hkusa.com

Canada: Human Kinetics
475 Devonshire Road Unit 100
Windsor, ON N8Y 2L5
800-465-7301 (in Canada only)
e-mail: info@hkcanada.com

Europe: Human Kinetics
107 Bradford Road
Stanningley
Leeds LS28 6AT, United Kingdom
+44 (0) 113 255 5665
e-mail: hk@hkeurope.com

Australia: Human Kinetics
57A Price Avenue
Lower Mitcham, South Australia 5062
08 8372 0999
e-mail: info@hkaustralia.com

New Zealand: Human Kinetics
P.O. Box 80
Torrens Park, South Australia 5062
0800 222 062
e-mail: info@hknewzealand.com

E5498

Several years ago my daughter Karen asked me what my life's goal was. Without really thinking about it, I answered, "To change the way riding is taught at the novice level." She said, "I'd like to help you." And so, with her help, the non-profit organization What Your Horse Wants was born. Whether I will attain my goal in my lifetime remains to be seen, but whatever work toward that end is accomplished through this book owes much to her help and support. And so I dedicate this book to my wonderful daughter, Karen Stoddard Hayes.

Contents

Preface

Riding is a sport that differs in many ways from most other sports, both in our understanding of it and in how it is performed.

To begin with, riding is not one sport, but many, each with its own levels of competition. For example the two major disciplines in the United States, English and Western, are further subdivided into many categories. Dressage, hunter, and saddle seat are English categories; reining, cutting, and barrel racing are Western. The enormous field of pleasure riding, with all its variations, rounds out the myriad activities that fall under the general term *riding*. Almost unique in the sport world, in nearly all disciplines women compete on an equal basis with men, and age is not a factor. In fact, being older can be an advantage.

The most important way in which riding differs from other sports is rarely considered. If you take up kayaking and paddle so badly that you drift all over, the kayak doesn't care. If you play golf badly, slicing the ball into the water hazard, it doesn't hurt the ball. But if you ride even a little bit badly, you make the horse uncomfortable. If you ride very badly, you damage the horse both emotionally and physically, often for life.

Although horses, taken separately, are every bit as individual as humans, they all share certain characteristics. By understanding the horse and how to relate to him physically, mentally, and emotionally, you will find that learning the fundamentals of riding can be relatively simple, confidence inspiring, and fun.

On the assumption that you care about horses, the goal of this book is to help you to ride well, not just after years of training, but right from the start. Or if you have been riding and are not satisfied with your skills, this book will help you to improve as quickly as possible. Instructors, especially of novice riders, will find that following this method not only is horse friendly but also produces a *good* rider in the shortest possible time. (This does not mean 6 months, but less than 5 years, as opposed to the 25 years that tradition says is the time needed.)

Before we go on, we need a definition of a good rider, one who is riding correctly. It simply means that the rider can ride in a way that is *comfortable for both rider and horse* and do all the basic movements—walk, trot, canter, and make turns and transitions—plus anything that both have been trained to do, without difficulty or resistance by the horse. In current mainstream riding of any discipline, the first few lessons for a novice student go something like this: She is introduced to the horse in the somewhat threatening confinement of the stall, then to grooming, tacking, and leading. Next she is mounted in the saddle and given stirrups and reins. She is shown how to ask the horse to go, stop, and turn and often how to trot and post. Occasionally she is put on the longe (the horse is on a long line held by the instructor, around whom he circles) so that she does not have to try to control the horse. But often, especially in camps and similar programs, several beginners are turned loose together to struggle with all this new information.

Attempting to take in such a tremendous amount of material in a short period is a bit like learning your numbers and how to add and subtract, all in the same one-hour lesson. Add in the psychological aspect of working with an extremely large and strange animal, *which you are expected to control,* and on whom you are trapped like a cat in a tree, 6 or 7 feet above the ground. It speaks volumes for the kindness of horses that so many people, after this sort of experience, continue to ride.

I learned to teach many years ago using this method, along with the accompanying maxims like "Horses are stupid," "Don't be a passenger; show him who's boss!" and "You have to fall off three times before you can call yourself a good rider!" (This last statement is like saying you have to be in three fender benders before you can call yourself a good driver!) Then about 35 years ago I started to realize that there had to be a better way, and I've been working to develop a better system ever since.

> There is only one kind of mistake, that is, the fundamental mistake. Regardless of how advanced the exercise, if the performance is defective, one can directly trace that fault to a lack in the fundamental training of either the horse or the rider.—Erik Herbermann

Taking a Different Approach

My approach is called "How Horses Want You to Teach." In this system, *the horse is the real teacher.* Only he knows whether what the rider or handler is doing is correct, that is, whether she is making it easy for him to perform the desired action. The corollary to this is that if the horse *doesn't* perform the desired action, or performs it incorrectly, that means that *the rider* is asking incorrectly.

If a rider continues to incorrectly ask the horse to perform an action, she is practicing her mistakes, which is confirming her bad habits. *This is the primary reason most people take so long to learn to ride well.* The second reason is that there is an element of fear in riding for all novices, often unrecognized by both the student and the instructor.

Upon meeting the horse, the rider has fear of the horse himself—a large, unfamiliar animal. The instructor knows that old Buddy is a gentle, safe creature, so it doesn't occur to her that anyone could be afraid of him. But to the novice, Buddy is more like a bear—a tame bear, but nonetheless a bear—and scary. Often the first thing the rider is told is that she must never go behind him, because he might kick! Once she is mounted, the rider now has the fear of being trapped up there, with no safe way to get back to the ground. A psychologist friend tells me that it is a kind of claustrophobia. This creates a physical reaction of clutching to hang on, especially with the seat and legs. The innate fear of the animal and of being trapped or falling leads to the typical tense, awkward beginner seat, which, if not dealt with at the very start, can be extremely difficult to change. Just as being able to move while remaining grounded and in good balance is a necessary skill for most sports, so a good seat, which allows the rider to be centered and grounded, is the foundation of correct riding. Conversely, everything that is built on an incorrect beginner seat will be wrong!

In the excitement of the moment, the rider might not be consciously aware of her fear. But her body senses it and doesn't like it. I call it the roller-coaster mentality. People are often smiling or laughing as they board a roller coaster, but their bodies are screaming and clutching the handrails in sheer terror during the ride. When the ride is over, boosted by the adrenaline rush, they go back and do it again. But, no matter how much fun they are having, *they can't stop their bodies from going into panic mode.* You sometimes see riders doing quite advanced things, such as barrel racing or fox hunting, from very tense positions. Their bodies have never gotten over the initial fear, and their minds have never recognized it. But you can be sure the horse is aware of the fear!

Obviously, then, a student's early experiences on the horse have a major impact on how long she will take to learn to ride well. This book gives you a proper foundation and helps you advance more quickly through the process.

If you can sit up, you can learn to ride a quiet horse correctly and safely. To do so, your body must be able to follow the movements of the horse's body. You have all the tools you need preprogrammed into your body and brain. The action of the horse's back under your seat bones duplicates the movements that are created by your own legs while walking or running on your own, so following the horse's movements when riding is as natural to humans as walking and running.

In addition to following the horse's movements, you must be able to relate to and understand other beings and be willing to learn. We use these skills all the time to function in human society. In fact, one advantage of learning to ride, especially when young, is that it is excellent training in executive skills and parenting. Because of the horse's size, it is impossible to totally control him physically. You can use force, but if your demands are too great or you cause too much pain, he can react in ways that can severely injure or even kill you. You can only truly control a horse to the extent and in the same way you control other people (that is, by earning his affection, trust, and respect so that he *wants* to please you).

Laying a Proper Foundation

In my program, the basics are a major departure from common admonitions to sit up straight, keep the heels down, and so on. Correct position comes as a *result* of correct basics and arises from a centered, grounded seat. The path to becoming a good rider, as defined previously, begins with the three basics of riding and a series of exercises called the seven steps.

My three basics are to develop a good relationship with the horse based on mutual affection, trust, and respect; learn to move around on the ground and to sit on the horse in a way that is comfortable for you both; and learn to communicate with the horse, including and especially understanding what *he* is saying to *you*.

The seven steps are a series of exercises based on yoga and similar disciplines. They are a proven method of dealing with stress resulting from fear. The seven steps help you quickly center and ground in case of trouble. Among the keys to the success of my riding program, these steps are introduced in the first lesson and rehearsed until they become second nature.

The three basics and the seven steps are explained in detail in chapter 2 and are explored and applied throughout the book. If you dedicate yourself to using these tools, following the order of instructions in the chapters, and following the guidance of experienced horses and instructors, you will almost surely become a good rider and enjoy the process as well.

Acknowledgments

A great many people have contributed to *The Gentle Art of Horseback Riding*. The members of the board of directors of What Your Horse Wants (WYHW), Karen Hayes, Meg Kluge, and Kim Mastrianni contributed many ideas and much hard work. My agents, Mike and Pat Snell answered all my questions, even the stupid ones. My editors, Tom Heine and Carla Zych, put up with my foibles patiently and supported me at every stage of the publication process. I am grateful to Charlotte Kneeland, Jessica Jahiel, and George Morris for taking time from their busy lives to provide kind remarks for use in the promotional materials for the book and to Bill Steinkraus for allowing me to quote him in the jumping chapter.

The photo shoot involved many people and horses, all of whom performed above and beyond the call of duty. It was a massive job, and the fact that we got it done in three days with little or no friction was miraculous. Photographer Neil Bernstein deserves many thanks for coming to the wilds of Vermont and being serene and good tempered from the first shot to the last. In addition to Neil and the WYHW board, I want to thank Caryl Richardson and Stone Gate Stables for making sure everything was picture perfect, and the models and horse tenders who pitched in cheerfully whenever needed: Hayden Bunker, Maela Chatal, Amy Fletcher, John Gagnon, Blythe Kessuk, Morgan Mastrianni, Ruth Sessions, Stella Silverman, and Kit Whallon. My thanks to the owners of the horses, Meg Kluge, Caryl Richardson, and Wendy Underwood, and even though they probably won't read this, special thanks to the patient, hardworking horses: Boomerang, bay, Welsh Cob, age 21; Fable, chestnut, Morgan, age 30; Domino, black (mostly), QH/Percheron, age 7; Dyna, dark bay, TB/Percheron, age 4; Jack, grey, Hanoverian, age 21; and Laurel, dark bay, Paint, age 13.

I'd also like to thank those whose contributions to the photo shoot were not as obvious but every bit as important. Marianne Hamshaw and The Cheshire Horse, Jess Sisto and Locust Hill Farm, and Cara Stickney and the Putney School generously loaned equipment. The Putney Food Coop provided wonderful food, and the Riding With Confidence e-group provided me with answers when no one else could, especially Lif Strand, who helped me with some of the Western details.

Thank you once more to publisher J.A. Allen & Co., Ltd., and Eric Herbermann himself, for allowing me to again include the quote on page x from the 1999 book *Dressage Formula, Third Edition*.

And last, but by no means least, love and thanks to my husband, Sam Bunker, for his kindness and patience during the long process of getting a book ready for publication.

Author's note: In the interest of clarity, through-out the book horses are referred to with male pronouns and humans with female pronouns. My apologies to any female horses or male humans who might be offended by this convention, which I borrowed from Mary Wanless. Those who think horses should be referred to as "it" will not understand this book.

Starting Out Right

Welcome to the world of horses. Horseback riding is a wonderful way of life. I call it that because it becomes a way of life for those who have learned to love it, and I'd like to make it as easy as possible for you to become one of us.

As noted in the preface, riding encompasses Western and English styles and numerous subcategories, such as jumpers, dressage, and saddle seat for English riders, and cattle cutting, reining, and barrel racing for Western, which involve their own goals, horses, and equipment. Non-competitive riders have many opportunities for riding just for the fun of it. So once you've perfected your basic skills, you can find an area that suits you. Refer to the appendix at http://tinyurl.com/d8pv7nz for information about many of the more common disciplines.

One of the best things about riding is that you don't have to be an outstanding athlete to ride well or even to compete effectively. There are two reasons for this. First, it is the horse that is the athlete! The bulk of the rider's job is to communicate to the horse the nature of the task and then to make it as easy as possible for the horse to perform it by riding in such a way that she doesn't interfere with him. You'll learn how to do this as you work your way through this book.

The second reason is that the human body is born knowing how to ride. Unlikely as it sounds, human skeletons and horse skeletons are very similar and are programmed to move in much the same way, even though horses move on four legs and humans on two. So when you are sitting on the horse's back, with his and your spines more or less connected, your body receives the same messages from the horse's hind legs as it would receive from your own legs. Therefore, following the movements of the horse comes naturally. You need to take other factors into account, though, if you are to become a good rider, and we'll deal with those at some length.

Because riding is so natural to the body, anyone who can sit in a chair can ride. Therefore, people who have physical disabilities can enjoy riding. In fact, in the 1950s, Lis Hartel, a Danish woman paralyzed by polio from the knees down, as well as being affected in her arms and hands, won the silver medal in dressage in the 1952 and 1956 Olympics. The year 1952 was the first that women were allowed to compete, and Ms. Hartel was the first woman to share the Olympic podium with men. She later founded Europe's first therapeutic riding center, and riding is now a recognized form of therapy for those with physical disabilities. Riding can also be enjoyed well into old age. I have known many people who rode actively, even cross country and over fences, in their 80s and 90s. Riding correctly requires far less effort than walking, which of course is why people started riding in the first place and one reason people still enjoy it today.

Body Type and Riding

Having a body with a low center of gravity makes balancing, and thus riding, much easier for both rider and horse. The ideal body shape for riding is shortwaisted and long legged, with calf and thigh nearly equal in length, of moderate weight, with not too much of it above the rider's center. However, by no means do all successful riders have the same, perfect build. There are many choices of disciplines, and with the desire to learn, accompanied by good instruction, virtually anyone can learn to ride well enough so that both she and the horse enjoy it. Add to that determination and patience and the result can be a successful competitor as well.

Why You Need Professional Instruction

Although this book will guide you in your riding career, riding is definitely not a sport that you can learn solely from books, especially in the beginning. When you are starting out, somebody knowledgeable has to be there to communicate with and guide both you and the horse until you develop several basic skills. If you and the horse are to be safe and comfortable, you will require many hours of fairly constant supervision followed by regular checkups for some time thereafter.

You should plan to take at least one lesson per week, and two would be better in order to keep your body from forgetting too much in between. However, taking lessons too often usually means that you are trying to learn too much too fast, which results in confusion. Also, your mind and body do a lot of learning in the "empty spaces" between lessons. You can finish a lesson having not really been able to perform as you wished, and then find in the next lesson that your body has figured it out in the interim. Your early lessons should involve a lot of repetition using different exercises so that you learn various aspects of the same skill before moving on to the next. Because every horse is unique in the way he feels and responds, you should also ride the same horse while learning the basic skills before changing to a new mount.

Private lessons are usually offered either for one hour or a half hour. I think that as a beginner, you get the most benefit from a one-hour private lesson, which allows some time for working on the ground—an important part of developing confidence and a good relationship with the horse. Also, getting mounted and getting everything adjusted correctly takes about 10 minutes, so a half-hour lesson doesn't leave much time for new work. A lesson that runs much longer than an hour, unless you are fairly advanced, is probably overkill in terms of information input. Later on, once you have a good understanding of your basic seat on the horse, an hour-long semiprivate lesson is more congenial and allows you and the other student to observe each other's learning processes.

It is difficult to say exactly how much riding lessons should cost, and there are enormous variations in what they do cost. Maintaining healthy and well-trained horses and buying appropriate insurance in today's litigious society make riding an expensive proposition, so it is understandable that equestrian sports are never cheap. An unscientific survey of barns around the United States found prices that ranged from $25 to $200 for a one-hour lesson; those on the upper end of the range generally are for specialized upper-level skills rather than introductory lessons. There are regional variations, because the costs of feed, hay, and land vary according to location. Barns in urban areas typically charge more than those in rural districts. People with more elaborate barns and arenas sometimes charge more in order to maintain their fancier facilities. In areas with lots of competition, some barns keep prices down to attract customers. The quality of horses and the quality of their care vary enormously from stable to stable. At some barns, the beginners are taught by less experienced instructors who charge less per hour but might not have as much to offer. But keep in mind that those who charge the most are not always the best teachers.

We can make some generalizations, however. Private lessons are generally the most expensive, followed by semiprivate and then group lessons. Group lessons, which include more than three

Lessons for Children

Except for some of the early exercises, the techniques presented in this book are generally more appropriate for children older than 7 or 8. For younger children, leadline or longeing, especially on a bareback pad, will develop balance and confidence, as will vaulting games such as jumping off at the walk or riding sidesaddle. I have found that children who try to learn control work, especially using the reins, at an early age, because of changes in their growing bodies and the intellectual aspects of riding, almost always form bad habits that are difficult to change. I learned to ride very young and didn't develop good hands until I was in my 30s. On the other hand, children who started control work later generally catch up to and pass their contemporaries who started young. This is not true, of course, of the child whose parent is an instructor, since she is exposed to riding and horses continuously and gradually rather than in a weekly or semiweekly lesson.

riders, mean that each rider gets much less individual attention, so they might not be a bargain. If you are a beginner, you should take either private or semiprivate lessons. In the case of the latter, if at all possible in the early stages there should be a qualified assistant so that each horse is under the control of an experienced handler.

Finding the Right Instructor

Probably the most important choice you will make in your riding career is your first instructor, so you need to spend adequate time and research to find the best one available in your area. This is also true if you have ridden before, things didn't go well, and you need help to get back on the right track.

Unfortunately, the traditional method of teaching basic skills, used by many instructors, has made riding one of the worst-taught sports at the basic level. Typically, riders are introduced to many skills before either their minds or their bodies are ready, resulting in bad habits that are very difficult to change. As a consequence, students often spend many years trying to unlearn reactions and behaviors they developed in their early lessons, and many never do learn to ride correctly, or, more important, safely!

In most sports, your instructor will take you at a pace that allows you to learn one basic skill fairly well before trying to build on it. When I took up golf, for some time I was allowed to use only one club until my swing was reasonably consistent and correct. Unfortunately, in riding it is not uncommon to see a student trying to learn to use the reins before she has balance, one of the first basic skills. In an attempt to get her own balance, she frequently pulls on the reins in a way that hurts and unbalances the horse and at the same time interferes with her ability to develop her own balance correctly. Because she is hurting the horse and sending incorrect messages as well, the horse will not respond as she expects and might even resist aggressively, which negatively affects her attitude toward the horse and riding.

Not every instructor will teach in the manner I describe in this book, but that does not mean she is not a good instructor. Gather information from reliable sources, and evaluate the instructor in person.

Do Your Research

Many people think they have to choose a discipline right at the start, but there is very little difference between English and Western at the basic levels. All horses walk, trot, canter, turn, and stop; these basics are taught in all disciplines (except in some gaited horse disciplines where the trot is usually replaced by one of the smoother four-beat gaits). It's best to find out what discipline is most common in your area, because it is most likely to have the best instructors.

You can look up stables online to get started because most reputable stables and instructors will have websites. If at all possible, find a stable that teaches Centered Riding, which is used in all disciplines and uses your body's innate skills, resulting in the most correct and secure position. You can find certified instructors in your area as well as other information at the websites of the American Riding Instructors Association (ARIA; www.riding-instructor.com) and Centered Riding (www.centeredriding.org).

Another good way to find more information is to visit your local tack shop and get into a conversation with the owner or one of the salespeople who seems knowledgeable. They should give you several choices rather than being too insistent about any one stable, unless the choices in your area are very limited. Ask not only about larger stables but about any smaller, "backyard" stables that they would recommend. Occasionally you find an excellent beginner instructor who for one reason or another is not associated with a large stable but prefers to teach on a few trustworthy horses she keeps at home. You do need to be careful, because some people with very poor teaching skills offer lessons to help pay for the upkeep of their horses.

It is not always a good idea to ask for recommendations from your friends who ride, especially if they are more experienced. Your requirements for an instructor might be quite different from your friends' requirements, and it could cause some ill feeling if you reject their choices. Unless you have had a good deal of recent experience, beware of the friend who offers to take you riding on her other horse. Very often the horse is not accustomed to strangers and reacts accordingly. I can't count the number of people I have met who, when we got on the subject of riding, related horror stories of being thrown or otherwise frightened on borrowed horses, which resulted in their giving up riding altogether.

Visit the Stables

When you call to arrange to visit the stables, ask about the program. Look for places with certified instructors who talk about getting to know your horse and developing correct basics, starting with balance. In any case, ask about the teaching experience of the instructors who teach beginners. Many staff members at stables think that the instructor with the least experience should be in charge of the beginner program, whereas in reality, because of the importance of developing confidence and a secure foundation, the instructor of beginners should be mature and very knowledgeable.

Be sure that the stable teaches many people in your age group and at your level of experience. Ask about the number of students in a group lesson. Even if you start with private lessons, you should eventually join a group both for the social aspects and to learn from watching others, but the group should be small if you are to get the attention you need, and also for safety. Be careful of stables that seem to emphasize competition because the tendency might be to hurry you to get you into the show ring.

If you rode as a child or teenager but have not ridden for many years, plan on going back to the beginning and starting again, even if you were quite advanced. You will progress more quickly than someone with no experience, but if you try to pick up where you left off, you might be in for a rude awakening. Both your body and mind are very different, and things that you found fun and easy as a child might be terrifying and difficult for the adult you have become.

Try to visit the stable during the week in mid- to late morning to get a feel for the atmosphere, or call and see when lessons at the level you are interested in will be taking place. Arrive early so that you can see whether students get their own horses ready or the horses are brought out to them. If the latter is the case, are arrangements in place for instruction in horse handling on the ground? If they are preparing their own horses, ask how many lessons they have had. Do they seem comfortable with what they are doing, or do they seem to expend a lot of energy trying to control the horses? Are they being supervised or is qualified help available nearby? Do they lead their horses to the riding area? If so, do they look comfortable?

Ask for a tour through the barn area and notice how the horses respond when spoken to. Your guide should treat the horses as friends, and they should come to the door of the stall in a friendly manner. One angry horse doesn't mean much, but if they are all unfriendly it does not speak well for the way they are treated.

The riding ring, and in fact the whole stable area, while it doesn't have to be new or fancy, should be organized and uncluttered. A horse that gets tangled up in loose equipment can panic and become extremely dangerous to anyone nearby.

Watch a Lesson

Because the horse is the athlete, it is essential that he be comfortable and happy. A jumper rider was once asked, "How do you get a horse to jump a six-foot fence?" (Six feet is much higher than most horses can jump easily.) The answer was "You make it the easiest thing for him to do." This is a far more serious answer than it appears at first: *Making it easy for the horse to do what you want is what successful riding is all about.* Therefore, you should look for horses who seem to be doing what they are told and seem to be happy about it.

At the same time, the *riders* should not appear to be struggling. They might not look absolutely perfect, but they should look balanced and comfortable with whatever they happen to be doing. They should also look as though they are enjoying themselves and feel safe and successful. A rider who can only walk but does it correctly is riding better and will become a good rider sooner than one who can canter but does it badly.

The instructor's approach should be quiet and positive. Aggressive instructors create a fear reaction in the best riders, and fear is a notable block to learning.

When the students are ready to ride, pay particular attention to the way they mount. Mounting can be a very dangerous part of riding, especially for the novice. Part of this is due to the way the horse is handled, and part of it is due to the way the rider mounts. A beginning rider should always be assisted during the mount. The horse should be held, and for most riders and horses, a mounting block should be used. This is more for the benefit of the horse than the rider because, with all the pull on one side, mounting is tricky for the horse even if the rider is skilled.

It is customary and necessary to tighten the girth just before mounting, but it should not be done aggressively or with too much force. A very tight girth is unnecessary and very uncomfortable

When watching a lesson, look for an instructor with a clear plan, calm and happy horses, and engaged and comfortable riders.

for the horse. If many of the horses show signs of being frightened or angry when the girth is tightened, either in their facial expressions or by attempting to kick, this shows lack of consideration and understanding on the part of the staff, and such insensitive treatment can predispose the horse to aggressive behavior when the rider makes a mistake.

I prefer to start students on a horse wearing a bareback pad rather than a saddle because it is easier for most students to find balance and relaxation without worrying about stirrups. However, this is not current practice at most stables, so if the riders are in the saddle, the instructor should spend time making sure everyone's stirrups are correctly adjusted and even.

All the riders should be settled before they start. If there are other riders in the ring, they should not ride in any way that threatens or interferes with the less experienced riders. This is partly a matter of safety and partly one of courtesy. You might not think the latter important, but if lack of consideration of others is tolerated, it will affect everyone's enjoyment.

The instructor should have an obvious lesson plan, which she may discuss with students beforehand. Generally the first part of the lesson is spent reviewing and making sure everyone is riding as correctly as possible. Nobody should look either unsafe or insecure. The second part of the lesson might be new work or continuation of something that the students are working on. The lesson should end on a positive note for all concerned.

It is a good idea to visit several stables before making up your mind, since once you are committed to a program it can be difficult and perhaps awkward to change. Observe carefully and let your common sense guide you. First and foremost, the program should look and feel safe because it is almost impossible to learn to ride correctly if you're scared. However, the students should not seem bored, although sometimes a lesson might appear rather slow to the observer. There is an enormous amount to learn about horses and riding, and a good instructor can impart information that challenges the students without pushing them beyond their abilities. Remember that choosing an instructor is probably the most important decision you will make about riding, so it is well worth taking the time to get it right.

Riding Attire

Nearly all teaching stables have some sort of dress code because safety has a lot to do with what you wear. However, you should be able to dress safely and comfortably for your early lessons without a big outlay of cash.

Helmets and Shoes

The most important safety item and (except for show clothes) often the most expensive is the helmet. Although disciplines in which jumping is not a part often do not require them, I consider this unsafe. Of the three people whom I knew personally who died of head injuries incurred while riding, none were jumping, and one was riding her own old quiet horse at the walk. A teaching stable that takes beginners should have safe, adjustable helmets available for loan during your early lessons.

Shoes are the other safety item both while riding in the saddle and while on the ground. They should support and protect your feet while allowing flexibility in the ankles. The soles should be fairly smooth, and they should have low heels. If the soles are leather, the heels should be rubber to avoid slipping on the ground. If possible they should just cover your ankle, offering both protection from the stirrup and some support. If you buy taller ones, which cover your ankle and lower shin, be very careful about the way you adjust the laces. If they are too tight in the ankle area they will interfere with flexion, making it hard for you to follow the horse's movements. Although some riders think they look cool, I advise you to avoid high rubber riding boots, for the same reason. If your instructor will be starting you on a bareback pad, you can wear any solid footgear that ties or straps on because stirrups are not a factor.

Clothing

Pants should be stretchy and loose enough in the seat area to allow for following the horse's movement. Their second purpose is to protect the inside of your lower leg from being chafed by the stirrup leather, especially in English saddles, so the lower pant leg should be fairly snug. Avoid pants that have a thick inseam for the same reason. Stretch jeans or leggings work well for most people. If you are very sensitive, you can wear tights or knee socks to protect your lower legs. Be sure to tell your instructor if you have discomfort because the tension it causes can lead to further problems. Once you have committed to riding, there are many articles of clothing to choose from for comfort and leg protection, but most of them are expensive and unnecessary for beginners.

There are lots of scratchy things around a stable, including some horses who like to nibble lovingly on you. For that reason it's best to wear a shirt that has sleeves that cover your shoulders and upper arms.

Cold-Weather Gear

One of the more dangerous things you can do is to ride when you are cold. Cold produces tension, which you are often unaware of until the horse, who is also cold, makes a sudden move that you can't follow.

Your jacket should be warm but not so bulky that the instructor can't see what your body is doing. Layering with long underwear, vests, and sweaters keeps you warm and also allows you to strip down if necessary.

Most people forget about keeping their legs warm, which is a big mistake because legs have a lot of skin area relative to volume and therefore lose a lot of heat. Cold legs also make your feet cold, which prevents your whole shock-absorbing mechanism from working well. Wear layers on legs and feet under your pants and footgear sized to fit over the layers—tight shoes make your feet really cold. If you are using stirrups, make sure that they are large enough to accommodate larger footwear. Many products are made specifically for riding in cold climates. They are expensive. but worth it if you are committed to riding and want to be comfortable and safe.

Underwear for Women

If you are large breasted, working at the sitting trot can be uncomfortable, so you should have good support. Bras are made specifically for riding, which you can find on the web.

Your seat area must be free of tension in order for you to ride successfully. Underpants should fit snugly so that they do not bunch, and if you are wearing tight breeches you might not want to show a panty line. Again, there are specific garments for riding. Just be sure that they are not uncomfortably tight or restrictive of movement.

Too Tight to Trot

Tight undergarments designed to streamline the silhouette have no place at the stables. In the 1960s, I had an adult rider who just couldn't seem to learn to sit the trot, even on the gentlest gaited horse. As a last resort, since in those days it was considered rather personal, I asked her what she was wearing for underpants. Turned out she was wearing a very tight panty girdle because she was afraid of chafing. I suggested that she try something different, and at her next lesson she sat the trot without difficulty. So we learn!

One thing you should *not* need in underpants is a padded crotch, such as athletes wear for bicycling. Your riding saddle, and the way you sit on it or on a bareback pad, should not cause any pressure whatsoever under the pubis (crotch) bone, which is not constructed to take pressure. If you have discomfort in that area, you need to change either the saddle or the way you are sitting on it.

Underwear for Men

Obviously I have no firsthand experience with this subject, but my late husband was an excellent rider and lifelong horseman. He advised that men should wear boxer shorts, not jockey shorts. If the sensitive parts are supported in front of the crotch bone as with jockey shorts, you can be injured either by being thrown forward against the back of the pommel or by coming down on top of it. Boxer shorts allow the parts to lie to one side, in the hollow of the thigh, where they are far less exposed to risk. Most of the time, discomfort or injury to this part of the body stems from the mistakes that men make in their efforts to protect themselves.

Although the actions outlined in this chapter may seem like a lot of trouble, as with any new endeavor, the effort you put into preparation will pay off later. The time you spend learning about riding and how to do things right is time well spent.

2

The Real Tools for Success

*I*f you are reading this book, chances are that you either haven't had much experience with horses or the experience you have had has not been successful. As you prepare to get close to the horse you will ride, physically and emotionally, we'd like to introduce you to some unique tools that will help you make riding a successful experience from the start.

We begin with the three basics, the foundation on which all your lessons are constructed. Then we explain the seven steps, a set of physical and mental preparations that will help you cope with the tensions that are inevitable in a sport unlike any other. We close out this chapter with some safety rules that will guide you in this new world you are entering.

You might be tempted to skip by this theoretical stuff and get to the fun part, but I assure you that you will have a lot more fun with the horse—*and he with you*—if you read this chapter pretty carefully, and bookmark it for reference, before going on.

Three Basics

If you have taken riding lessons before, or even read other books, you probably think of the basics as often-repeated commands such as "sit up straight," "head up," and "heels down." These and similar instructions for beginners are actually the *result* of correct basics, because they are actions that your body does naturally when it is comfortable and secure, rather than guiding principles. So, what are the real basics? There are three of them, and your commitment to applying them will significantly affect what and how you will learn:

1. Build a partnership with the horse based on mutual affection, trust, and respect.
2. Move around the horse and sit on him, at all gaits and activities, in a way that is safe, comfortable, and nonthreatening to both you and the horse.
3. Communicate with the horse first by listening to him and then by talking to him so that you both understand each other's needs and desires.

The Confrontational Colleague

I was attending a seminar at a large facility where other lessons were taking place at the same time. I was in the stall tacking my horse when a girl of about 10, obviously inexperienced, entered the stall next to mine. She attempted without success to put the bridle on the horse, who was quite tall and simply raised his head up so that she couldn't reach. After a few minutes, an older child entered the stall, yelled at the horse and slapped him, and he then allowed her to put the bridle on. Although her method succeeded, it did nothing to establish a basis for a working partnership—in fact, it did just the opposite.

Basic 1: Build a Caring, Trusting Partnership

This is by far the most important element in riding. Safety is always a major concern when horses are involved. By building a good relationship, you teach the horse that he can trust you to care for his welfare. In time the horse will learn to trust your motives in spite of your mistakes. A horse that feels his rider loves him will put up with all kinds of abuse resulting from ignorance and incompetence.

I used to meet a woman around town who always told me what a wonderful horse she had, how much she loved him, and how well behaved he was. I eventually saw her ride and was appalled at what a bad rider she was. She bounced on the horse's back at every step, and her hands jerked the reins. The horse looked terribly uncomfortable, but never in any way did he show it except by his rather sad, resigned expression. He knew that she wasn't hurting him on purpose, so he forgave her for her mistakes.

To work successfully with someone, you need to know what he is like as an individual and what his background is. If you were working with a person from another culture, you would want to know his traditions and the kinds of things that make him comfortable or uncomfortable in a relationship. The same is even truer with a horse because he can't explain to you in words how he feels about things. If you don't make the effort to understand him, his efforts to explain how he feels can be very disturbing.

In chapter 3 I talk more about the general characteristics of the horse and how you can become better acquainted with the horse you ride. The important message here is to develop an equal partnership in which the goal of each partner is to give the other the freedom he needs to feel comfortable without the need to sacrifice his own freedom or safety.

When you begin working around horses, you should have an experienced person with you at all times. Since you have not yet established a good relationship, and the horse is much bigger and stronger than you, once he knows you aren't going to eat him, his next step is to try to place himself above you in the pecking order, something a beginner doesn't have the skills to deal with.

A common, and I think mistaken, way of dealing with this is for the instructor to tell the student that she must 'be the boss' and not let the horse 'get away with that.' Without experience and knowledge, the student tends to resort to aggressive behavior. A kind horse usually will not respond with equal aggression, but a behavior pattern has been set up that is bad for both parties. An experienced handler can use nonaggressive body language and tools to establish a respectful relationship that will extend to you as well. As you gain knowledge and thus confidence, you will be able to earn the horse's respect on your own.

Basic 2: Move Around and Sit on the Horse Comfortably

If the horse isn't comfortable, you won't be, either. Tense horses respond awkwardly and often overreact. Comfort starts with building a good relationship, so that's where we begin. A poor relationship involves some degree of fear on one or both sides. I talk more about fear later in this chapter, but for now let's just say that fear can arise and create problems in many situations, and it is contagious. So it is important for you to learn how to move and be around the horse in ways that don't make either him or you nervous.

Everything you are taught in this book is based on doing things in a carefully planned way. Learning in small steps builds your confidence and helps both you and the horse to be comfortable with each other and what you are doing at all times—maintaining a level of comfort is important both for your safety and your enjoyment. Practicing those steps until they are securely rooted in your muscle memory creates a strong foundation on which further steps are built. From the horse's point of view, as well as your own, you will make fewer mistakes, so his job will be much easier, more pleasant, and less stressful.

Basic 3: Communicate With the Horse

The traditional emphasis is on the rider learning to tell the horse what to do and often how to *make* him do it when he doesn't want to—not an approach that leads to a pleasant relationship. This forceful approach is the result of a lack of understanding on the part of the instructor about why horses are "disobedient." Put simply, when a horse does not behave in the desired manner, it is often because the rider is sending a confusing or incorrect message. It could be a matter of the rider's poor timing or the horse's lack of physical ability or preparedness—he isn't able or ready to perform that task at that moment. It might be a lack of trust—the horse might feel insecure and might not trust his rider enough to try. These are situations we can all relate to and learn to resolve by understanding that the most important part of communication is *listening to the horse*. This means learning his language and the kinds of things that make tasks easier or more difficult for him.

Part of communication is the use of aids such as the reins, and leg pressure. Most people think these aids tell the horse *what* to do. To an extent they do, but when used correctly, they should tell him *how* to do it. They should aid the horse, that is, they should *help* the horse to perform the task in the most efficient and easy way. When rider and horse have a good relationship and have developed their skills, telling the horse *what* you want is more a matter of intent, that is, having a very clear idea of what you want and also what he needs to do with his body to accomplish it. The aids are used as necessary to help him. A very skilled horse–rider partnership can accomplish advanced movements with little or no apparent use of aids. Riders in this type of partnership are said to be using invisible aids, and being able to communicate artfully is the ultimate goal of every rider.

During your riding career, you will be continually learning about all three of these basics. You will never learn everything there is to know about them, because every horse is unique both in himself and in his life experience. Part of the joy and excitement of riding is the constant learning process. You keep progressing, and it never gets boring because there is always more to know.

The Seven Steps and Grounding

The seven steps are a series of movements that place your body and mind in the best frame for riding. Grounding is a physical activity that results in a feeling of security that is essential for learning to ride correctly. Grounding can be achieved by using the seven steps. The steps are based on yoga and Centered Riding and similar disciplines. I have found this selection of exercises to be the easiest and most useful for students at all levels. I consider them an essential tool and recommend and use them not only for riding but for many other aspects of life.

To understand the need for the seven steps and how they work, you need to understand something about tension, which is *the* major block to comfort on and around the horse. Fear is a key cause of tension, and overcoming fear is an important part of riding. For reasons we'll discuss later, no matter how brave you are and how much you love horses, when you start you are going to have some fear, no matter how well and safely the lesson is conducted. If you are excited about this new experience, you might not even be aware of the fear, but it will be there, and you must deal with it early on if you are to progress. Fear is also contagious, so the horse picks up on it as well, which affects your relationship.

Emotions originate not in the conscious brain but in the body, and thus in the reflex brain. The body takes in signals through the senses and reacts by laughing, crying, or jumping away. The conscious brain recognizes this behavior. It doesn't have to think, *I'm happy, unhappy, or frightened;* it simply knows based on what the body is doing. What the conscious brain *can't* do is talk directly to the reflex brain because there is no direct connection between them. So if you are tense, having the instructor say, "Relax," or saying to yourself, "Get over it," doesn't work because the reflex brain doesn't react to words or thoughts. What it does react to is what the body is doing.

When I was little, if I fell and hurt myself and ran to my mother, crying, she would dust me off and treat my injury. Then, if I was still crying, she would say, "Now smile," and she would smile at me. I would smile back and it would all be over. If she had said, "Get over it," I might have continued crying, but the physical act of smiling had a positive effect on my emotional state. In the same way, the seven steps are a way for your body to tell your mind that things are okay so you don't have to be afraid.

Each emotion affects the body in its own way, and each has a characteristic physical appearance. If the emotion is fear, the body tries to assume a protective fetal position (chin down and legs drawn up) while at the same time the feet prepare themselves to run, the muscles become tense, breathing almost stops, and the eyes become hard and focused. Confidence, the polar opposite of fear, has a completely different appearance. The body and head are erect but not tense, the feet are solidly grounded, breathing is normal and regular, and the eyes are soft and far-seeing (figure 2.1).

Figure 2.1 A confident posture makes the rider and the horse comfortable.

While your conscious brain can't control your emotions by thinking about them, it *can* control your body. If you teach yourself to put your body in confident mode when tension appears, the tension and fear will go away. The seven steps are designed to put you in a relaxed, confident state so you and your horse will both feel comfortable.

The seven steps are as follows:

1. Growing
2. Shaking out
3. Breathing
4. Using soft eyes
5. Longitudinal centering
6. Following the movement
7. Lateral centering

Each step leads to the next, so you should practice them in order, but don't overdo. Pushing your body to the point where you are uncomfortable defeats the purpose. Over time you will find them easier both to do and to remember.

Before you begin the seven steps, you must first find your "bubbling spring." Sit in a low chair with one shoe off. Cross your leg so your shoeless foot is resting on the opposite knee. Use your fingers to feel the sole of your foot. Run your fingers partway across the back of the ball of the foot. Behind your second toe you will feel a hollow. That is your bubbling spring point and is the place where your body connects with the ground (figure 2.2). You will find in step 5 that if your bubbling spring starts to come off the ground, you lose your balance.

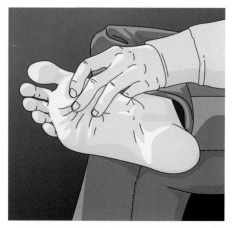

Figure 2.2 The bubbling spring.

Preparatory Grounding: Creating a Base

Begin each of the seven steps with this exercise.

Stand with your feet shoulder-width apart and at the same relative angle to the ground. Wiggle your toes for a minute to relax the muscles in your feet, then imagine that you have feet like a duck: wide and flexible to give you a good platform to stand on. Picture where the bubbling spring point is and connect it to the ground. Think about your legs and try to release any tensions you feel. Imagine the tension turning into water and melting away.

When you complete the seven steps, you will repeat the grounding exercise. With practice, you will notice that your body feels significantly more connected with the ground, and thus more secure, when you do the grounding exercise after performing the seven steps. The preliminary grounding exercise, though not as comprehensive, is also useful by itself in an emergency.

Step 1: Growing

Gentle Stretching Exercise

a. Stand in the base position previously described. Begin with your left arm. Bend your elbow and bring your left hand up so that your thumb is in front of your nose (figure 2.3a).

b. Following the movement with your head and eyes, raise your hand until your arm is fully extended (figure 2.3b).

c. With your arm still raised, drop your chin until your face is vertical. Think of looking over granny glasses. Continue to reach up with your arm until you feel a pull at your waist (figure 2.3c). Keeping your body tall, allow your arm to drop to your side.

d. Repeat steps a through c with your right arm.

e. Keeping your body tall, bring your right hand down and tap yourself on the top of your head, in line with your nose and directly between your ears (figure 2.3d). Allow your arm to drop to your side. Imagine that there is a string fastened to the top of your head, where you were tapping. Then imagine the string fastened to something above your head. It can be a fixed object or a floating object such as a balloon. Imagine that you are hanging suspended from the object so that your body gently stretches out and gets as long (tall) as it can.

f. Finish by growing with your left arm, and while it is still over your head, growing your right arm up to it so that both sides are equally long. Let yourself ground into your feet (figure 2.3e). Bring both arms down.

Figure 2.3 Growing.

Step 2: Shaking Out

Releasing Small Unperceived Tensions in Your Body

a. With your hands dangling at your sides, imagine that they are wet and you are trying to dry them by shaking them. Begin by thinking about just your fingers, then your hands, your wrists, your forearms, your elbows, your upper arms, and finally your shoulders (figure 2.4*a*). Return your hands to your sides.

b. Hold a chair or other support with one hand for balance. Start with the opposite leg. Hold your foot slightly out in front of you. Working from your knee, focus first on shaking your foot, then your ankle, and your shin (figure 2.4*b*). Then work from your hip to shake your knee and thigh. Repeat with the other leg. Be sure you use a jiggly shaking movement, not a twist.

c. With your feet shoulder-width apart, allow yourself to bend from the waist with your arms dangling loosely as far as you can go without straining (figure 2.4*c*). Take a little time and allow your body to stretch gradually. Don't bounce or otherwise try to force the stretch. Hang there for a few seconds.

d. Now shake all over like a dog coming out of water. When you are finished, come up slowly to an upright position and ground (figure 2.4*d*).

e. Repeat part *f* from step 1.

When you're in a situation that makes you a little tense all over, such as waiting to enter a competition, a little shakeout is very helpful for releasing the excess tension without experiencing a letdown.

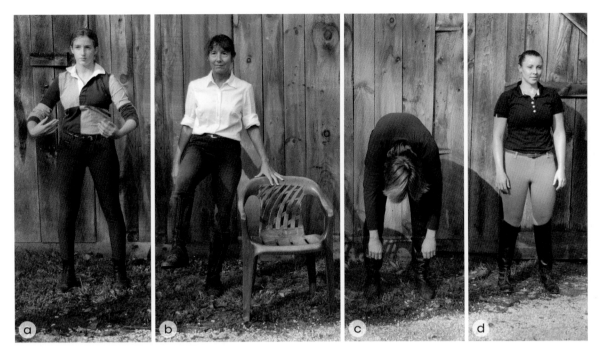

Figure 2.4 Shaking out tension.

Step 3: Breathing

Relaxation as Nature Intended

There are three ways you can breathe: Inhale longer than you exhale, inhale and exhale the same, and exhale longer than you inhale. The first tends to be energizing; the last tends to be relaxing and is the one you're going to learn.

a. Stand straight and grounded, hands hanging by your sides or lightly clasped in front of you. Keeping your shoulders quiet, breathe in, thinking about using your diaphragm (see Breathing With Your Diaphragm sidebar). Allow yourself to exhale. Repeat several times until you feel comfortable.

b. Now breathe in through your nose, then exhale *slowly* through your mouth, making the exhalation last as long as is comfortable—about twice as long as the inhalation. Count to yourself, "In, two, three; out, two, three, four, five, six" or whatever amount is easy for you.

c. As you breathe, begin to notice what your whole chest area is doing. As you start to breathe in and your diaphragm moves down, your lower rib cage expands front, side, and back. At the end of the inhalation you can feel your upper rib cage expanding. As you start to exhale, the process reverses.

Breathing is the most useful, and the most used, I believe, of all relaxation exercises. It can be done unobtrusively anywhere, in any situation, and it always helps to relieve stress.

Breathing With Your Diaphragm

Many people, especially children, breathe consciously by lifting their shoulders and breathing from the chest instead of the diaphragm. This exercise will help you overcome that. Lie on the floor on your belly and elbows on a rug or blanket, not a bare floor. Adjust your arms so that they drop vertically from your shoulders to your elbows, with your forearms side by side under your neck. Let your weight rest on your arms.

Now think about breathing in and out either through your nose or through your mouth. You can try both to see which feels more natural. You will find that you cannot move your shoulders. Start to feel how your diaphragm presses against the floor with each inhalation and comes away as you exhale (figure 2.5). This is the healthy, effective breathing that you want.

Figure 2.5   Learning to breathe from the diaphragm.

Stand up, grow from the top of your head, and think about breathing in by pushing your diaphragm down and out into your abdomen, then letting it come up by itself to exhale.

Step 4: Using Soft Eyes

Changing the Focus

The concept of soft eyes is new to most people but has many uses. Soft eyes help you to find yourself in space. When you are frightened, your body wants to find control, so it goes into hard-eyes mode. But hard eyes have a very narrow range of vision and can't see what's going on around you. When you are dealing with balance and motion, it is important to know exactly where you are relative to your surroundings because everything is moving.

Finding your soft eyes is quite easy:

a. Standing in an open space, find an object nearby (5-10 feet, or 1.5-3 m, away), focus on it, and try to block everything else out of your vision and your thoughts. This is called hard eyes.

b. Without moving your eyes or turning your head, allow your scope of vision to widen so that you can see all around the central object: up, down, and in both directions in a panorama. This is soft eyes.

c. With your eyes still soft, hold your arms out to either side and a little behind you. Wiggle your fingers, stop, and wiggle them again. Notice that you can see them wiggle and stop. Look to see how far back they are.

d. If you have someone with you, ask her to walk past you from front to back, about five feet away. As soon as you can no longer see her, call out, "Stop," then turn your head to see where she is. It's quite surprising how far behind you can see with soft eyes.

Soft eyes help your body to be aware of itself relative to your horse and help you to be aware of other objects around you. But being aware of yourself in space is only one of the uses of soft eyes. Here are the attributes of both soft and hard eyes:

Hard Eyes	Soft Eyes
Left brain	Right brain
Verbal	Nonverbal
Linear	Holistic
Controlling	Noncontrolling

Hard, or focused, eyes are associated with learning. When you are taking any sort of lesson, someone is usually talking to you, so you will be in left-brain, or verbal, mode in order to take in the information. Your hard eyes will be on to keep you focused. The person talking will be giving instructions, one step at a time, which is linear, like a list: "As soon as you are in the car, adjust the seat and mirrors. Put your foot on the brake. Put the key in the ignition and turn it to start. When the engine is running, move the shift lever to drive." The left brain needs to keep everything organized, so it is controlling.

Soft, unfocused eyes also are necessary to the learning process but in a different way. Once your brain has taken in all the information, it needs to process it holistically—that is, put it all together so that rather than think about each step, you get into the car and drive away with no real conscious thought at all. The process that takes care of this is in your right brain, which you turn on with your soft eyes. The right brain can become so skilled that your body will react in an emergency without conscious thought and often no memory of reacting even after the emergency is safely over. This has saved me from serious harm at least three times in my life.

Humans use soft eyes all the time without being aware of it. If you are trying to remember how something looks, you tend to look off into space for a moment, not in an intense way, but more like *Hmmm, I wonder*. That's your right brain working, and very often you will see the answer in your head. Your eyes focus again and you continue with the task. If you are really in right-brain mode, if someone speaks to you, you might not hear her, and even if you do, it will be a moment or so before you can switch back to left brain and answer her. Right brain is noncontrolling, which means that rather than being tightly organized, it allows creative thinking.

Both left- and right-brain thinking have practical applications, so it can be helpful to know how to switch from one to the other, which you do by consciously going from hard (focused) to soft (unfocused) eyes or vice versa.

Soft Eyes Save the Day

I was riding a young horse in the field late one afternoon. Suddenly my horse heard the sound of the other horses being fed. Afraid he would miss a meal, he spun around suddenly and took off at a gallop toward the barn. I found myself hanging off one side of him with only my hands on his mane and my calf over the saddle keeping me from falling. At the same time, I thought, *I should try to see whether the gate is closed or open*, which would affect what the horse did when he got there. I looked up with soft eyes because I wasn't sure where I was and suddenly found myself back up in the saddle again! I have no recollection of how I got there, but I have to assume that when the soft eyes told my body where it was, it knew what to do and did it with no conscious effort on my part.

Step 5: Longitudinal Centering

Staying Over Your Base

Longitudinal centering has to do with keeping your center, which is located within your pelvis, over your base, which would be your seat bones if sitting or your bubbling spring point if standing (figure 2.6). If you are exactly centered, there is minimal muscular effort and thus minimal tension.

a. Run quickly through the previous steps so that you are as straight and free of tension as possible. Then stand with your feet fairly close together with your hands by your sides.

b. Keeping your body completely straight, and *bending only at the ankles*, sway forward slowly until you lose your balance and have to take a step.

c. Repeat, but this time, stop just *before* you lose your balance. Notice that your bubbling spring is still in contact with the ground. Now slowly sway forward until your bubbling spring leaves the ground, trying not to let your toes curl (figure 2.7*a*). You will have to take a step, or sway back so that your bubbling spring is on the ground, to keep your balance.

d. Try the same exercise, but this time sway backward rather than forward. Notice that again you lose your balance when your bubbling spring leaves the ground (figure 2.7*b*).

e. Sway forward again, but stop before you lose your balance. Notice the tension in your lower body and legs. Sway back and again look for tension (figure 2.7*c*). Then sway forward very slowly until you feel all the tension leave your body (figure 2.7*d*). You are now longitudinally centered.

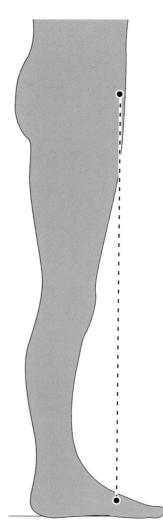

Figure 2.6 For longitudinal centering while standing, your pelvis must be over your bubbling spring.

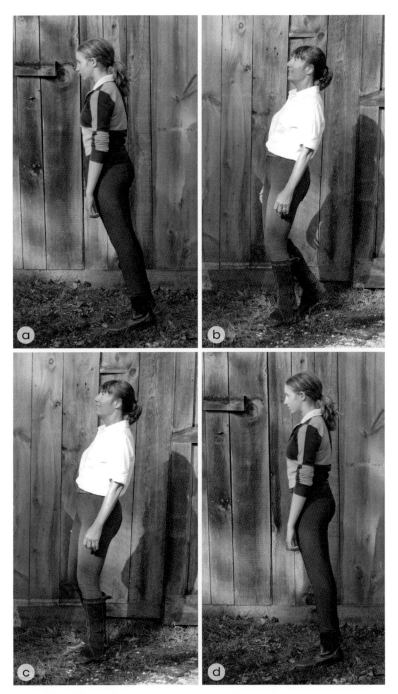

Figure 2.7   Finding your longitudinal center.

Step 6: Following the Movement

Becoming Part of the Horse

When you are sitting on the horse's back, you can feel it moving underneath your seat bones. To keep from bouncing on the horse, which would be uncomfortable for both of you, your body must learn to follow the movement. You can start working on this on the ground by becoming aware of how your own leg movements affect your body, since the movements are the same.

a. Begin by grounding and growing. Place your hands lightly under your buttocks so you can feel how your seat moves. Then, with your feet fairly close together and keeping the balls of your feet on the ground, start to walk in place by pushing your knees forward and lifting your heels one at a time (figure 2.8a). Do not sway from side to side or twist. Notice how each side of your seat drops and lifts as each knee bends and straightens. If you were on a horse that was walking, your seat would be dropping as the horse's hind leg on that side lifted up (that is, when his knee bent).

b. Start to swing your arms as though you were walking (figure 2.8b). If your arms are swinging naturally, on the horse they would be swinging in time with his front legs. This becomes important when you start using the reins so that you can follow the motion of his head.

c. Still without lifting your toes, try jogging in place while swinging your arms, and notice that everything moves slightly differently because the gait is actually different, not just faster (figure 2.8c).

This exercise is also fun to do on a small trampoline, where the additional springiness is more like being on the horse. Here the trick is to keep your feet solidly on the trampoline and not let them bounce up as you walk and jog in place. This is important when you use stirrups.

Figure 2.8   Following the movement.

Step 7: Lateral Centering

Learning to Keep the Horse Underneath You

Because the horse is fairly narrow side to side, it is easy to lose your lateral balance. This also unbalances the horse, so it is important to be able to control it.

a. Begin by growing as in step 1 with your feet shoulder-width apart. Then place one hand on your abdomen with your thumb on your navel and the other hand opposite it on your back (figure 2.9a). Your center is located between your hands.

b. *Keeping your spine vertical*, move your pelvis and your center to the left so that they are over your left foot. Your weight will also be over your left foot. You are moving your weight and your center together (figure 2.9b).

c. Return to the original position, then repeat to the right. Notice that shifting your weight to one side with your center makes it difficult to move the foot on that side but allows you to move the opposite foot easily.

d. Now repeat the exercise, but instead of thinking about keeping your spine vertical, think about keeping your weight even on both feet. To do this, your spine will have to tilt in the opposite direction from your center (figure 2.9c). Now you are moving just your center. In order for either foot to lift up, you will have to shift your weight as well.

e. Finally, move your center and weight over to the left until your center is to the *left* of your bubbling spring (which will start to come off the ground). You will lose your balance and either have to move back to the right or take a very awkward crossover step to the left. Try it to the right as well. Finish by grounding.

Controlling your lateral center and weight are important both for keeping you on the horse and as aids. An old cavalry maxim says that you can't fall off with one leg on one side, one leg on the other, and your head in the middle.

Once you have learned grounding and the seven steps, try to practice them fairly frequently to fix them in your muscle memory. Having them at your command will make the process of learning to ride both faster and easier for you and the horse.

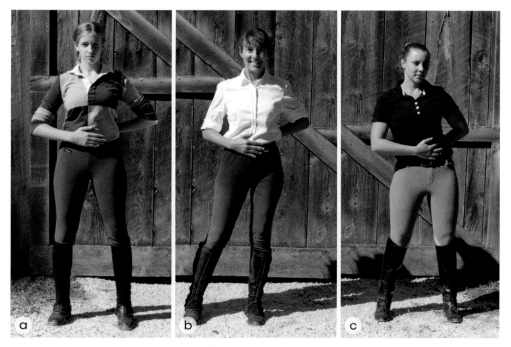

Figure 2.9 Maintaining your lateral center.

Safety Guidelines

The principal reason we concern ourselves with safety around horses is their size and strength. Being stepped on by a horse is not going to hurt you as much as being run over by a car, but it can break your foot, and it hurts a lot. However, just as the average driver will not run over you on purpose, so the average horse will not bite, kick, or otherwise try to hurt you on purpose. Most accidents involving horses are the result of someone's poor judgment and are avoidable.

The only really safe horse is the one that doesn't want you to get hurt and will make every effort to protect you from harm. This means he must love you and care about your welfare, which in turn means that you must love him and care about his welfare. Everything you do with a horse should reflect this philosophy.

Every well-run stable has safety rules that apply to all clients. It would be impossible to list every scenario that might be dangerous, but it is possible to list some general rules that will keep you safe in most instances:

1. Begin by taking lessons from a reputable, experienced professional.
2. Wear proper clothing, especially a helmet.
3. When working near the horse on the ground, stay in the safe area, near his front legs, unless you have reason to work elsewhere.
4. Just as you would get to know a person before going for a long drive with her, so you should get comfortable with the horse before mounting. In both cases, the other individual is in charge of the vehicle!
5. Never touch a horse on his hindquarters when you first approach. Always approach from the front. If you can't do that, attract his attention to establish contact first so that he knows you are there. If he shows no signs of fear or aggression and you feel comfortable. walk promptly to his head without touching him elsewhere.
6. Never approach an unknown loose horse in a field without some sort of a defensive device such as a lead rope in your hand. For a variety of reasons that have to do with protecting himself or his herd, he might try, not to hurt you, but to drive you away, and he can run faster than you can.
7. When two horses are together, sometimes their behavior can get a little rough. They won't intend to hurt you, but they won't realize that you can't get out of the way easily. Pay attention, and be ready to separate them if necessary.
8. When you try *anything* with a horse that you have not done before *yourself*, be a little careful until you're sure he's okay with it.
9. Listen to what *your* body tells you. If you feel really nervous about something, don't do it if you can possibly avoid it. Walking home on your own two feet is better than being carried home on a stretcher.
10. Try not to ride alone. If you must, make sure that someone knows you're out and will check to make sure you are safely home.
11. Don't buy a horse until you are pretty comfortable, and keep him with a professional for at least the first few months. Better yet, lease a horse to make sure you have the time and the desire to work by yourself. Learn about your and the horse's equipment. Know how it should fit and how to use it, and keep it in good shape.
12. Bear in mind that horses are living creatures and therefore by definition unpredictable. Just as a person can never be counted on to show exactly the same behavior under a certain set of circumstances, neither can a horse. Also remember that a horse that is comfortable with someone else might not be comfortable with you. Paying attention to your horse's state of mind at all times is the *most* important factor in keeping both of you safe.

3

Getting to Know the Horse

Our relationship with horses is different from our relationship with most other domestic animals. This is because it is, for most of us, a working relationship. You and your horse work together to perform all kinds of tasks, depending on your needs and the horse's capabilities. He is the athlete, the worker, and you are the guide. Many people take this to mean that you must be the boss and the horse the servant, but that's a little like thinking that the coach of a football team is the boss and the players are servants. In both cases, the athlete is the one who actually has to perform the task, so he must always be allowed a certain amount of freedom and input.

In addition, when you are riding, *the horse is the one who is actually in control of the vehicle.* No matter what your skills might be, no matter what you use in the way of equipment, if the horse really wants or doesn't want to do something, there is very little you as the rider can do about it. Therefore, your concern should be not how you can master the animal so you can make him do what you want but rather how you can get this animal to like and respect you so that he *wants* to do what you want. And the answer to that question brings you back to the first basic, which is outlined in chapter 2. A horse that has a positive and trusting relationship with his rider is motivated to do as the rider wishes. Building this type of relationship begins with ground work and takes place over time as you put the pieces together.

As a novice, you shouldn't look for respect from the horse right away. The horse knows more about riding than a beginning rider does and knows that he has this advantage, so you have to depend on his kind nature until you have the skills to gain his respect as well.

Knowing something about a horse's essential character will give you some guidance as you get to know your particular horse. The information that follows will get you started, but there is just as much to know about horse psychology as there is about humans, and in many ways they aren't that different.

First, he is a prey animal, so he has well-developed survival instincts and abilities.

- He thinks of the human as a predator until he has learned to trust.
- He is easily frightened.
- He has fast reflexes.
- When his head is aligned with his body, he is able to see almost 360 degrees around himself (figure 3.1*a*). However, he has a cone-shaped blind spot directly in front of his nose and directly behind his rump.
- He sees in a limited horizontal band rather than a sphere. He must raise or tilt his head (and thus his band of vision) to bring objects into view (figure 3.1*b*).
- He tends to run away from surprises.
- He is curious and likes to explore strange objects cautiously but thoroughly.

Second, he is a herd animal, and since he depends on the herd for survival, he needs to get along well with others.

- He is nonaggressive unless threatened or trapped.
- He is very responsive to body language.
- He needs companionship.
- He wants a good place in the herd pecking order, so he might try to dominate.
- He accepts leadership well from someone he trusts and respects.
- He enjoys physical contact—grooming, scratching, and similar attention.
- He likes being ridden, when it's done with knowledge and consideration.
- He enjoys working, learning, and experiencing new things when approached with care.
- He responds well to positive reinforcement and quiet handling.
- He responds poorly to harsh punishment and aggressive handling.

As you start to work with the horse, first on the ground and then riding, you will see how these characteristics apply and how you use this knowledge to get along with him. The initial instructions for the introduction are described here as taking place in some sort of enclosure—a barn for ground work and an arena for riding.

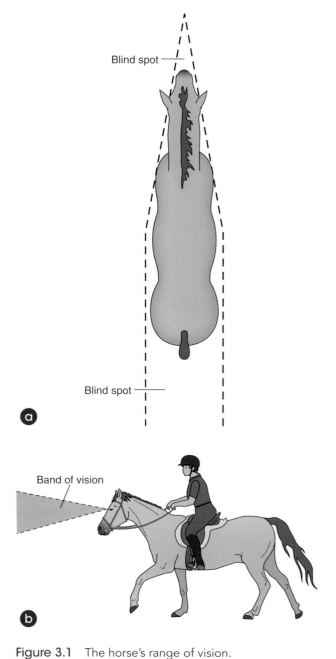

Figure 3.1 The horse's range of vision.

A good rule when you're starting out is not to make any moves around the horse without being told to. This includes reaching out to pat him or walking up into his space or any of the things that, if you think about it, would bother you if a stranger did them to you. Wait and follow the instructor's lead, but, on the other hand, if you are asked to do something that makes you really uncomfortable, you should say so. Trying to do things you don't feel ready for usually ends unsuccessfully.

The first part of your first lesson, and of most lessons thereafter, will be on the ground. Begin by doing the seven steps, on your own if necessary (see chapter 2), to get your body as relaxed and secure as possible.

Handling the Introduction in a Closed Space

The first time you meet your first horse, he should be in his stall with the door closed, or some sort of gate that he can put his head over, but prevents him from walking out. The instructor will probably tell you his name and perhaps a little bit about him: "This is Billy. He's 14 years old, his color is chestnut, he's a quarter horse. I've owned him for about 5 years, and he's a wonderful, safe horse to start out on." She might also go over some safety and behavior rules, such as not making loud noises or sudden moves.

Having introduced you to Billy, her next step is to introduce Billy to you. Since your eyes are placed on the front of your head, this classifies you as a predator. Until you have shown that you are not a predator, he will be a bit cautious. Horses, like most animals, identify others primarily by smell, so the horse needs to sniff you and touch you a little, and the most comfortable way for you is to have him sniff your hand.

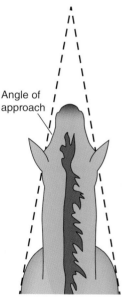

It is important to approach the horse in a way that is not threatening. That means making sure he can see you easily. As with all prey animals, the horse's eyes are on the sides of his head, and he is quite accustomed to seeing something with only one eye. However, it means he has a blind spot directly in front of his face (figure 3.2), so you should avoid approaching a horse directly from the front. The polite thing to do is to approach at a slight angle from the front, usually from his left side because most horses are accustomed to being approached and handled primarily from that side. You should also use soft eyes to avoid staring at him, which would be the action of a predator.

I have found that almost every novice's initial reaction to having the horse reach out with his muzzle to her hand is to jerk her hand away. That's because her body interprets the horse moving his mouth (and perhaps his teeth) toward her as possibly aggressive. Similarly, a horse that is not accustomed to people jumps away when a person reaches out her hand to touch him.

Figure 3.2 Avoid the horse's front blind spot by approaching at a slight angle.

A student once told me about her very first riding lesson, with a different instructor, which was almost her last. The instructor talked for a minute or two, then took her over to a field, pointed, and said, "There is your horse. Go get him!" Um, how?

Nice to Meet You

Humans use hands to explore strange and possibly dangerous objects because we can reach out with them, thus keeping the strange object at a distance, and jerk them back quickly if necessary. The horse uses his muzzle in the same way and for the same reasons, plus he has the added advantage of having his sniffing apparatus in the same area. Therefore, shaking hands in humans, and touching muzzles in horses, are the least threatening ways to start a friendship.

To overcome this, I have the student shake out the right hand and arm thoroughly to remove any tensions. If the rider seems very timid, I might suggest running quickly through the seven steps. Then we approach the horse while I show the correct way to hold the hand, palm down with fingers curled. I put my left hand over the rider's right hand and bring it to a point where the horse can reach it (figure 3.3). By putting my hand on top, I give the horse a chance to smell our hands while still making the rider feel protected. Of course you should not reach out, especially to a strange horse, and shove your hand in his face. That's like a stranger grabbing your hand and shaking it before you offer it.

After the horse has had a good sniff, and if the student seems relaxed, I demonstrate how to use the back of curled fingers to rub the horse's muzzle just in front of the corner of his mouth. You hold your hand this way because it is not threatening, as

Figure 3.3 Being introduced to the horse under the guidance of the instructor eases fear and builds confidence.

holding up the flat of your hand would be. If you hold out your hand palm up, the horse might think that you are holding a treat in it and accidentally nip you. Rubbing the horse's muzzle is nonthreatening to both of you and feels nice and soft.

Getting Acquainted Out in the Open

Now the instructor should bring the horse out of the stall and put him on crossties. That is, the horse will stand in the aisle with a rope fastened from the wall to his halter on each side. This allows him to move his feet in any direction, but not turn around, which makes it easier to work around him.

Although it is the safest way for a novice to work around the horse, not all stables and situations allow for the horse to be on crossties. Depending on how the horse is tied, you may have to move around him in slightly different ways; for example, not walking under his neck if he is tied with only one rope, and being aware that he can move his body around more freely . Your instructor should guide you carefully, and you should wait to be shown before trying different approaches.

Having introduced yourself, you should continue to show the horse that you aren't going to harm him and that you have at least some knowledge of polite behavior. Again, it is similar to the way you present yourself to other humans, and it begins with respecting their personal space. You would not like a stranger to touch your face with a hand, but putting a hand on your shoulder is all right. Your face is personal space; your shoulder probably is not as much. A horse's personal space begins above his muzzle and runs back to just in front of his shoulder.

After you run through the seven steps again, your instructor should walk you around to the horse's left side and stand just behind his front leg, inviting you to stand as close to his shoulder as you feel comfortable—about as close as you would stand to carry on a conversation with a person. Check yourself to make sure you are well grounded and secure.

The next step is to place your right hand on the top of the horse's shoulder. Again, the instructor might assist you with her hand the first time (figure 3.4). Take a step forward if necessary so that you keep your longitudinal balance and thus your grounding. It's important to do this, because if you are unbalanced forward, you will curl your toes, which sends a message to the horse that you are getting ready to run, meaning that something scary is nearby. He does not, of course, realize that the something scary is him! If you feel a little uncomfortable, you can quietly bring your hand down, wait a few seconds, and put it back, leaving it a little longer.

Figure 3.4 Standing by a cross-tied horse's shoulder with the instructor's hand on top of the rider's creates a nonthreatening experience for both the horse and rider.

When a doctor gives a new patient a checkup, he often begins by putting one hand on her shoulder and letting it rest there for a moment. He doesn't pat or rub or stroke her arm, which would be invasive; his hand just sits there and says, "I'm going to be in your personal space, but I'm not going to be aggressive about it or hurt you." If she were a nervous patient and pulled away, he would probably talk to her a little longer and explain what he was going to do and why. Horses respond well to the same signal, and their response also tells you whether it's safe to proceed. If the horse pulls back from your touch, you know that he is afraid of you and thus potentially unsafe.

Being close to the horse can be scary if the horse moves in such a way that you are afraid of being stepped on, so you must learn how to move out of the way without scaring the horse or yourself in the process. It's not very difficult providing you are standing balanced and grounded. Simply let your arm fall smoothly to your side and take a quiet step back. Practice stepping up close to the horse and away again a couple of times, thinking about your seven steps. Using soft eyes, breathing, and shaking out very subtly might be necessary the first couple of times. It might seem like a silly thing to have to do, but it will help your body to feel comfortable around the horse very quickly and make the next steps much easier.

Watching His Step

Horses are a very ancient species. Eohippus, the earliest horse, was quite small and had soft feet. He also tasted good, so if he couldn't run fast he became somebody's lunch. To run fast, his feet had to be in good shape, so he was particularly careful never to step on anything strange that might injure his feet.

My mother was riding down a road one day and came to an intersection with the word *STOP* painted in large white letters across the road. Her horse immediately stopped, refusing to step on this odd-looking surface. The student who was riding with her said in a very surprised voice, "My, I didn't realize horses could read!"

This instinct to protect his feet still exists in modern horses with hard hooves, so horses will generally try to avoid stepping on you.

Ask your instructor if the horse likes to be gently scratched any special place. Many horses really enjoy being scratched in the little hollow behind the withers or at the base of the neck just above the shoulder point. The facial expressions and movements they make when you hit that sweet spot can be very entertaining. You can almost hear them saying, "Ooooooh. Right there." This is a wonderful way to start to appreciate the horse as an individual with a personality all his own.

Grooming

Now that you are starting to be comfortable touching and being close to the horse, the next step is hand grooming, in which you learn how to position yourself as you move around the horse to groom him without worrying about the various tools just yet. Sometimes a horse will have a tender or ticklish spot and might react with a defensive reflex. If you make a habit of standing in the right place and paying attention to your horse's reactions, you will greatly reduce the chance of injury. In my 70-plus years of working with all kinds of horses, I have never been injured by one I was working close to.

You start almost all activities from the horse's left side because he is accustomed to this and therefore less likely to be startled. The safe area is beside or a little behind the horse's front leg. From there it is difficult for the horse to catch you unawares with a nip or a kick if you accidentally hit a sensitive place. Make a point of always moving back to the safe area after finishing whatever task has taken you out of it. If you are consistent in this, eventually you will condition yourself so that a little alarm will go off in your head if you are out of the area without a reason. As an instructor, my alarm goes off if I see anyone doing it.

Hand Grooming

Hand grooming will teach you what moves are comfortable for the horse while still keeping you safe and comfortable. The general rule is to face either the horse's head or his tail, rather than his side, with the hand nearest the horse resting on him while you groom with the hand farther away. You might find working with your left hand a little clumsy at first, but much of riding requires you to be somewhat ambidextrous, so the more practice you get, the better.

Work from the safe area down his front leg, forward toward his head, back toward his tail, and down his hind leg. Then move to his other side and repeat. For hand grooming, you always work with the grain of his hair. Working against the grain is the source of the saying "He just rubs me the wrong way."

Instructions for Hand Grooming

Here are the steps to hand grooming. Figure 3.5 will help you find your way around.

1. Right hand is on top of the horse's withers or shoulder, as you face the horse's head.
2. With your left hand, stroke down the horse's shoulder, across his chest, then down the outside and front of his front leg as far as his knee, bending your knees and moving your right hand down as necessary. *Keep both feet on the ground.* Do not get any part of your body in front of his leg except your hand, in case he picks it up unexpectedly.
3. Stand up again and stroke the base of the horse's neck, starting about one-third of the way up his neck and stroking back toward his shoulder. Cover the whole lower third of the neck from top to bottom, then move up to the next section toward the side of his head.
4. As you approach his head, you are getting more into his personal space, which might bother him. Make your moves slower and smaller, using an advance-and-retreat approach, and watch his responses. If he moves his head up or away, back off to his neck and finish there. Be especially careful about approaching his ears and eyes, and stroke only where he seems comfortable.

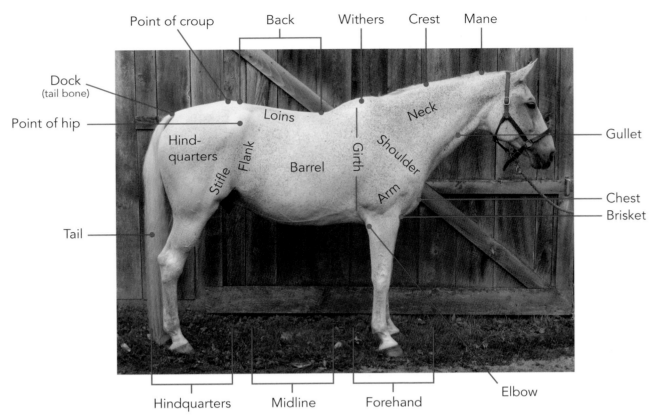

Figure 3.5 Parts of the horse.

5. Go back to the safe spot and turn around so that you are standing by his front leg facing his tail. Now your left hand will be on his withers or back and your right hand will be grooming.

6. Start stroking with your right hand on top of his back near the withers. Stroke back as far as you can easily reach, then gradually move down his barrel. Just go as far as where his barrel turns to go underneath, because some horses are very sensitive farther under. Also stroke the back of his front leg as far down as the knee

7. Now move farther back, and note the area between his barrel and his hindquarters where the hair grows the opposite way. This is called the flank, and it can be sensitive—on you it's a very ticklish place. Stroke gently but firmly with the grain of the hair, and stop if he fidgets.

8. Finish with the hindquarters, standing by the flank and working back around the corner to his buttock and down the back and side of his hind leg to the hock. Don't try to do the front of his hind leg just yet, but return to the safe spot.

9. Move to the other side of the horse (see Walking Around the Horse's Head) and repeat. The positions will be facing front, left hand on withers, right hand grooms shoulder, front leg, chest, neck, and head; return to safe spot; facing the rear, right hand on withers, left hand grooms back, side of barrel, back of front leg, flank, hindquarters, side and back of hind leg, return to safe spot.

Walking Around the Horse's Head

Usually when you want to go from one side of the horse to the other, you walk around his head. This is not so much because of the possible danger of walking around behind him—which you will also learn how to do safely—but because most of the time you are holding on to him by something attached to his head that you don't want to let go. When he is tied, your principal concern when walking around his head is not to accidentally pull on his rope, or if he moves, not to get stepped on or struck by a front foot. Again, keep in mind that that sort of thing is virtually accidental and usually the result of the person's own carelessness.

To walk around your horse that is cross-tied, you must lift up the ties and walk underneath them. You just have to be very careful not to lift them in such a way that they pull on the horse, which could cause him to pull back. Pull only on the end that is fastened to the wall and as lightly as possible.

If by chance your horse is tied by only one rope, it is best not to try to go around his head until you are more experienced. If he gets frightened and pulls back you may be trapped. Also, sometimes a horse is tied in such a way that he can put his head down so that the rope is lying on the ground. Never, ever, try to step *over* a rope that is attached to the horse! He will instinctively throw up his head, catching and tripping you and scaring him badly, in the course of which you could easily get stepped on. This is a perfect example of accidents being caused by carelessness on the part of the rider, not malice on the part of the horse. If there is no reason that he might kick (such as another horse nearby), it's usually safer to go around his hindquarters, but you should wait for guidance by the instructor if you aren't sure.

Walking Around the Horse's Hindquarters

If the horse is relaxed and calm, it is perfectly safe to walk around his hindquarters as long as you do so correctly. However, you need to consider some things in order to avoid accidents.

The chances of your meeting up with a horse that kicks at people are pretty small and extremely unlikely if you are a beginner. However, many people worry about it, so it's good to talk about it ahead of time.

A horse's kicking is nearly always the result of his feeling threatened and at the same time trapped so that he can't get away. Horses have a fairly large blind spot directly behind them (see figure 3.1), so they might be frightened by something because they can't see it clearly. *Kicking at humans on purpose is rare in horses who have been trained with kindness and understanding.* Horses are very aware of the difference between hurt inflicted intentionally and hurt that results from clumsiness and ignorance, and they are very forgiving of the latter.

The horse can kick either with one leg (cow kick) or with both. He can kick quite far forward with a cow kick, which is why the safe area is up by his front leg, where he can't reach without turning. It is also one reason to be aware of his discomfort if you are grooming in a sensitive area anywhere behind the safe area. Signs that he felt threatened might include pinning his ears back, showing the whites of his eyes, moving restlessly, swishing his tail rapidly (when there are no flies present), and raising a hind leg for no reason. If any of these behaviors are present, stop what you are doing and ask for help.

A very dangerous sign, if he feels really threatened and is preparing to kick with both hind legs, is the horse clamping his tail firmly against his hindquarters and tucking his hind legs up underneath him (figure 3.6). Since he might be very frightened, he won't necessarily show any of the signs of aggression described

Figure 3.6 Regardless of whether he shows other signs of aggression, such as pinning his ears back and showing the whites of his eyes, a horse that clamps his tail and tucks his hind legs is preparing to kick.

previously. The behaviors that might cause this reaction in an insecure horse include a person running up behind him, especially in his blind spot; coming up behind him with a strange-looking or strange-sounding object; and coming up behind him leading a horse that he is afraid of. On the positive side, he can't kick with both hind legs *unless* his tail is clamped. Until you have more experience, if you have to work behind a horse you aren't sure of, get help from your instructor.

So when would you walk around the horse's hindquarters? If you were grooming back there, you might step over to brush somewhere on the opposite side, or you might be back there and need another tool that is nearby but on the other side of the aisle. You might be grooming the horse in the stall, which is often the case in a stable where there are many horses and not enough aisle space. A horse in the stall will often stand with his head in the corner, perhaps eating. It is much easier to walk quietly around the horse's hindquarters than to try to push past him in front.

There are two keys to walking safely around his hindquarters, which are based on awareness of the effective distance a horse can kick and respect for his blind spot. As it happens, he cannot kick back effectively with both hind legs at things that are very close to him, and his effective long range is about his own length. Therefore, if you are working close to him and want to get to the other side easily without going around his head, you want to stay as close to him as possible. You also want to keep in contact with him so that as you walk through his blind spot he knows where you are.

The technique is as follows: Starting from the safe spot, face the rear and rest your near hand on his back. As you walk to the rear, keep your hand on his back and just let it slide gently along as you walk. When you actually walk around behind him, stay close so that your body rubs lightly against his (figure 3.7). Think of the way a cat rubs up against your legs. Continue all the way up to the safe spot on the other side, but remove your hand from his back once you "turn the corner" so that you don't stroke him the wrong way.

The first time or two you do this, it is best to let your instructor lead the way,

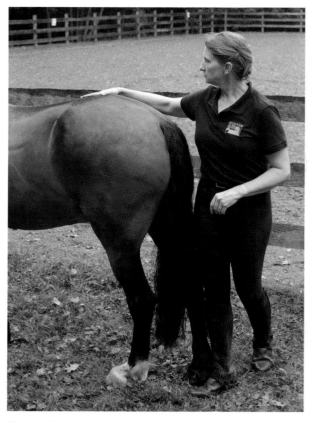

Figure 3.7 To pass safely behind the horse, stay close to him and maintain contact with him.

which will give you confidence. Again, if in the early stages of your experience you don't feel comfortable, ask to wait until a later time. If you need to walk around and behind a horse in the aisle, and you're not sure about the horse, stay close to the wall until you get well clear of him, about 8 to 10 feet (2.5-3 m), then walk quietly across to the other wall and your destination.

Excuse Me, Please

Some stables permit riders to leave their horses unattended in the aisle for long periods, forcing other riders to figure out a way to get by with their horses. I consider this an unsafe practice and a credit to the kind and forgiving attitude of most horses that very few accidents result. Leading a horse under the crossties to which another horse is fastened is extremely dangerous.

Some people don't understand about the horse's kicking range, but know they are supposed to keep a hand on him so he knows where they are. So they put one hand on him, and then walk an arm's length away, which is exactly the *worst* place to walk, since this distance puts them close enough to be in his blind spot, but not close enough to be safe from a dangerous kick.

Grooming With Tools

Once you start to feel comfortable around the horse on the ground, which is to say after one or two more lessons, the next step is learning how to use the grooming tools to improve his appearance and health. Horses should be groomed on a regular basis for several reasons, including the following:

- To keep them clean and avoid injuries such as chafing
- To look for injuries
- To massage muscles and enhance circulation
- To develop understanding and improve the relationship

Horses have fairly thick fur that holds dirt, which they love to roll in. They also sweat all over when working in hot weather. If not washed off, the sweat becomes crusty as it dries. Tack rubbing against dirty or sweaty hide increases the likelihood of chafing and sores. Regular grooming keeps the exterior coat clean and reduces the amount of dirt in the undercoat, so the horse is less likely to develop sores.

Horses' bodies have a lot of surface area and many little hidden crevices. Quite severe wounds can pass unnoticed and become seriously infected. Only with regular careful grooming can you avoid problems that might result in the horse's being laid up or even suffering long-term damage.

A horse, like any athlete, is subject to stiffness and soreness. Thorough, knowledgeable grooming, especially before and after heavy work, during cold weather, or if the horse is unable to exercise, will help maintain his circulation and muscle health.

Grooming is something the horse should enjoy, a concept that is frequently overlooked by professional grooms. Highly bred horses of the type often used for competition are especially likely to be sensitive both physically and emotionally, yet one often sees them responding with tension and anger to unnecessarily rough grooming. I cannot help but think that this must affect their performance adversely.

Even if you don't compete, and especially if you are a novice, spending time with your horse and grooming him in a way that shows your caring and consideration for his feelings and needs are never a waste of time. Unless absolutely necessary, having somebody else attend to the grooming is a loss of an important relationship-building tool.

There are many grooming tools and special techniques related to various disciplines. However, to start with, for grooming the horse's body you need to know about only two tools and their use. These are the brush and the curry comb. Later on when you start asking the horse to move around on the ground, you will learn to clean his feet (see chapter 8), which is an important part of grooming.

Brushing the Horse

You will begin by using just the brush, which is the one indispensable tool. Other tools do certain things better, but a brush can be used for everything—body, mane, tail, even the feet if necessary. The two basic brushes are the dandy brush, also just called a brush, and the body brush (figure 3.8). The dandy brush is the most common and the easiest for most people to use. The long oval shape is comfortable for most hands. The bristles range from very stiff to very soft, but for most uses a medium grade is the best. If you apply it with care, you can use it every place on the horse's body. It is nearly always used with the hair, although it can be used to gently scrub a sticky spot.

Because the bristles are long and tightly packed, if you put the dandy brush firmly straight down onto the horse's body, he most likely will find it uncomfortable. Try it on your own bare arm and you'll see what I mean. Instead, *start each stroke by putting the brush down at an angle, sweeping it in a long, rolling stroke* as firmly as the horse finds comfortable and ending in a flick that lifts the dust off and away.

The body brush is a wide, oval shape with a strap for your hand. It has shorter bristles, often with two degrees of stiffness, one for picking up the dust and the other for sweeping it away. It is applied in more of a flat stroke but should still be tilted slightly at the beginning. Because it is usually larger than a dandy brush, it covers more area at one stroke. However, because of its size, it can be clumsy for a woman or child. It does come in a smaller size for smaller hands.

If you are about to touch a horse's body with any object for the first time, let him inspect it first. Approach him the same way you did when you were being introduced: Hold the brush by your side, then quietly bring it up and hold it where he can easily reach it with his nose, but don't shove it in his face.

After he has inspected the brush, rest the

Figure 3.8 Two commonly used and easy-to-handle grooming brushes are the dandy brush (top left, top right, and bottom left) and the body brush (bottom right).

hand that is holding it on his shoulder, then roll your hand over until the brush is resting on him. If he seems quiet about it, you can go ahead and start brushing him in the same sequence as your hand grooming: slowly and gently at first and then more firmly and briskly if he seems to like it.

Now that you're more comfortable around the horse, you can brush the front of his hind leg, which you do by standing beside it facing his head. This is a slightly unsafe position if he should kick at a fly, so you should be sure that he is relaxed and quiet. While you're standing on his left side, your right hand will be on his rump and you will use your left hand to brush the front of his hind leg. To brush the inside of the opposite leg, both front and hind, reach around the near leg.

This careful approach will probably be overkill with the sort of horse you will meet as a beginner, but think of it as on a par with learning to say *please* and *thank you* and *excuse me*. You can never go wrong using those phrases, but you can sometimes get in trouble if you don't!

Using the Curry Comb

The curry comb is a fairly small, flat oval or round tool with little teeth or nubs on the bottom and a strap or handle across the top to slip your hand through. It lifts the dirt out of the horse's undercoat and brings the dirt to the surface where it can be swept away with the brush (figure 3.9). Curry combs come in rubber or rubberlike material and in metal. For all practical purposes, metal curry combs should *never* be used anywhere on the horse's body. They are far too severe and can easily scratch or otherwise make the horse sore or at least uncomfortable. They are really only useful for cleaning brushes.

The rubber curry comb is used in a circular scrubbing motion across and against the hair, very much like scrubbing a table or a pot. The curry comb is used only on soft tissue; that

Figure 3.9 The rubber curry comb is used for deep cleaning soft tissue areas. The combs at the bottom are for sensitive horses.

is, it should not be used to scrub hard, bony places, where it could actually remove the hair if the spot is very dirty or sticky. As a general rule, never use the curry comb on the horse's head, below his knee in front, or below the upper leg behind.

Since you use it more vigorously, it is especially important that, until you know how that particular horse responds, you start slowly and gently on a safe place such as the front of his shoulder. As you work around him, over time you will find areas where he is more or less sensitive. Usually his barrel and hindquarters are the least sensitive. Unless the horse is very clean, currying brings a lot of dust to the surface, leaving the horse looking very dirty. But when you follow up with the brush, he comes up clean and shiny. Generally you curry one section, brush it clean, and move on to the next. Some people like to keep the tool they aren't using in the other hand, but I find this clumsy. I prefer to keep my free hand on the horse, as I do for hand grooming, for communication and for maintaining my balance.

When you are grooming, you might miss certain places because you can't see them easily. One is his brisket, the area between his front legs. Another is along his midline, under his stomach in the very center. And another little area is the backs of his pasterns, just above his hooves. It's a good idea to run your hand over these areas before and after grooming to see whether they feel clean, and in the case of his midline, to see how he reacts.

Also notice that he has no hair in the area up high between his hind legs and under his tail. These areas don't generally get very dirty, but if they do, they need to be cleaned with a damp sponge and under supervision the first time because they can be sensitive.

Because you are just starting out, you should observe and learn while someone more experienced than you does any further preparation for riding.

4

Overcoming Your Natural Fear of Falling

Now that you're at least somewhat comfortable with the horse on the ground, you're ready to sit on him. All your early lessons from this point on will be bareback or on a bareback pad. Although starting in the saddle might look easier and safer, starting on a bareback pad with a ground person controlling the horse is the easiest way for your body to get comfortable and learn to relax while on the horse at the walk. Once you can do that, moving to the saddle and stirrups, which are used partly because they help your lateral balance, will be easy.

In the lesson that follows, you will learn how to get on and off the horse and how to sit on him comfortably while standing still and moving a few steps with someone holding him. The horse will not need to wear a bridle because you will not try to control him in any way, so he can continue to wear his halter and lead rope. Other than that, he will not need anything because learning to get on and off is easiest with nothing in the way. He will not be moving more than a couple steps, and you will have constant help, so the less equipment you have to think about, the better. Because he is not wearing any pads and you will be lying across him at one point, remove any bulky items you are wearing such as a large belt buckle or large buttons or slide them around to your left side or back.

Later you will learn to mount and dismount from a horse wearing a bareback pad and eventually to dismount safely from a moving, saddled horse.

A Learning Experience

Some years ago, before I understood a lot about fear and tension, I had a young student who had a great fear of riding. Her mother owned horses, so the student was used to having them around but was afraid of riding, and I didn't help. She finally stopped taking lessons from me altogether. Some time later her mother told me that she had started taking vaulting lessons, which involve a lot of jumping on and off a moving horse that wears a special apparatus, making it easy to hold on with the hands. As a result of these lessons, she gained a great deal of confidence and was enjoying riding again. Her experience contributed to my understanding of this problem.

We have said that riding is natural and easy for your body. However, as with many things, if you're nervous and tense you will find yourself unable to do things that should be easy. We mentioned in chapter 2 that getting ready to actually sit on the horse brings up fear, separate from fear of the horse himself, that you should deal with right at the start to avoid forming bad habits. Sitting up on a horse brings on a sort of claustrophobic reaction that causes your body to clutch the horse with your legs and hands and hang on for dear life. As long as the horse stands still, you're all right. But as soon as he moves, the tension prevents you from following his movements, so you feel even more insecure and thus tend to clutch even harder. Horses who are used to having strangers and beginners on their backs can deal with this calmly, but many other horses cannot. This can cause an accident as the frightened horse reacts—an accident that is completely preventable by taking time in the beginning to solve the problem.

The solution is quite simple and obvious. Because the body is mostly worried about not being able to get down safely, that should be the very first thing you teach your body how to do. In essence, you teach your body that there is an open door to safety.

Of course, in order to get off, you must first get on. But rather than do so all at once, you'll mount in a series of very small steps. This will also initiate the process of learning how to get down.

Mounting in Baby Steps

There are several ways to mount without a saddle depending on the size of the horse and rider and the equipment available. The basic challenge is getting your body high enough so that you can bring your leg easily across the horse's back.

The first method, if there is no mounting block or if the horse is too tall for you to use the available block alone, involves the instructor assisting you by giving you a 'leg on' or 'leg up.' The second and simplest method is with a high mounting block, if one is available. This is a platform with steps to bring you up to a level where you can swing your leg over with the help of your hands and perhaps a little hop. The third method, if you are taller or more athletic and the horse is not too tall, is to mount from a smaller mounting block using the 'belly-over' technique. Either mounting block can also be used along with the leg-on method. The method you will use depends on the equipment available and the relative sizes of the instructor, you, and the horse.

The most important things during both mounting and dismounting are to maintain your balance and grounding and *to stay centered over the horse* as long as possible throughout the process.

No matter which method you learn, you will learn it one step at a time, repeating the previous steps so that they start to become established in your muscle memory. Besides returning to previous steps, you may repeat each step several times until you feel comfortable.

Using this baby-step method will also force you to learn to stay centered. The instructor or an assistant will hold the horse in position for you. The horse might take a step or two, but not more, if you accidentally unbalance him.

Holding the Mane

Unlike you and me, the horse does not find it painful to have his mane pulled on. Therefore, using it as a handle to help you with mounting and dismounting, as well as with your balance when riding, is entirely acceptable and much better than losing your balance and pulling on the reins instead.

Holding the mane sounds as though it's a no-brainer, but there are some important tricks for efficiency and safety, especially when dismounting. First is the way you place your hands: Your thumbs *must* point upward toward the mane rather than try to grasp the horse's neck. If they are pointing sideways or down, it is all too easy to sprain them as your hands rotate during the dismount. Second is the placement of your hands, which depends on your size and the horse's size. Your right hand will be somewhere near the top of the withers and your left hand farther up the horse's neck. The goal is to find a position that you can keep throughout, since it is essential not to let go. The horse doesn't have any handles anywhere else, and saddles can turn if pulled hard enough. During the mount when you are bellying over is the most likely time for you to let go, leaving you with no support if the horse should move suddenly.

When learning to mount, use the seven steps detailed in chapter 2 at the beginning of all of the mounting methods and at any time during the process if you feel at all tense. *After each step* in the mounting process, *return to the ground*, make sure you are grounded, then go to the next step. In this way your body learns how to get off as well as on in small steps.

Mounting With a Leg On

If the person giving the leg on is experienced, this is a very effective way of mounting and is often used when a mounting block is not available. If you have never had a leg on, it's helpful—and easier on the horse—if you can practice the jump upward on a fence first. (Don't try to sit on the fence.) A three-rail post-and-rail fence is about the right height. This is also helpful for mounting-block belly-over mounting as well. You can modify the following instructions when practicing on a fence.

Instructions for Mounting With a Leg On

1. Stand with your hands on either side of the horse's withers if you are ready to mount (figure 4.1*a*) or with your hands on either side of a fence post, where the fence is strongest, if practicing.

2. Keeping your thigh vertical, your back straight, and your eyes soft and level, bend your left knee so that your calf is horizontal (figure 4.1*b*). The person who is lifting you will put her left hand under your knee and her right hand under your ankle.

3. Bend your right knee slightly. The lifter will also bend her knees slightly. She will count to three.

4. On three, jump straight upward, keeping your hip straight and your knee bent (figure 4.1*c*). *Do not try to get your body or your leg over the horse.* Try to jump up *above* the level of the horse's withers (or the fence), then center yourself over your hands. If you collapse your hips or try to scramble on, the lifter should let you back down again. The lifter must be careful to lift straight up, not pull your leg out away from the horse.

5. When you are centered over the horse, supported by the lifter as well as your own arms, bend your right knee, turn to face the horse's head, and bring your right leg over, being careful not to kick the horse (figure 4.1*d*). Make sure you are fully facing forward before you bring your leg down, and sit gently on his back.

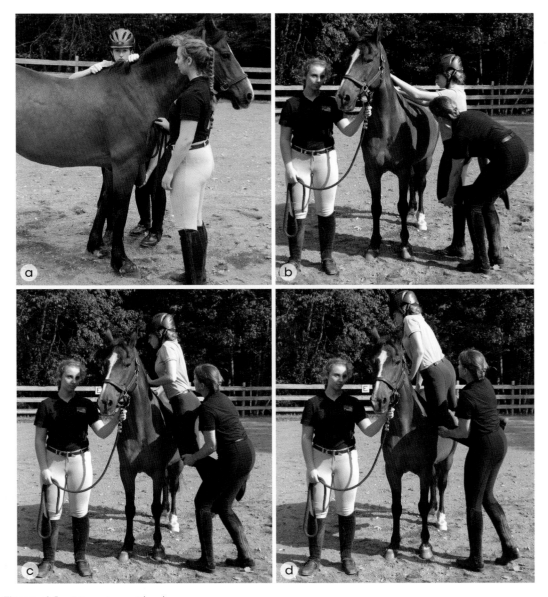

Figure 4.1 Mounting with a leg on.

> The secrets to getting a leg on are to keep your hips locked so that you don't collapse as you are being lifted and not to swing your right leg over until you are centered over the horse's back.

You can do the leg-up from the ground or from a mounting block. If the block is low, the lifter can stand on the ground beside it and still lift high enough. If the block is high, it needs to be large enough so that both you and the lifter can stand on it, unless the lifter is tall. Obviously you must take care not to slip off the block.

If the horse is very tall, you can give the rider a leg up high enough to reach a belly-over position. She can then continue the mount as if mounting from a low block.

Giving a Leg On

Giving a leg on (being the lifter) does not require as much strength as coordination and timing. If you're experienced at lifting, you can give a leg on to someone much larger and heavier than you. The danger with being a strong but inexperienced lifter is that you can throw the rider right over the horse! The other and very serious danger can occur if no one is holding the horse during the mount. Should the horse move forward, the rider can easily land behind the saddle or pad, on the horse's loins. This is a very sensitive area, and landing on it suddenly causes many horses to run and buck. There is no safe way to dismount from this situation, therefore, if there is no helper, the lifter should put her left hand through the rein so she has some control if the horse moves.

Mounting From a Low Block, No Leg On

After each of the following steps, return to the position in step 2.

Instructions for Mounting From a Low Block

1. Step on and off the block.
2. Stand on the block close to the horse, facing his withers.
3. Place your hands thumbs up on either side of the horse's withers.
4. Stroke the horse from his lower neck to his croup on both sides. Take your time.
5. Using your hands on the withers for support and keeping your body erect and eyes level, bend your knees a little, then jump *straight* up as high as you can (figure 4.2a). *Do not try to put any part of your body over the horse at this point.* Come straight down, being careful to land back on the block. Your instructor might have to steady you.
6. Grasp the mane with both hands thumps up.
7. Place your right forearm on the other side of the horse's withers. Find a comfortable solid support with your arm.
8. Starting with your hands holding the mane, jump up, bringing your forearm over and using it to help you reach a position where you are lying on your belly, *centered over the horse* (belly-over position, figure 4.2b). *Do not try to put your right leg over the horse's back when you're first learning.* Trying to swing your leg over when you aren't centered and balanced triggers a sense of fear: "I'm going to fall! I have to scramble up on top where it's safe!" Let go of the mane and let your arms and head dangle and rest in this position for a minute. Feel how secure it is when you are centered over the horse.

   8.A (Note: This exercise should be skipped the first time you mount, and may wait until the next lesson if you are feeling insecure.) Wiggle around as necessary to be sure you are as centered as you can be. The instructor will now ask the horse to move a few steps so that you can feel the movement while you are centered but unable to grip with your legs. Because you are lying over the horse's back rather than sitting up, you feel closer to the ground, and your whole body is involved in the centering. It's another way to boost your body's confidence. Finish by shaking out your feet and wiggling your toes to relax them, then allow yourself to slide gently to the ground.

9. From the first belly-over position in step 8, holding the mane with your forearm over the withers, turn to face more forward, bring your knee up, and hook it over the horse's back (figure 4.2c).
10. Continue to turn forward. Finally, when you are lying along the horse's midline, bring your right foot down on the horse's right side and sit up.

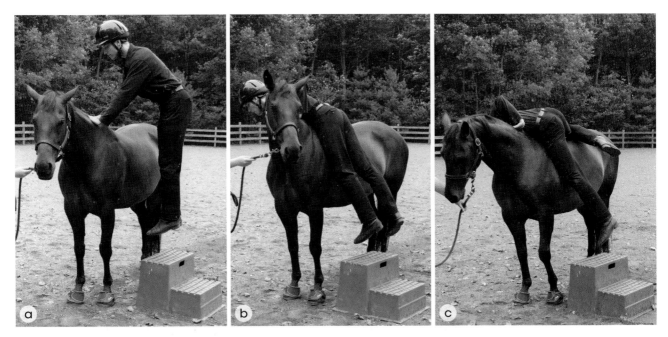

Figure 4.2 Mounting from the low block.

Even if you will be using a high block, you should go through steps 1 to 8 of the low-block method first, including the exercise in 8A, and using a leg on if necessary. This is because step 8 is an integral part of the dismount as well.

Mounting From a High Block

For the high-block method, when you stand on the block beside the horse, your crotch should not be more than a few inches lower than his withers.

Instructions for Mounting From a High Block

1. Step up onto the block, then step down. If you feel at all uncomfortable standing in mounting position on the high block, repeat steps 1 to 3 until you feel secure. Thereafter, return to step 4 after each succeeding step. Stand on the block close to the horse, facing his withers.

2. Place your hands on either side of the withers. Stay balanced and look out, not down, with soft eyes (figure 4.3a).

3. Stroke the horse's shoulders, back, and croup. Stroke both sides as far down as you can comfortably reach. Stroke across his croup with your hand as though you were sliding your leg across him. Take time with this stroking exercise until you both feel comfortable.

4. Grasp the mane firmly with both hands thumbs up.

5. Using your hands on the withers to help you, keeping your head up, and holding your body as erect as possible, hop up high enough to bring your crotch just above the horse's back. Turn to face somewhat forward as you jump up. *Do not try to get on.*

6. Holding the mane, lift your right leg, bend your knee, and raise your foot. Keep your left leg straight and grounded.

7. Holding the mane, turn to face almost forward. Lift your right knee and foot and bring them over the horse's back if you can, touching it lightly. Bring them back and down.

8. Start from the position in step 6, then jump up as in step 5. Turn as you jump, bring your leg over the horse's back to his other side, and use your hands to help you land softly (figure 4.3b). Sit up.

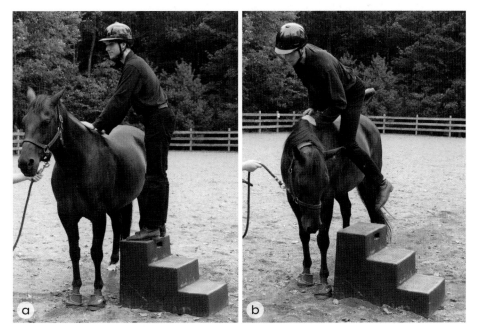

Figure 4.3   Mounting from a high block.

And there you are, sitting on a horse at last! But not for long, because, don't forget, you're supposed to be learning how to get off. The next thing that should happen, while you breathe and keep your eyes soft and keep hold of the mane, is that someone should move the mounting block if it is small and easy to move. If the block can't be moved, then, with someone steadying you with a hand on your lower thigh and someone holding the horse, the horse can be moved instead—only a step or two, just enough to get clear of the block.

Dismounting Safely

While mounting, either bareback or into the saddle, is fairly complicated, dismounting is much easier. There are two important things to remember. One is to have a firm, correct grip with both hands on the mane, or the mane and saddle, and hold on as long as you can. This is because *if you're holding on with your hands, you cannot go off headfirst*, which is the most dangerous way to fall. The second thing is to stay centered and balanced either over the horse or over your feet throughout the dismount. The reason for that is if you lose your centering, you will become tense, which makes it harder to dismount and more likely that it will hurt if you should slip and fall.

Safe at Any Speed

I learned my dismounts as a child playing games with my siblings on our ponies. We dismounted at all speeds with the reckless abandon typical of our age. My body learned the technique so well that at an advanced age I can still dismount quickly and safely from a moving horse. If I take a fall in the process, I rarely even get a bruise because my body relaxes completely. I have taught the dismounting skill to many adults over the years, and their bodies also pick it up surprisingly quickly.

Quick Dismounts

Quick dismounts, or emergency dismounts, will be useful throughout your riding career. If a situation starts to feel unsafe and you can dismount quickly and without harm before you lose control of either yourself or the horse, you will be in a much more secure position on the ground. Unfortunately, some people don't understand this and think that if you dismount, you are some sort of loser. Ignore them if they happen to be riding with you. You might someday find them in a hospital after their efforts to "master" an upset horse result in a serious fall.

Preparing for the Dismount

You are now sitting up on the horse. Grow, breathe, and soften your eyes. Next, with the instructor holding your leg to keep you steady, take your hands off the mane and put them back on several times. You can look down the first time or two, but then try to do it with your head and eyes level. Be sure you get a good, firm grip each time with your hands in proper position.

The next step is to loosen up your right leg, which might be somewhat tense and gripping.

Instructions for Preparing for the Dismount

1. Hold your leg out a little away from the horse and shake it out, starting with your foot and going as far as your knee, then let it dangle down loosely.
2. Without lifting your knee, swing your foot gently forward as far as you can. (If you swing it hard, you might scare the horse.) Then let it swing back and hang down again.
3. Swing your leg back, but try to keep your foot from hitting the horse (who is wider behind) because he might take it as a signal to move.
4. Repeat the leg swings several times, being sure to stay centered and *not allow your buttocks to slip off to the left.*

Dismounting

You are now ready for the dismount. Don't forget to take one step at a time and go back and repeat before moving to the next step.

Instructions for Dismounting

1. Take a firm grip of the mane with both hands and *don't let go* (figure 4.4a).
2. Swing your right foot forward.
3. Start swinging it back, bending your knee, and at the same time lean forward over your hands, keeping your eyes level.
4. Pivot your whole body to the right while *staying centered over the horse's back.* You will want to start to slide off but that will unbalance you. Your upper body should swing to the right while your bent right leg comes up over the horse's back (figure 4.4b).
5. The instructor may have to help you bring your right leg across the first time. Then let it fall down beside your left leg so that you are in a belly-over position.
6. Wiggle your toes to relax your feet and ankles. Use your hands to push yourself a little away from the horse and allow yourself to slide slowly to the ground, letting your knees and ankles bend a little as you touch the ground (figure 4.4c). Let go with your hands. If the horse is tall, the instructor should be ready to catch and steady you.

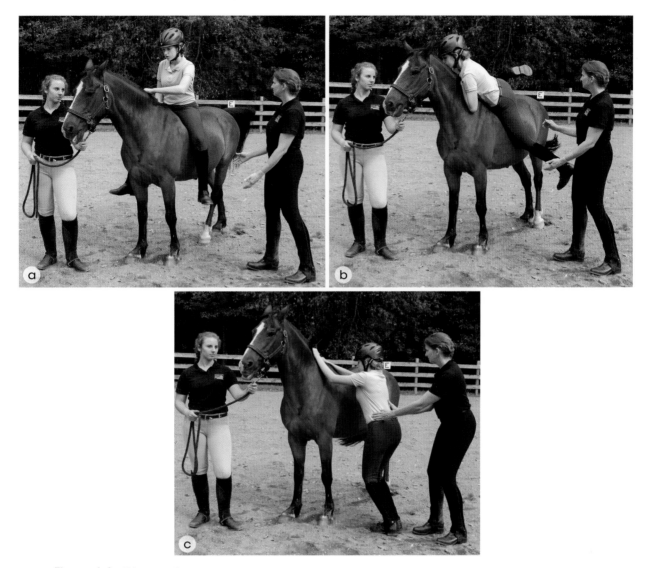

Figure 4.4 Dismounting.

Go through the entire mount–dismount procedure again, but this time go right from one step to the next, as long as you feel comfortable. At some point many instructors like to teach riders to dismount from either side in case a circumstance arises where the left-side dismount would be dangerous. But at this point you are mostly doing it for psychological reasons, and the left side is more comfortable for the horse.

Getting Comfortable on the Horse

Now that you have been on and off several times, you're going to get on once more, go through the seven steps, and see if you can finish in good style by finding a comfortable and correct position at the standstill.

> Hold the mane, or the grounding strap if there is one, with at least one hand at all times. This makes you feel much more secure and makes it easier for you to relax your lower body.

Instructions for Getting Comfortable on the Horse

1. Start by shaking out your lower legs. It's a little different when you're sitting on the horse. You can shake out both legs as far as the knee at the same time. During the shakeout, hold your feet a little out in front of you, where you can see them. This will help to relax the gripping muscles in the backs of your thighs.

2. Lift one knee up and away from the horse just a little, and swing your foot forward so it's hanging straight. If you feel uncomfortable, ask the instructor to steady you with her hand on your other knee. Shake your thigh as best you can, thinking about helping it to loosen up. Repeat with the other leg.

3. Shake out each arm one at a time, holding on with the other hand, starting with the left arm and finishing by growing on each side.

4. Breathe and soften your eyes, imagining that you are working any tensions out of your body with each breath.

5. With both hands, hold the mane or grounding strap, which should not be too short. Grow from the top of your head.

6. Keeping your back straight, sway backward a little with your center, letting your arms stretch as much as necessary. The instructor can offer you a handhold if necessary. Your back should be flat, not arched at the waist or rounded in the shoulders. Lift your knees up slightly until you can feel your tailbone against the horse's spine. Swing your feet forward at the same time. *Your weight should be on your seat bones, not your tailbone, and there should be no pressure under your crotch bone at all.* Unless the horse is very bony, this position should not be at all uncomfortable (figure 4.5).

Figure 4.5   Getting comfortable on the horse's back.

If you feel very comfortable and secure on the horse, you can ask the instructor to lead you for a few steps on the straight line, just to see how it feels.

Do one more dismount, maybe even a little faster than the one before, and you're done. Congratulations on a good job!

Horse With a Prominent Spine

Most horses are comfortable to sit on bareback for a short time, but the occasional horse, either from age or from lack of muscle, has a very prominent spine in the area where you sit, that is, the low point of his spine just behind the withers. If this is the case, you should wait to work on position until the horse is wearing sufficient padding to make him comfortable to sit on.

5

Taking Your First Real Ride

After two ground sessions—one at the previous lesson and another today—plus the dismounting work, your body should be fairly comfortable with the idea of actually riding a horse. However, especially if you are recovering from a bad experience, it's possible that you might feel more tension than you would like. If that happens, don't be afraid to say so. It takes time to build trust, so if you need more, your instructor can adapt her approach to suit you. It might help to know that when the United States had a cavalry, each recruit, no matter what his previous experience, spent a full two weeks on ground work with his horse before he ever got to ride.

But in any case, the day will come when you are ready. Needless to say, you won't be galloping, jumping, or bronc riding right away, but if you took up tennis you wouldn't be playing at Wimbledon right away, either. As in any sport, there are many basic skills you have to work on if you are going to become competent.

> The goal of these early lessons is to help you to feel safe and secure on the horse so that your body doesn't tense up. This will also help you to learn your skills as quickly and easily as possible while keeping the horse comfortable and happy.

You must always have the instructor or an experienced handler on the ground controlling the horse until you have developed a centered, grounded position and the confidence that must accompany it. Our assumption in this book is that this is the case. The point in your learning at which you can dispense with the leader will be made very clear. If you are asked to control the horse before you're ready, it will be very difficult for you to learn to use your riding aids correctly, which will be painful for the horse and frustrating for you.

Using the Bareback Pad to Achieve a Secure Seat

You will be starting out, not in a saddle, but on a bareback pad, and you should understand why. Why not start out in a saddle? Wouldn't that be easier? Isn't that the way most people ride? Yes, it is the way most people ride, and it is easier for both horse and rider when riding for long periods or doing fast work. But what makes the saddle easier to ride in is primarily the stirrups. In fact, the saddle was invented as a device to hold stirrups.

For centuries people rode on pads, or bareback, without stirrups. Then someone figured out that you could throw a spear or shoot an arrow more effectively if you had something solid under your feet. They also figured out that to keep the stirrups in place, they needed a framework that fit over the horse's back in such a way that the saddle couldn't slip off to one side if they stood on one stirrup. The saddle has an interior metal and wood device— called the 'tree'—which serves this function.

For reasons we'll talk about later in the book, the stirrups themselves hang loose and swing from the saddle, and beginners have problems keeping their feet in them. The way to keep your feet in the stirrups is neither difficult nor complicated. If your legs hang down without tension, their weight resting on the stirrups is enough to keep your feet in them without any other effort. However, as we learned in the last chapter, your legs don't want to hang down relaxed when you first start, and we have to spend some time overcoming that reflex before we try to use the stirrups. How long this will take varies tremendously from rider to rider, but there is a great deal that you can learn easily and safely on the bareback pad while your body is learning to be relaxed and comfortable on the horse.

Using the Grounding Strap

After your ground work, once the horse has been groomed, the next step will be to tack him up, which means to get him dressed for riding. The instructor or a qualified helper should do this until you have more experience. What you can do is watch carefully as the instructor dresses the horse and ask a few questions.

Ask if you can help with the tacking by passing the instructor various items so that you start to learn their names and the order in which they are put on the horse. From now on, in addition to his halter or bridle, he will be wearing a pad and a grounding strap, which will help you to find a more secure seat. The grounding strap is a *very* important tool, especially when you are starting out.

> Using the grounding strap correctly means the difference between developing a centered, grounded, and thus confident seat in the shortest possible time and perhaps not developing it at all.

When your body feels insecure, having something secure you can hold on to with your hands helps you develop good balance and confidence. Remember learning to ride a bicycle? You really needed those handlebars at first! Using the grounding strap also helps to correct the tendency to crouch over the horse's neck, which we discuss at little later. Most of the time, you will have a very light, lifting contact with the strap—just enough to help you ground. Pulling hard makes you tense, which is the last thing you want. Think of using someone's arm or hand for security if you are walking across an icy patch. Grounding is really nothing more than allowing gravity to pull you down, which is achieved through relaxation.

The way you hold the grounding strap and establish a connection between it and your body is critical. Hold the grounding strap with the first two fingers of each hand, which will leave your remaining fingers free for such things as the reins and the stick. The backs of your hands should be approximately parallel to the slope of the horse's shoulders. As you look down on your hands, your thumbs should point toward the opposite sides of the horse's muzzle. Your hands will be about 6 inches (15 cm) apart, although that varies with the size of both horse and rider.

Using your hands for grounding is directly related to your hand and wrist position. If you cock your hand upward from the wrist, with your thumbs pointing up, which seems natural to many people, the pull will go up the top of your forearm then to the back of your upper arm and down your front, tipping you forward onto your crotch and into an insecure and ungrounded position (figure 5.1a). However, if you hold the grounding strap so that your thumbs are pointing downward and your hand and wrist juncture is flat, the pull will go the other way: up the underside of your forearm, up the front of your upper arm, down your back, and into your seat bones where it belongs (figure 5.1b). *Only if you hold your hands this way will they help you to ground.*

Figure 5.1 *(a)* Incorrect, *cocked* hand and wrist position and *(b)* correct, secure hand and wrist position. When the wrists are cocked, the rider will lean forward, but when the wrists are flat, the rider can sit solidly on her seat bones.

Finding the Proper Hand and Wrist Position

The best way to find and feel this hand and wrist position at any time is as follows.

1. Grow and shake out your arms, beginning at the fingers, so that they hang relaxed and naturally from your shoulders (figure 5.2*a*). Then think about your right arm being completely dead weight, with no resistance.

2. With your left arm, reach over and pick up your right arm just above the wrist. Lift it up until your right hand is in front of you and a little off to the right. Your hand should hang down from your wrist, your wrist should be slightly lower than your elbow, and your elbow should be a little in front of your rib cage (figure 5.2*b*). Try to keep your right arm completely relaxed. Let go with your left hand, keeping your right elbow bent, but let your hand and wrist continue to hang down naturally.

3. Curl your fingers slightly, but don't make a tight fist (figure 5.2*c*). The classic description is as though you were holding

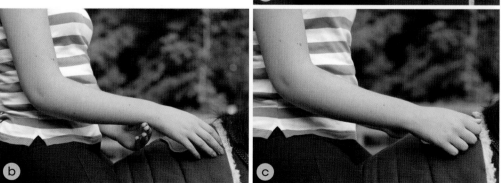

Figure 5.2 Finding the proper hand and wrist position.

a little bird. You don't want it to get away, but if you hold it too tightly, it will die of fright. Your thumb will rest on top of your index finger, pointing slightly downward.

4. Finally, shake out your left arm once more and bring your forearm and hand up so that it matches your right hand. Think to lift your wrist, and let your hand follow it. Your hands will be somewhat apart, depending on your conformation.

Take hold of the grounding strap in your first two fingers, one hand at a time, so you can use the other as a reminder of the correct position. The higher you hold your hands, and your wrists, the closer together they will be. The height will depend on a number of factors, such as your upper-body position, the height of the saddle when you start using one, and, when you start holding the reins, the position of the horse's head. For now, wherever you are comfortable holding the grounding strap will determine the level at which you hold your hands.

Using the grounding strap properly will also start teaching your body how to use the reins in a way that helps both you and the horse to ground, a skill that will prove essential as you become more advanced.

Mounting: Getting It Right From the Start

Begin by mounting step by step as outlined in chapter 4, going back a step or two if you get confused or you or the horse feel tense. Take your time during this learning period. If you get it right, it will be in your muscle memory correctly for good; but if you get it wrong, you'll have to undo your mistakes and start over, which takes much longer. Do one dismount, using assistance as you need it and remembering the importance of staying centered. Then remount, moving from one step to the next without hurrying but without delaying unless you need to correct something.

When you are mounted, take hold of the grounding strap with both hands. Go through the first four of the seven steps outlined in chapter 2 (growing, shaking out, breathing, using soft eyes). When you get to step 5, longitudinal centering, take both hands off the grounding strap and hold them out in front of you. Be sure the horse is being held, and if you start to feel insecure, hold the strap for a moment and ask the instructor to steady you with a hand on your lower thigh. Continue the exercise when you feel secure again.

Keeping your head level, begin to sway your torso forward and back, *using only your hip joint*— don't let your shoulders round as you sway forward or your lower back arch as you sway back. If you have trouble with this, and most people do, first arch your back so that it is locked in that position, then sway back and forth until you can feel that you are moving only from your hip joints. Now allow your back to return to normal position, cross your arms behind your back so that you can feel if it moves incorrectly, and see if you can move just from your hip joints. Sway with them in that position until you can rock back and forth without your back changing. This is a skill you will need quite a lot later on for other purposes, so try to get it right from the start.

The goal is not to see how far you can sway but *how quickly you can feel the tension that tells you you're out of balance.* When you sway forward too far, your inner thighs will start to grip; when you sway back too far, the tension will appear in your lower back and buttocks. As soon as you feel the tension, stop and sway the other way. Finish by swaying back and feeling the tension, then very slowly sway forward until you feel the tension in the lower back disappear. Drop your arms. You should now be sitting with your center over your base (seat bones) and your body vertical but not stiff.

Think about your seat bones for a moment. Almost everyone sits on the seat bone on the left side but a little back on the cheek on the right, which makes a little twist in the body. It doesn't sound very important, but it will create problems later. To correct it, place your right hand on the top front of your right hip bone, just below your waist, and then push your hip bone forward against your hand until you are sitting squarely on both seat bones. Add this little move to step 5 of the seven steps when you're mounted.

Take your grounding strap, and without losing your centering, check that you still feel grounded. Use your breathing and soft eyes if necessary. The instructor will give you a final check and you're ready to start your first real ride.

Following the Movement

All through your riding career, you will hear people talking about a rider having a "good" seat or perhaps a "weak" seat. What they mean is that the way you *sit* on a horse—which starts with the way your seat connects to the horse's back—is basic to whether you ride badly or well. By looking at that facet of riding from the very start, you are starting the process of building a solid foundation.

At first the instructor should steady you with a hand on your lower thigh as the horse starts and as you make turns, which in this lesson will be only to the left because left turns are easier. Once the horse is walking smoothly, think about what the movement of his back feels like under your seat bones. Some people feel it as up and down, some forward and back, and some side to side. It's a combination of all these, but whatever you feel is okay. Now the horse should be stopped for a moment. While he is standing still, slide your left hand palm up under your seat and feel your left seat bone, just so you are conscious of where it is, which is quite far under you. Take your hand out and put it back on the grounding strap. Imagine that your seat bone has a strip of Velcro on it, with the other half on the pad, so that the two are firmly stuck together.

Start walking again, and think about your seat bone being stuck to the pad as the horse's back moves underneath you. Then just *allow* his back to lift you up and gravity to bring you down again; that is, don't make any *muscular* effort to follow the movement. The pressure should be constant—the same all the time. Keep your eyes very soft and lift gently on the strap to help you stay grounded. Be sure your hands and wrists are as described earlier. You might also want to shake out your lower leg a little. When your lower leg is relaxed—called a loose leg— you can easily see your toes in front of your knees. Once you feel that you're following with your left seat bone, think about your right seat bone as well and feel how they move in rhythm but separately. The movement is like a bicycle being pedaled backward. You should feel even pressure between the two seat bones.

Don't make any sharp turns yet. As you go around a corner, notice how the pressure between the two sides changes, but don't try to correct it right now. Practice the following seat until it starts to feel easy and natural, which, since it is much like walking, doesn't usually take long.

Lateral Centering

When you are sitting on the horse correctly, he is directly underneath you—that is, his body is between you and the ground. *As long as you can keep the horse underneath you, you cannot fall.*

A very common kind of fall occurs if the horse makes a sudden turn and you don't. However, you can easily teach your body how to avoid this kind of fall by teaching it how to stay centered. You have a kind of built-in automatic recovery system; you just have to activate it. It's the same thing you learned when you learned to ride a bicycle. And it's important to learn because your centering affects the horse and thus your communication with him. The first step is to become conscious of how your body reacts to lateral thrust, that is, the kind of movement that pushes you sideways.

Reacting to a Left Turn

1. At the standstill, use the first five steps to check your position (growing, shaking out, breathing, using soft eyes, longitudinal centering). Sit evenly on both seat bones and lift up lightly on your grounding strap to keep you grounded. Try to keep your eyes up and soft throughout the exercise.

2. The instructor will turn your horse sharply to the left in a tight turn. She should watch you carefully and be ready to steady you if you lose your balance too much. Your goal is to try to feel which way the sudden movement throws you. So try not to resist the thrust, but let it move your body and just notice what's happening. The turn should not be more than one circle and probably less. Pay particular attention to the pressure on each seat bone. You can repeat the turn one or more times if you want to understand it more clearly.

3. What you should feel is that your body is thrown to the *outside* of the turn—in this case, to the right. The law of inertia says that a body will continue to travel in the same direction unless force is applied to change it. So as the horse turns, your body (that is, your torso, which is not directly connected with the horse) tries to keep going straight ahead. To put it another way, you started out over the horse's center, then his center moved to the left and yours did not, so your center was no longer over his (figure 5.3*a*).

4. Again at the standstill, slide your seat bones to the left as far as you can without slipping off. Do *not* grip with your left leg to pull you over. Instead, use your hands on the horse's withers and your abdominal muscles to lift your seat up a little, give a little hop, and push your left leg *down* until your right seat bone is almost directly on top of the horse's spine, just slightly to the right. You will end up sitting more on your left seat bone and will feel as though you are almost falling off to the left. Try not to hang on with your right leg, but let it fall down on the right side, shaking it out if necessary so that both legs are loose. Use your grounding strap to try to make everything the same as it was before, except that you are off to one side.

5. Now the instructor will again spin the horse to the left while you observe what is happening before, during, and after the spin. Don't forget to use the grounding strap and soft eyes. You will observe that while the horse is being spun, you will feel centered (figure 5.3*b*); but when he stops, unless the spin has moved you over, you will again feel as though you are falling to the left. So this time, at the start your center was not over the horse's. When he spun, his center moved under your center; but when he stopped, he was no longer under you. Because the process is a bit different, we'll talk about maintaining lateral balance during turns to the right later on, in chapter 6.

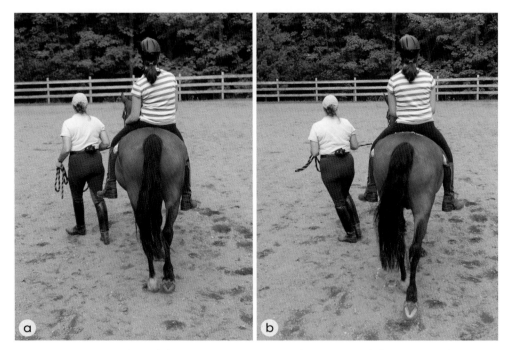

Figure 5.3 Reacting to a lateral thrust in *(a)* an uncentered position and *(b)* a centered position.

The conclusion is that if the horse is turning, you must move your center in order to stay over his. Of course, the horse's center and yours are fixed in your bodies, so another way of thinking about this is to speak of it as the horse's center of motion moving to the left so that you must move your center left to stay over his center of motion rather than over his physical center.

Putting It All Together

The final step in this exercise is to put the last two steps—following seat and lateral centering—together so that you understand how they relate to each other.

Combining Following Seat and Lateral Centering

1. At the standstill, practice moving your center a little bit to the left. Use the same technique as you used earlier to move your center (see the section Reacting to a Left Turn) but move only a small amount. Let your shoulders go a little to the right to help you balance. Reverse the moves to get yourself back into the center, this time keeping your right leg loose and pushing it down as you hop over.

2. The horse's leader should start walking in a long, straight line while you think about your following seat and keeping the even pressure and grounding (figure 5.4a).

3. When you approach the turn, look across it, turning your head about 45 degrees. As the horse begins the turn, move your center to the left as in step 1, and find a place where you feel even pressure on both seat bones as they follow the horse, and your legs can hang free. Be sure you reach *down* with the leg that you are moving your center toward, rather than letting it grip and ride up. Your spine should stay vertical, not lean either way (figure 5.4b). If possible, someone should walk directly behind you to check it.

4. As the horse comes back to the straight, move your center back over his. Continue in this way, combining straight lines with gradual left turns.

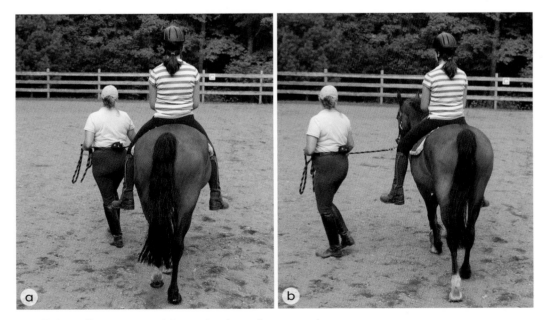

Figure 5.4 Following seat while staying laterally centered.

Caley and Tommy

Some years ago I was giving a lesson to Caley, a fairly experienced rider who had recently started with me. We were working on sitting a slow trot on Tommy, who usually trotted along very willingly. This time, however, he would trot a short distance and then come back to the walk. He would start right up again when asked but would soon stop again. Caley wasn't falling forward, which is the usual cause of this behavior, so I watched carefully to see if I could see the reason. After a minute I noticed that Caley's inside leg would get tense after a few trotting steps, and Tommy would then walk. What was happening was that Caley was losing her balance and sliding a little to the outside, then gripping with her inside leg—the leg toward the center of the ring—to keep herself on. Tommy would then tense up and stop. I showed Caley how to tell when she lost her centering and how to move her center to the inside. As soon as she figured it out and corrected the problem, Tommy settled down into a nice, steady, slow trot.

Distinguishing between following seat and lateral centering can be a bit confusing since they both involve your seat.

> Following seat is something that your body should be doing at all times. In order for your seat to follow both sides evenly, you must be centered.

When the horse's center of motion changes, which in the case of lateral centering means when he is turning, your center must move laterally so that you can stay centered. If the pressure of your following-seat bones is not equal on both sides, it means that you are not laterally centered.

Another indication of loss of lateral centering is tension in your legs, which will try to grip to keep you on if you are slipping to one side. Your right leg will grip if you are slipping to the left and vice versa. Unfortunately, this reflexive response just makes things worse because your tense leg tends to slide upward in the same way that your fingers slide off a basketball when you try to squeeze it to hold on. It also tends to make the horse tense.

If you don't learn how to remain centered while following with your seat now, it will be more difficult to learn to canter correctly because of the complicated lateral movement involved. You can continue working on your following seat, perhaps walking over some poles on the ground or down a slight slope, both of which exaggerate the motion. Work on your lateral center can continue with some large circles and spirals (only to the left for the moment.) With enough practice, lateral centering and following seat will become fixed in your muscle memory and you no longer have to think about it.

Releasing Physical Tension

Your body will not immediately get over its fear of being on the horse. It will take some miles of safe, successful experience before you develop a well-grounded, relaxed seat. Here are two exercises that will speed the process a little bit.

Grounding on Your Seat Bones

When you're sitting on the horse, especially without stirrups, which is the best way to start, you have to be grounded not on your feet but on your seat bones. Unless you are, you will develop tensions that will not only give you problems now but also make it very difficult to ground onto your stirrups when you start with them later on. Because of the tendency of your thighs to grip the horse, which we'll deal with next, you may have trouble finding that grounding. However, if you can take your legs out of the equation for a little while, grounding in your seat becomes quite easy.

On the bareback pad, you might need some assistance from your instructor or the person who's holding the horse, but the procedure is simple. Begin with a nice grip on the grounding strap, grow, and allow yourself to lean back slightly, using the strap for support. Then, instead of allowing your legs to hang down, bring them up, one at a time, until your knees are almost touching above the horse's withers. Swing your feet slowly forward until your calves are hanging straight down or a little forward. As long as you are still leaning a little back, not crouching forward, you should now be able to feel that you are sitting on your seat bones. Without letting go of anything, just think your way through the first four steps—growing, shaking out, breathing, and using soft eyes—which will help you to feel more grounded.

Focus on how this feels. Then, one leg at a time, bring each leg down, very gradually, trying to let gravity do most of the work. At some point you will feel that you're starting to lose that contact with your seat bones. *And that is as far down as you should bring your legs.* Any farther will lift you up and you will literally lose your seat.

In some disciplines, riders are told that they should force their legs down to lower the center of gravity and allow them more "leg" on the horse. It is true that you do want your legs to drop down, but that is something that happens by itself as the muscles and ligaments in your pelvis get softer and more forgiving. Forcing it doesn't work.

Breathing Away Body Tension

Different people have different areas of their bodies in which they hold tensions. Often a person is so accustomed to being tense in a particular way that she doesn't even know she does it. The most common areas where a rider feels tension when on the horse are the hip and thigh areas and the shoulder and neck areas, but the jaw and the feet are also areas of consideration.

Here is a simple way to locate and release tensions. You can do just one area, or you can do them sequentially, starting from the bottom up.

Begin by deliberately creating tension in the area you want to work on. In each area there is a sort of control point that tenses up the muscles around it as well. For your feet, curl up your toes tightly; for your hips, squeeze your buttocks together; for your shoulders, draw them up around your ears; and for your jaw, clench your teeth.

After you have tensed up the control point, notice what other muscles in the area are tense. Hold the tension until it becomes uncomfortable. Then, using long, slow exhalations, gradually release the tensions over the whole area. When you're finished, mentally check the whole area again to see if it feels free of tension. The more you do this exercise, the more aware you will become of areas of tension and the more easily you will be able to release them.

Another benefit of releasing your tensions is that what you do with your body is reflected in the horse's, so calming your body will help the horse to feel more comfortable as well.

6

The Indispensable Halter and Staying Centered During Turns and Transitions

The one piece of equipment virtually every domestic horse has is a halter. He wears it on the ground when you are doing almost anything with him, to give you some way to keep his attention. You're not ready to learn to control the horse on the ground by yourself yet, but with some assistance you can learn how to put the halter on and take it off. This will help prepare you to put on the bridle (see chapter 14).

Since each horse's halter has to fit him reasonably well to be safe and comfortable, many sizes and proportions are available, and most horses have their own. The two basic types of halters are rope and leather or nylon. On most rope halters, you can attach a rope only under the jaw, while leather and nylon halters have metal rings to which you can attach a lead or tie rope on both sides as well as under the jaw.

When you're learning to put on a halter, it is easiest if the horse is put on crossties and his current halter is partially removed and slid back behind his ears (figure 6.1). His head is then free but he can't go anywhere.

Rarely, you meet a horse who is frightened by pressure around his neck, so it is a good idea to test his response before tying him this way.

Figure 6.1 The horse in a safe position for putting on the halter.

Rope Halter

The rope halter opens by unfastening on the left side with either a loop on the cheek piece and a long double tail on the crown piece or, less commonly but most simply, with a loop on the crown piece and a metal hook on the cheek piece.

Putting On the Rope Halter

1. Even though he is familiar with the halter, the horse might not be sure what *you* plan to do with it. Before you start, then, allow the horse to look at and sniff the halter, and gently rub it across his shoulder. After you've put it on him once or twice, this will no longer be necessary.

2. With the crown piece unfastened, hold the halter as follows: Left hand holds the top of the left cheek piece and also holds the crown piece just above its juncture with the right cheek piece. The rest of the halter hangs down. Note your hand position, with your thumbs up.

3. With the horse fastened to the crossties, stand just behind his head facing forward and reach over the horse's neck with your right hand, as high up his neck as you can reach comfortably. Bring your left hand under the horse's neck until you can take the end of the crownpiece in your right hand (figure 6.2a).

4. Bring both hands up, guiding the noseband carefully around his nose until it is just under his cheekbone (figure 6.2b). At the same time bring your right hand across so that the crownpiece is behind the horse's ears.

5. Bring your right hand down on his left side (figure 6.2c) and use both hands to fasten the crown piece to the cheek piece as described in the section Fastening the Rope Halter.

Figure 6.2 Putting on the rope halter.

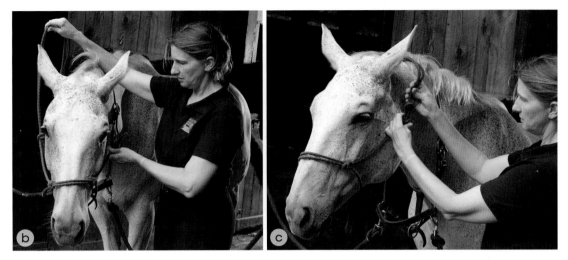

Figure 6.2 (*continued*) Putting on the rope halter.

Fastening the Rope Halter

If the halter has a metal loop and hook on the cheek piece, fasten it by slipping the crown piece loop through the metal loop from underneath, then around the hook. Pull up on the crown piece to set it firm.

If the halter has no metal fastening, insert the long tail of the crown piece from underneath through the loop on the end of the cheek piece. Take the tail to your right (figure 6.3a)—toward the horse's tail—then pass it under the lower part of the cheek loop and all the way around to the front (outside) (figure 6.3b) and run it under itself where you first put it through. Snug it up by holding the top of the cheek loop while you pull on the tail (figure 6.3c). Be sure the knot is tied *around* the cheek loop, not above it.

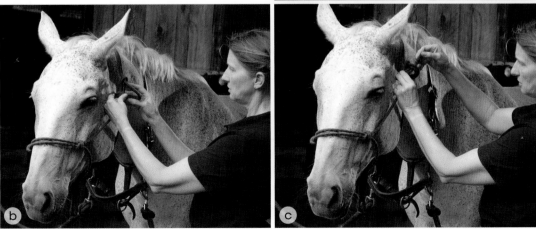

Figure 6.3 Tying the knot to secure the rope halter.

Taking Off the Rope Halter and Turning the Horse Loose

1. Stand on the horse's left side, a little in front of him but close enough to reach the halter fastening without losing your balance. If the halter has a hook fastening, push the crown piece down a little and undo it, then go to step 3. If it's a knot fastening, loosen the knot by pulling a little slack down from the crown piece.

2. Carefully pull the tail out of the knot with your left hand, and hold the cheek piece up by the loop in your right hand until you get the tail out of the loop.

3. Let go of the crown piece and, holding the cheek loop in your left hand, quietly bring the halter down until it falls off his nose. If the crown piece doesn't slide off easily, either lift it off from behind his ears with your right hand or reach under his neck and gently pull it down until the halter slides off.

4. Turn to face his tail and step backward so that you are facing him but backing away. Often a horse will wheel away from you when turned loose and bump into you if you don't step back.

Leather or Nylon Halter

Nearly all leather and nylon halters can be put on in one of two ways, since, unlike rope halters, many of them unfasten in two places. Use figure 6.4 as a guide to the relevant parts of the horse.

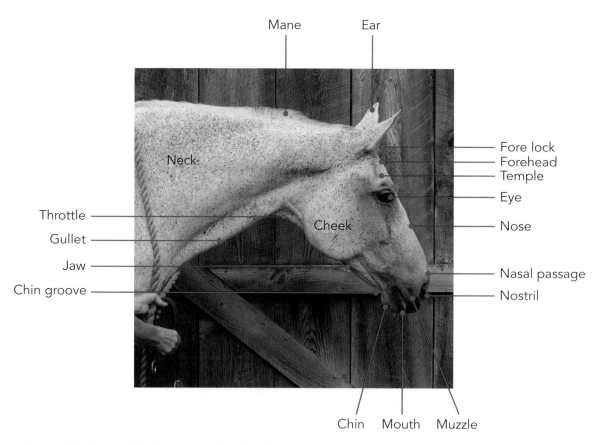

Figure 6.4 Parts of the horse's head and neck.

Putting On the Leather or Nylon Halter That Fastens With a Buckle

If the crown piece is unfastened by unbuckling it on the left side, you can put it on just as you do with the rope halter, finishing by fastening the buckle and tucking in the end of the strap. This method of putting on the halter is best for a horse that is ear shy or that raises his head high to avoid being haltered. You should also use this method the first time you put a new halter on the horse so that you can adjust the fit. Remove the leather or nylon halter in the same way as the rope halter.

Putting On the Leather or Nylon Halter That Fastens With a Snap

The other method, where the crown piece remains fastened and the throat latch snap is undone, is much faster both to put on and take off, since the snap is faster to manage than the buckle. However, it is a much easier method to abuse, and many people do so without realizing it. For that reason it needs more careful explanation.

1. With the crown piece fastened and the throat latch undone, hold the top of the crown piece in your right hand with your fingers on top and your thumb underneath and the front of the halter facing away from you (figure 6.5a).

2. Stand just behind the horse's head, and bring your right hand either over the horse's poll between his ears or over his temple so that your hand is about in the middle of his forehead. Hold the halter carefully so it doesn't bang on his face or get in his eye. Note: If you are not tall enough to get your hand at least over his temple, or he raises his head to prevent you from doing so, use the rope halter method until you are more experienced (see Slipping on the Halter If You're Short).

3. Using your left hand to guide the noseband, carefully pull the halter up until the noseband is just below his cheekbone (figure 6.5b). His left eye will be between the two sides of the crown piece.

4. Switch hands so that you are holding the top of the crown piece in your left hand with your fingers underneath and your thumb on top.

5. With your right hand, gently hold the horse's right ear by the base.

6. While lifting up on the halter with your left hand, guide the ear forward and bring the crown piece back over it until it rests behind the ear (figure 6.5c). *The horse's ears do not move straight forward and backward. Instead they move out to the side and around.* Be aware of how he responds to the pressure and do what seems easy for him. You can also gently play with his ears during grooming so that you become familiar with how they move.

7. If you can reach across easily, take the horse's right ear and guide it through the crown piece in the same way. The crown piece will lie behind both ears and the poll when you are finished. If you can't reach, walk around his head to the other side until you are facing front, keeping the halter in place with your hand as you do so. Then reverse the procedure so that you guide his ear with your left hand while moving the crown piece with your right. The horse's ears are very sensitive, and dragging the halter over them without consideration can be very uncomfortable for the horse, leading to resistance and possibly aggressive behavior.

8. From your original position on the horse's left side, take the throat latch snap, check to make sure that nothing is twisted or caught, and fasten it to the upper ring on the left cheek piece (figure 6.5d).

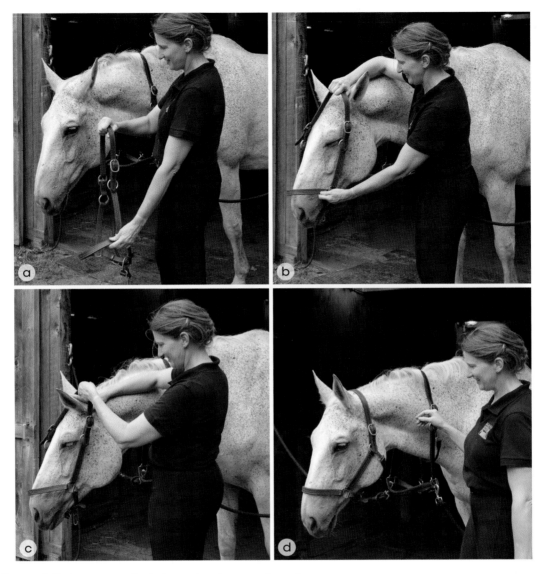

Figure 6.5 Putting on the halter using the snap fastening.

Slipping On the Halter if You're Short

Many short people are taught to stand under the horse's head and reach up from underneath to slip the halter over his ears. The problem with this is that it tends to make the horse raise his head even more. Tipping your head back to look up because you are under him also causes head raising because of his tendency to copy your body movements. A better solution is for the horse to be taught, using positive reinforcement, to drop his head for the halter. Some horses learn to almost put on the halter by themselves.

Removing the Leather or Nylon Halter

1. Stand on the horse's left side just behind his head, unfasten the snap on the throat latch, and let it drop.

2. Turn to face forward, and slip your left thumb under the crown piece, just below the horse's left ear (fingure 6.6a). You can rest your right hand on the top of his neck to steady him—and yourself—if you like.

3. Lift the crown piece up and slip it over just the horse's left ear, carefully pushing the ear forward with the crown piece to do so.

4. Still holding the crown piece, if you can do so easily, reach across and lift it forward over his right ear with your left hand (figure 6.6b). Doing one ear at a time allows more slack in the crown piece for each ear, so it avoids pulling or chafing. Again, if you aren't tall enough to reach, make sure the halter isn't in his eye. Then let go of it so it is hanging from his right ear, walk around, and carefully lift it off the other ear with your right hand.

5. Keeping your forearm across his face, slide your arm down until the halter and your hand drop below his head. This prevents him from throwing his head up and getting caught in the halter as you are removing it.

6. Turn to face his tail and step backward so that you are facing him but backing away.

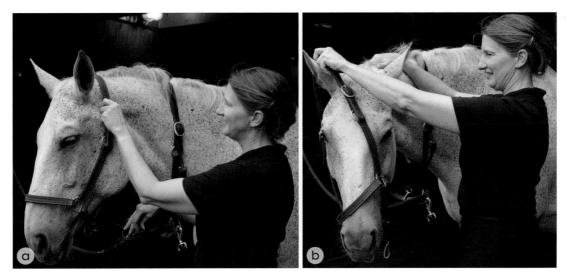

Figure 6.6 Removing the halter.

You can always remove leather or nylon halters by undoing the crown piece, as with the rope halter, but it is much simpler to undo the throat latch instead. Again, it is very important to consider the horse's comfort, that is, his ears. I have seen people stand in front of the horse, grab the halter by the center of the crown piece, and drag it over his ears. This is really uncomfortable for the horse and will make him resistant and ear shy.

Checking the Fit of the Halter

Since horses often wear halters for long periods, it is important that they be properly fitted and adjusted. The noseband should hang well above the horse's nostrils. His nasal passages continue up under the skin for a couple of inches, with unsupported bone in between them, which is very sensitive, so the noseband must lie above that area if he is to be comfortable. The side of the noseband should be a couple of fingers below the cheekbone.

The noseband should be loose enough around his lower jaw for him to eat and chew comfortably, but not so loose that he or a playmate could get a foot caught in it. The throat latch should lie up close to his throttle, where his head and neck meet, but should not be tight (figure 6.7). A general rule is that you should be able to insert your fist between the throat latch and the horse's throttle.

Figure 6.7   Properly fitted halter.

You can make most of these adjustments by lengthening or shortening the crown piece, and some leather halters also have adjustable nosebands as well. But sometimes the proportions of the halter straps are wrong, so he needs a different size or type. As you use halters you can become familiar with the various types of rings and adjustments.

Staying Laterally Centered

We talk about turning to the right separately from turning to the left because, in my experience, the body doesn't do exactly the same thing in both directions. Right turns are more difficult. When you learned the seven steps, you stretched the left side first because it tends to be less flexible than the right side. When a part of the body is inflexible, not only does it not want to stretch because the muscle is tight, but it also doesn't want to compress and bend. When you stretch it, it becomes softer and bends more easily.

So before you can turn—and move your center—to the right, your left side has to get softer so that it will give, and allow the right side to stretch in a smooth curve. Since softening and giving on the left side are hard for your body, instead of bending as it should, it makes what is called an S-curve instead (figure 6.8). It feels balanced, but your center has not moved to the right as it should to keep you over the horse's center.

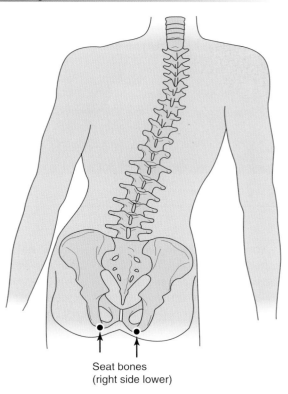

Seat bones
(right side lower)

Figure 6.8   The S-curve.

A Natural Imbalance?

In the 1960s my wonderful trainer, William Hillebrand, who was trained in Germany, taught me that horses tend to have a slight longitudinal curve in their bodies. The left side is longer but less flexible than the right. He called this natural crookedness and considered it to be universal among horses and people. No reason for this is known, and it is not affected by right- or left-handedness. In the many years I've observed it, I have never seen either horse or rider who did not fit the pattern. With proper training, especially stretching, it causes minimal problems. This knowledge has been invaluable to me.

Lateral Centering Exercise

1. At a standstill, sitting squarely on both seat bones, raise your left hand over your head and grow your left side as far as you can and still stay grounded in your seat.
2. Keeping your left hand up, raise your right hand up to it. Try to grow evenly on both sides. Remain grounded on both seat bones and not rolled back on your right buttock.
3. Put your left palm against the top of your pelvis on the left side and gently press your pelvis to the right, moving your center to the right as well. Imagine that your center is a big, rather heavy ball and let it roll to the side, opening up your right side as it rolls. Your hip should be farther to the right than your shoulder (figure 6.9a).
4. At the walk, the instructor should lead the horse from the right side and—since you won't be using your grounding strap—steady you with her hand as you repeat steps 1 and 2.
5. The instructor should begin a right turn while you go to step 3 (figure 6.9b). If you are over the center of motion, your spine will be vertical and both your legs should hang loose and free.

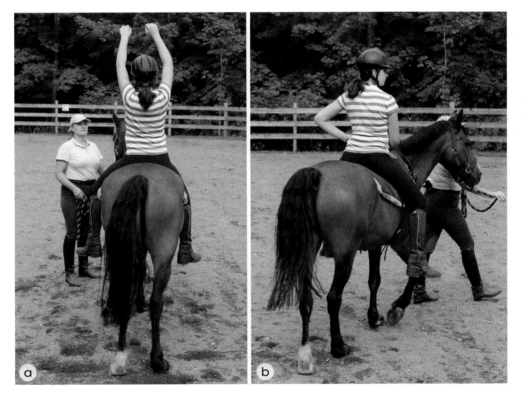

Figure 6.9 During the (a) preparation and (b) execution of a right turn, the rider must be laterally centered with freely hanging legs.

Practice lateral centering frequently, using exercises like those for left turns presented in chapter 5 as well as bending around cones, until you can stay centered easily at the walk in both directions without any tension, especially gripping with your thighs.

Longitudinal Centering During Transitions

In riding terminology, transitions refer to changes from one gait to another or changes in pace within the gait itself.

Increasing and decreasing pace (at this stage, going from the halt to the walk and back again), which involve your longitudinal centering, are the next two problems to solve. The challenge is similar to riding turns in that your center wants to keep doing what it's doing as the horse's center is doing something else. But again, your body has the tools (that is, the reflexes) to handle nearly all the longitudinal problems you will encounter.

As with the lateral centering, you are concerned not only with your own balance but also with the horse's balance. You are concerned in both cases with losing balance forward or backward. On level ground, because of the placement of the horse's center, it's virtually impossible for him to fall over backward, since his hind legs support him. It is also very difficult for you to fall off him backward because his hind legs are back there and because you don't bend backward very easily. Finally, nearly all the time you are holding something with your hands, either the grounding strap or the reins or both, which will prevent you from falling back very far.

Falling forward is a lot easier to do and is a very common way to fall both for the rider and the horse. In the case of the horse, his center is very close to his front legs, so if for some reason he can't get his front legs far enough forward—if he trips, for example—his center goes ahead of his feet and down he goes. Because of his length behind the center, most of the time he just goes down on his knees and then recovers.

In the case of the rider, there are several reasons for falling forward that are not immediately apparent when you first start riding. The first is a psychological one. As you sit on the horse, he has that nice long neck and head out in front of you, which should be enough to stop you, right? Let's play a little game and see.

Gaits

Most horses have three gaits. The walk and trot are functionally identical to our walking and running, so when riding is correctly taught, following the horse's movement is quite easy and natural. The third gait, the canter or gallop, is a little more difficult because it has a phase when all the horse's weight is on one front foot. Since our "front feet" don't reach the ground, we don't use this gait.

Besides the ordinary gaits, each gait also has two other speeds: collected, in which the horse's body is more rounded and his hind feet are farther underneath him so his weight is back and the gait is more up and down, and extended, in which the horse's body is stretched out and he takes longer strides. There are more subtle variations as well, but this is the general distinction.

There are also horses, usually called gaited horses, who have one or more additional gaits, usually sped-up variations of the walk but sometimes quite complex. These additional gaits are quite smooth and easy to sit to, even at speed, which makes them a popular ride.

Longitudinal Positioning Exercise

1. With the horse standing still and the instructor holding his head, take your hands off your grounding strap and hold your arms stretched out in front of you.

2. Keeping your arms out, lean forward from the hip joint as far as you can while still feeling safe.

3. The instructor performs this step: Using a treat if necessary, she gets the horse to quickly drop his head to the ground. Oops! With his head and neck no longer in front of you, leaning forward doesn't feel safe at all (figure 6.10a).

4. Lean back until you feel centered.

5. Now, with the instructor helping you, you'll lean back as far as you can. You can use the grounding strap if it's long enough; otherwise the instructor can hold your hands or you can place them behind you on the horse's back, whatever makes it easiest for you. Lean back slowly, and let your knees come up in front of you a little to ease the strain on your back (figure 6.10b). Keep going back as far as you can, and guess what! With no saddle in the way, you wind up lying flat on the horse's back! You can't go any farther back than that. And once you get accustomed to the idea, it's quite comfortable on a bareback pad. (Horses have to learn about this too, so don't try it on a horse you don't know.)

6. Sit up and try leaning forward and backward again.

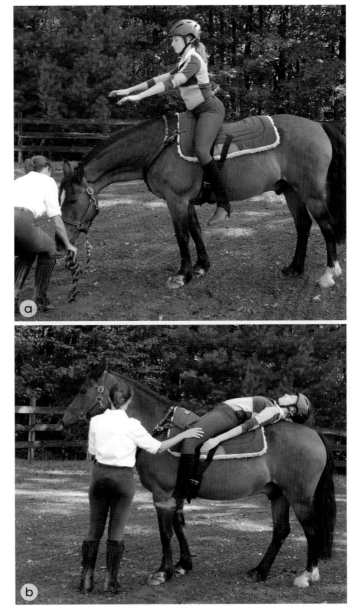

Figure 6.10 Leaning (a) forward feels secure until the horse drops his head. Leaning (b) backward feels scary, until you realize the horse is solidly behind you.

What you have begun to do is, first, to teach your conscious mind that, contrary to your instincts, getting ahead of the horse's center is not very safe, while getting behind it is okay. Second, you are teaching your body, that is, your reflexes, the same lesson. And this is very important, because in an emergency it is your reflexes that take over to save you. Your body's natural reflex in an emergency is to curl up in a ball, which means leaning forward. This is the physical reason why you tend to fall forward more easily than back. For the most part that makes sense because you can use your hands to save yourself. However, it doesn't work when you're sitting on a horse, and your body has to learn that. With practice it will do so.

Starting Up From the Halt

Try some simple transitions now. You should be settled and comfortable on your horse's back before starting the new work.

1. Begin at a standstill with a light feel on the grounding strap and centered over both seat bones. Unless it makes you nervous, close your eyes, which will help you feel the movement more easily. Just as you did when you were learning about lateral centering, try to allow your body to do what comes naturally rather than resist the movement.

2. The instructor will start the horse walking. As he starts, your body will sway backward a little bit. Since it doesn't like to fall backward, you might feel yourself trying to bend forward to recover. Try not to do this, but let yourself sway back a little and use the grounding strap to support you. The grounding strap helps enormously by giving your body the confidence that it isn't in any danger when it sways backward. Then quietly sway forward again just enough to recenter.

3. Try this several times, seeing if you can just let your body sway back a little bit as the horse starts, and then recenter.

You might ask, "Why don't I just lean forward when I want to start up? Then I won't fall back but just get centered as he moves." There are two reasons why not. First, when the horse starts up, he needs to lift his front end a tiny bit to stay balanced. Try this yourself. Stand square, then lean forward a little and take a step forward at the same time. You'll find that your foot hits the ground fairly heavily. Now try it again, but this time keep your weight a little bit back as you take the step. Your foot will hit the ground very softly and smoothly, like a dancer.

In the case of the horse, tipping forward is called going on the forehand. Besides being rather uncomfortable to ride, it puts a strain on his front legs that can lead to lameness.

The second reason, which you'll learn more about later, is that the horse is very responsive to where your center is relative to his. If you start to move your center ahead of his, it's as though you stepped out in front of him, and his reaction is to stop. This is a very common reason that a horse is thought to be stubborn or lazy or unresponsive. What he's really doing is responding very correctly to a signal the rider doesn't realize she is giving.

I once saw a horse running away backward with a man who didn't understand this concept. He was kicking the horse to make him go forward and at the same time leaning forward and pulling on him, so the only way the horse felt he could go was backward, which he did as fast as he could!

Stopping From the Walk

This is the one you really need to work on so that your reflexes do the right thing every time. Falling forward, even if you don't fall off, can get the horse in a lot of trouble.

1. Start out at a nice forward walk, centered, with your hands on the grounding strap keeping you solid and secure and your eyes closed as before.

2. At some point the instructor will stop the horse. As soon as you feel yourself swaying forward, lift your chest and use your back muscles to bring you back to a centered position. Shake out your legs to release any tension caused by the stop.

Practice starting and stopping until your body starts correcting by itself. You will never reach a point where you won't be caught off balance by a really unexpected sudden stop, especially from speed, but you can learn to recover from most of these without a fall. In addition, if you work on your emergency dismount, you're usually in a good position to use it if the situation is dangerous and get to the ground safely.

Preparing For the Emergency Dismount

Eventually you will learn how to dismount from a moving saddled horse. You need to consider two things: Your body will hit the ground at whatever speed the horse was traveling when you began the dismount; and there is more equipment to get caught on when the horse is saddled, and you are more likely to get caught on it if he is moving.

The solution to both these problems is the same and quite simple. It is also one of the reasons for staying centered until both your legs are on one side and you're ready to slide down.

When you reach that position, you will be belly over, but with your head up, and holding the mane. As you start to slide down, push yourself away from the horse a little with your hands, and simultaneously roll over onto your right hip so that you are facing forward. Now there is very little to catch on the horse's equipment, and when you land from a moving horse you can keep walking or running in the same direction. If you land facing sideways when the horse is moving, it's all too easy to break your leg.

Practice this at the standstill, taking a step or two forward when you land so that you end up a little in front of the horse's head—a good position from which to regain control of him if necessary.

Performing an emergency dismount from a moving horse is actually easier than when he is standing still because the movement from the gait helps to lift you up and off. The goal is to get your right leg up and over his back while keeping yourself centered, until you're in a position to drop safely. At some point you might want to learn to dismount on the other side as well, but it's less confusing if you learn to dismount just from the left at first.

Dismounting From the Walk

Practice steps 1 and 2 at the standstill first.

1. Holding your grounding strap, swing your right leg forward and back as far as you can without hitting the horse with your foot. Lean forward a little as you swing it back. Try to hold your thigh a little away from the horse so that your whole leg can swing freely. The idea is to build up some momentum so your leg will come over the horse's back easily.

2. Sit up straight again, let go of the grounding strap, and practice grabbing the horse's mane with both hands: right hand close to the withers, left hand slightly farther up the neck, thumbs on left side but pointing up. You'll have to lean somewhat forward to do so (see Holding the Mane in chapter 4). Practice slowly a few times until you're sure you're grabbing the mane correctly, then try it a little faster once or twice.

3. With the horse walking, put steps 1 and 2 together so that you grab the mane, lean forward, and swing your leg back and up all in one motion. The horse might stop as you swing forward. This is normal and he should be allowed to do so.

4. At the standstill, repeat step 3 slowly. Then bring your leg to the left over the horse's back, turning your head and upper body to the right as you do so. *Do not slide off*, but try to stay on top of the horse. It's essential to stay centered throughout the dismount, and this exercise forces you to be aware of whether or not you are. (You had a little taste of this in your first lesson.) Be sure you don't lose your hold on the mane at any time.

5. Wiggle your toes to make sure your feet and ankles are relaxed for the landing.

6. Without sliding off, bring your right knee up and hook it over the horse's back as you turn your body to face front again. This is the same step you use in mounting from the ground (chapter 4).

7. Sit up and let your right leg fall down on the horse's right side.

8. Practice these seven steps until you can partially dismount and then remount without too much difficulty. The reason for the exercise is that you can do it only if you stay centered over the horse the whole time, which is also necessary for a safe emergency dismount.

9. With the horse walking, repeat steps 4 and 5. Then with your upper body across the horse and both legs on his left side, start to slide down, rolling onto your right hip so that you are facing forward (figure 6.11a).

10. As you slide, push yourself away from the horse with your hands and release the mane. You should land facing forward about a foot (30 cm) away from the horse with your knees softly bent (figure 6.11b). Take a step or two to make sure you're balanced.

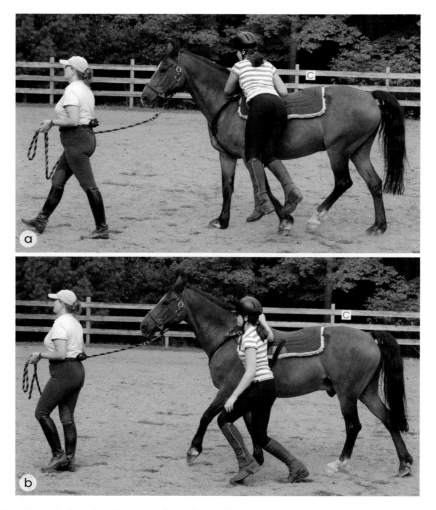

Figure 6.11   Completing the dismount from the walk.

Try to do at least two walking emergency dismounts in every lesson. When you're riding in a group, the instructor might know some games you can play to keep it interesting (see appendix at http://tinyurl.com/d8pv7nz).

You are now familiar with the basic skills you need in order to keep yourself and the horse comfortable and balanced. All you need to do is practice them, eventually at all gaits, until they are fixed in your muscle memory.

Negotiating Simple Ground Movements

By now you should have spent some time on ground work, getting comfortable with your horse, and getting to know a little about him. The next step is to start learning how to ask for simple moves, but try not to think about it as learning to control him. What you are looking for is the way to get him to *cooperate willingly*.

Let's talk first about *how* you get the horse to do what you want. Many people will tell you that you have to be tough and let him know who's boss—that you have to be the one in charge. But that's not easy if you don't have very much experience. Usually you just end up being aggressive, which is unpleasant for you and the horse.

Apart from the unpleasantness, why shouldn't you just be aggressive and bossy? Lots of people treat horses—and other people—that way, and to a certain extent it seems to work. That is, a nonaggressive person or horse may be willing to submit to being bullied or bossed around rather than risk a fight.

However, constant exposure to this kind of treatment will always have a less successful result over the long term or even the short term. If you live or work in constant fear of punishment, you'll be tense and resentful all the time. That means that there will be no trust, so in the case of the horse, any new experience will mean another fight. It also means that he will never perform up to his ultimate capabilities. A horse that has the potential to be a winner might well end up a loser instead. Furthermore, working in a constant state of tension has an effect on health and physical soundness, so the horse's working life may be shortened. Somebody once asked a famous veterinarian, "What's wrong with our horses that they go lame all the time?" The answer came promptly and firmly: "There's nothing wrong with the horses; it's the way you ride them."

Finally, sometimes the worm turns—the horse encounters a situation that he fears more than the bully. This is how people get hurt by horses that explode out of fear and frustration or even become dangerously aggressive in self-defense. Sometimes these results accumulate and show up years later, and the ultimate receiver is the innocent purchaser who bought a "bombproof" horse.

How do good horse people who *do* have experience control the horse? The answer is they don't. The best riders in the world do lose control of their horses—not very often and usually not for very long because they are good horsemen, but it does happen. A misstep causing a fall, an unrecognized soreness causing a buck or other resistance, an old fear causing an unwillingness to continue—any of these can occur and cannot be controlled. Recovered from, yes, but not prevented.

> Control, in the sense of being able to *make* the horse do whatever you want whenever you want, is not possible, no matter how experienced and skillful you might be.

Why You Aren't Leading Your Horse

Many beginners are given the horse to lead *and try to control* on their very first lesson. Since a beginner has no communication skills at that point, and no experience, the leading methods she assumes are usually very tense and can result in a leading technique that is ineffective and usually annoying to the horse. Because this is rarely addressed in the lesson, it is rarely corrected and so becomes a habit. I have seen some very experienced people using leading techniques that resulted in resistance and sometimes dangerous behavior from the horse. Once you have developed a comfortable relationship with the horse, leading correctly is an easy skill to acquire. We'll get into that in chapter 8.

In other words, there is no such thing as absolute control of the horse. Maybe that thought scares you, but let's put it into context. Your car, like your horse, is large. It comes with all kinds of built-in controls so that strength is not necessary. And, unlike the horse, it has no will of its own. Nonetheless, no matter how good and experienced a driver you might be, an unexpected blowout of a tire, a faulty brake line, or a patch of black ice can cause you to lose control of the car.

We all know that, but it doesn't stop you from driving. What it does do is to teach you to keep up the car's maintenance and to use good judgment and common sense about how, when, and where you drive. In the same way, the awareness that you can't be sure of controlling the horse should not prevent you from riding, and doing so safely and happily. But it should inspire you to use good judgment and continue to learn throughout your riding career.

Achieving Cooperation Through Communication

Learning how to converse with the horse and get the results you want is neither quick nor easy. It's much like learning to handle personnel or children. It is also another area where the seven steps are very useful, since they help you to feel and appear confident. Confidence earns respect from others and, unlike aggressiveness, does not create hostility.

Voice Commands

The two voice commands that almost every horse has been taught are the cluck and "whoa." The cluck is made with the inside of your cheek against your teeth and is really more of a clicking sound. The horse learns to associate the cluck with moving his feet in whatever direction he is asked, or moving faster. Most people can do it without difficulty if they hear someone else a couple of times, but a few people can't and usually resort to using the tongue against the roof of the mouth. Some people cluck just once and some a couple of times close together. The horse will respond to either.

"Whoa" usually comes out more as "Ho" and can be either a sharp and aggressive "HO!" (which means *stop* or *stop it right now!*) or a more drawn-out and coaxing "Ho-o-o-o-o" on a descending note, which means *it's okay* or slow down gradually. When you're around experienced horse people, listen to how they use their voices and observe how the horses respond. Horses respond as much to vocal tone and attitude as they do to a verbal cue.

Positive and Negative Reinforcement

Praising or rewarding the horse for doing what you wanted—called positive reinforcement—has been shown to be much more effective than punishing him for mistakes. The other half of this training method is called negative reinforcement, which is an often misunderstood title because it sounds aggressive or painful. However it simply means that something unwanted—such as pressure—is stopped when the desired result is achieved. For example, if you press on the horse's shoulder and he responds by yielding to your pressure, you immediately stop the pressure, thus rewarding him in a slightly different way.

There are many sources for more study of this technique (see appendix at http://tinyurl.com/d8pv7nz). Rewards usually take the form of tasty treats, but feeding treats is tricky and should wait until you have more experience. Meanwhile, you can use sincere words of praise such as "good boy" or "thank you" to convey your approval. Smiling is also effective, because it expresses happiness, an emotion he can pick up on. And finally, if he has a place that he enjoys having scratched, that is also a good reward.

We've spoken about the dangers of riding and working closely with the horse, but the real point is that if you are patient and willing to learn to work with him, the danger is minimal. Horses are not naturally malicious or aggressive; rather, they are loving and caring and wonderful companions and friends.

So let's get started with some simple ground work. You'll ask the horse to step over with his front legs (forehand) and—separately—his hind legs (hindquarters). The term *forehand* refers to the part of the horse from the shoulders forward, while the area from the hip point back is the *hindquarters*. We start with moving the hindquarters because that is easier for most horses.

Don't set too high a goal for yourself. That is to say, if you have trouble getting the horse to step over, don't worry about it. It's like trying to make yourself understood in a language you don't speak well. Lots of times you'll use the wrong words, but that's part of learning. At first your instructor should help you to figure it out. Something else to remember is that different horses respond in different ways, depending on how they were trained and how easy or hard something is for them.

The most important thing to understand about getting the horse to move in any direction is that *he must move himself.* Trying to move the horse by pushing on him is like trying to push your car uphill. It also makes him tense and resistant. Here's an example for you to try, which takes two people: You stand still with your feet together, while the other person tries to move you sideways by pushing on you at the level of your shoulder. At first you might take a not-too-awkward step as you are pushed off balance, but as the pusher continues to push without stopping, you will lose balance more and more and might even fall if the pusher doesn't stop. So be careful.

If you are much bigger and stronger than the pusher, when you start to lose your balance you will push back. If the creature being pushed happens to be a horse, and you're in the stall with him, you can get pushed against the wall. This is called crowding and is quite scary. (If you should ever get in this situation, just stand very still and don't try to push back. In a few seconds the horse will relax, too, and you can walk out.)

Now try the pushing game again. This time, as soon as you start to shift to take a step, the pusher must stop pushing, allowing you to rebalance. If another step is desired, you just repeat. The whole thing is to *ask* the other person to move, not try to *make* her move, and make it as easy as possible for her to do so.

But let's get back to the horse. For this work he should be lightly restrained in some way so that he doesn't just leave if you make a mistake. It's easiest if somebody experienced holds him for you, especially a horse that doesn't stand well on crossties. If he is on crossties, they should be quite loose because you will need to turn his head in order to learn to move his feet easily.

Earning Respect

My first experience with school was in a one-room schoolhouse, with 30 students ranging from first- to fifth-graders. Our teacher, Miss Kelley, was about five feet tall, so she certainly did not command respect with her size. I never heard her raise her voice in anger or say anything hurtful or unkind. But we would not have dreamed of disobeying her or talking back. We respected her, and she treated us with respect as well. I believe that another factor was her innate kindness: Since she did not inspire fear, she did not create in us a need for aggressiveness. Creating respect without fear is not easy to achieve, but it is a very worthwhile goal in all aspects of life, riding included.

Moving the Horse's Hindquarters

You are more likely to have to move the horse's hindquarters than his forehand when he is on the crossties. For some reason many horses like standing with their tails near the wall, which means if you want to work on that side, or get by, you have to get the horse to move. We're going to move his hindquarters to the left first, so when you're ready to begin, the horse should be standing so that the left crosstie is loose. He should be standing fairly square, that is, with his feet more or less evenly underneath him and balanced (figure 7.1).

Attach a separate lead rope to the horse's halter on the lower right side for you to use in this exercise.

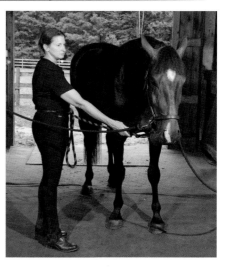

Figure 7.1 When the horse is ready to be asked to move his hidnquarters to the left, the handler begins to comb the rope so that the horse yields with his head.

Moving the Hindquarters

1. Stand on the horse's right side by his head. Holding the slack in your left hand to keep from getting tangled in it, take the lead rope in your right hand, close to the halter, and draw your hand along it, creating a light pull. This is called combing. You may want to comb first with one hand, then the other, repeating as necessary. The pull should be outward, not straight back. If the horse turns his head toward you, stop combing, praise him, and repeat. If he pulls away, release for a moment, then try combing even more gently and try to feel his response. Keep yourself centered and your arm very soft and yielding.

2. Using the combing technique, coax his head around as far as you can without creating a pull on the crossties. Take all the rope into your right hand, holding the slack in your fingers.

3. Gently hold his head with your right hand and place your left hand on the side of his hindquarters a few inches behind and above his stifle. Stroke him a couple of times to let him know you aren't going to hurt him. Be sure you are centered and grounded.

4. Press and release or tap with your hand against his hindquarters, giving a light tug on the lead rope and a cluck at the same time. *Do not lean into him.* If you feel him start to move, praise and release, then ask again if necessary. Experiment a little, as long as he seems comfortable, and see if you can get at least one step (figure 7.2).

Figure 7.2 The horse steps to the left with his hind legs.

5. Try it on the other side as well because one side might be easier than the other.

When asking the horse to move, the timing can be tricky. If you release too soon, he might think you've changed your mind. But if you push too long you might create resistance. It just takes practice and is why you don't want to have too high an expectation at first.

Moving the Horse's Forehand

You will ask the horse to move his forehand over to the right by stepping sideways with his front feet. He will step sideways with his right foot and should step in front of his right foot with his left, which means he has to be able to step forward a little as well as sideways. As before, he should be held if possible, should be standing square, and the left crosstie should be extra loose.

Moving the Forehand

1. Standing on the horse's left side, stroke his neck gently with your left hand and then the side of his face between his mouth and his cheekbone. *Be sure to stay centered and balanced over your feet; don't lean into the horse.*

2. Keeping your hand flat, gently press against the side of his face (figure 7.3a). If he moves away from the pressure, immediately release it and praise him. Wait a few seconds, then repeat. If he doesn't seem to even notice the pressure, try using a little more pressure. Hint: *If he responds in any way at all*, even if it's the wrong way, then you know he heard you but doesn't understand or can't respond. "Shouting" at him by using more pressure won't help.

3. If he resists the pressure, ease it a little until you find a pressure he accepts, even if he doesn't actually yield. Then try using little taps or pressing and immediately releasing, looking for even the slightest response.

4. Also try reaching around with your right hand and gently pulling on the other crosstie as you press against his face. Soften the pull if he yields, or release it and apply it smoothly again if he resists.

   Your main goal is not so much to get the horse to turn his head as to teach yourself to become aware of his responses and learn to avoid creating resistance. In any case, you don't want him to turn his head very much, or he will get in his own way when you ask him to step over.

5. When he has yielded slightly with his head, keep your left hand on his face and place your right hand on the side of his shoulder and apply the same sort of pressure. *Be very careful to stay centered and not lean into him.* You want him to yield to the pressure by taking a step sideways, or at least shifting his weight in preparation (figure 7.3b). You can also cluck to indicate that you want him to move (see the section Voice Commands).

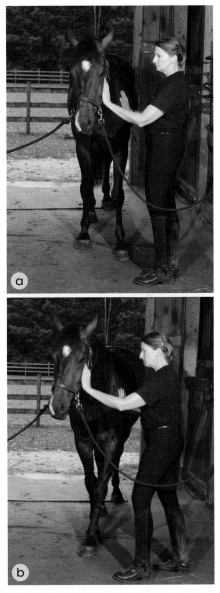

Figure 7.3 Moving the forehand to the right.

6. As before, if you get no response at all, you can increase the pressure, perhaps using the tips of your fingers rather than the flat of your hand to press with. Look for even the slightest yielding from the horse, and release and praise. Horses that are used by beginners are accustomed to their doing uncomfortable things that are meaningless and can get in the habit of ignoring a lot of what's going on, so it might take a little time to get his attention. Therefore, it is very important to praise the horse, which he pays attention to, rather than punish him with too much pressure.

If the instructor is helping you, she may give the horse treats by hand as a reward when he responds to you. Watch how she does it because it is important not to let the horse get in the habit of asking for treats by being pushy.

After you have finished working from the left side, try working from the right. As with moving the hindquarters, horses usually find one side easier than the other, so he might respond differently on the right side.

Moving the Horse Backward

Usually you want the horse to move forward or to take a step or two sideways, especially if he is tied, but there are times when you want the horse to back up, though usually only a few steps. It's useful to be able to get the horse to back a few steps on the ground. Sometimes he is too far forward on the crossties for you to be able to move him to the side easily, or he is in someone's way. Later on, when you are mounting by yourself, you may need to back him a step or two to get him at the right place next to the mounting block.

There are several techniques, but the following is fairly easy to learn. If possible, someone should be holding him, and you should not do this exercise on crossties if he tends to pull back against them. If he is on crossties, they should be very loose and he should be as far forward as is comfortable. Be careful not to back him so much that the crossties become tight.

Your goal is to use pressure on his nose, either directly from your hand or from the halter, to ask the horse to move back. Begin by standing almost directly in front of him facing him but a little to one side so that you can place your hand comfortably on his nose.

Curl your fingers softly, then using the back of them and starting at his muzzle, stroke downward, gradually moving your hand up until it is about at the midline of this face (figure 7.4). This reassures him that your intent is not aggressive. If he seems quiet and accepting of your touch, you're ready to start.

Figure 7.4 Stroking the nose in preparation for asking the horse to move backward.

Getting the Horse to Move Backward

1. With your palm toward the horse, place your thumb and fingers on either side of his nose bone, and again stroke gently downward.

2. With your eyes looking past his body and using your intent (see basic 3 in chapter 2) to communicate what you want the horse to do and how you want him to do it, close your fingers and press against his nose so that you are pushing gently back. As with the other exercises, do not lean into him or try to force him back. Think instead of how you ask a person to move in a crowded room. What you are looking for first is a slight yielding at his poll so that he gives with his nose (figure 7.5a).

3. If you get no reaction at all, add a little more pressure. If you feel him resisting—pushing back—release and then apply pressure again. Try to feel any tendency to resist, then release the pressure and immediately ask again. This might seem like rewarding him for resisting, but the pressure should not be enough to constitute "punishment," and the horse can always resist harder than you can push. By releasing, you don't offer him anything to push against, so he has to rethink his reaction when you continue to ask.

4. If you still get no response at all, rather than use more strength, try asking him to yield to one side and then the other, then ask again. Always use the lightest possible pressure each time you start, increasing only as much as necessary to get a response. That's how the horse eventually learns to respond to the light pressure.

5. When he gets the idea of yielding a small amount with his nose to a light hand pressure, then the next step is to get him to respond to pressure from the halter. Stand beside his head rather than in front, but face more or less toward his tail. Your left fingers should be just above the halter noseband, and your right hand should hold the lead rope fairly close to the halter. Use your finger and halter pressure together, following the same procedure as before, and gradually reduce the finger pressure until the horse is responding just to the halter (figure 7.5b). Don't forget to reward him.

6. Now you're ready to ask him to shift his weight back in preparation for moving. Follow the same procedure as before, but this time when he yields with his nose, praise with your voice, keep the pressure the same, and add a cluck to ask for movement. Do *not* try to push him back, and *do* use your eyes and intent.

7. Look for the slightest movement back with his body, release, and praise (figure 7.5c). If you get resistance, handle it in the same way you did before. Continue asking a few more times. If you don't get the beginning of a step, move toward his shoulder and use finger pressure in the area of his shoulder point, escalating in the same gradual way that you did on his nose and looking for movement. Eventually you should get at least one step, and with practice you should be able to get several with very little effort.

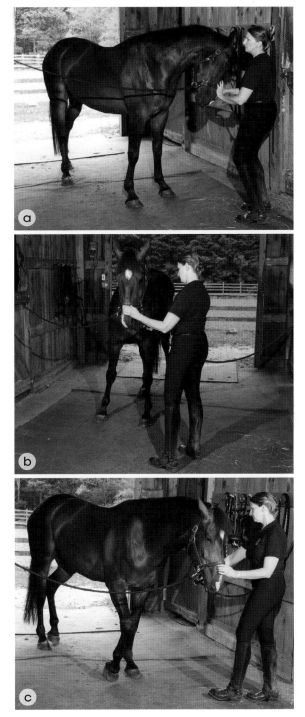

Figure 7.5 Moving the horse backward.

When you are finished with the backing, move the horse forward again by turning to face forward yourself, looking where you want him to go. Give a smooth forward tug on the halter while clucking. If you have a lead rope attached, you can comb it as previously in the direction you want.

This group of ground exercises is not something you do in one lesson. You should plan to work on getting the horse to move a few steps in different directions over time and with help from your instructor.

The important lesson you should take from this is to never use any force or strength to try to control the horse because that will only cause him to use strength in response.

8

Gaining Respect and Becoming the Leader

When you want to go somewhere with your horse, and you aren't going to ride or trailer him, you have to lead him. Leading the horse with a rope is another essential skill that is more difficult than it might seem and is often either not taught or taught incorrectly. Many horses develop bad habits such as dragging the person around if they see a particularly tasty bit of grass, or they spin and break away completely. Once a horse learns to use his strength to get his way, it is a very difficult process to reverse.

As with other control issues, your strength is not a factor in getting good results. That is, you do not *pull* the horse after you like a wagon (which is instinctive for many people at first). Rather, he follows under his own will. Since horses move in herds, following comes very naturally. You must learn two significant skills:

1. How to position yourself so that the horse perceives you as the leader
2. How to apply pressure to the rope so that you give a signal without creating resistance

For learning purposes, the horse should be wearing a halter with the lead rope fastened under the jaw. Work in an area free from tasty temptations such as grass. The horse should have no bad habits related to leading.

Holding the excess lead rope correctly is important for safety. If the horse should get frightened and pull back, and the rope wraps around you in any way, you can be badly hurt. Never tie, lay, or wrap the rope *around* any part of your body or clothing, especially around your neck. When you hold the end of the rope in your nonleading hand, the safest method is to lay it across your palm in flat loops, then wrap your fingers around them. If you have small hands, make fewer loops in the rope or get a shorter rope to practice with (figure 8.1).

Figure 8.1 Holding the excess lead rope.

Leadership Position

When you are first learning to lead, in order for you to be perceived by the horse as the leader, your head should be slightly in front of his head—you must be ahead of him—at all times. This is easiest to visualize in terms of the relationship of the horse's head to your shoulder. If you are leading from the horse's left, which is the normal way of doing it, as you look over your right shoulder the horse's head should not go past it. He should also be off to the side so that if something spooks him from behind and he jumps forward, he won't run into you. Later on, as you develop more experience and confidence, you can let a well-trained horse walk beside you or even in front and still have him respect and listen to you (figure 8.2).

While you are inexperienced, if his head gets in front of yours, the horse will feel that he is the leader. If he is feeling timid, without what he perceives as his leader to follow, he might be unwilling to keep going; if he is feeling bold, he might try to take charge. Some horses like to get directly behind you so they can sneak up and nip you, not out of maliciousness but as a horsey game.

Figure 8.2 When a horse is being led correctly, he will be slightly to the rear and to the right of the leader. A lowered head indicates his submission to the leader.

Dealing With Resistance

The horse uses his head and neck for balance. The kind of resistance we're talking about is what occurs when you pull on the horse's head in such a way that it *interferes* with his balance, or he thinks it will, or he feels trapped in some other way. In any case, instead of giving to the pull (and in this case following you), without pulling back actively, he simply doesn't respond.

Your immediate reaction will be to pull harder. This reaction is absolutely wrong for three reasons: First, pulling hard makes the horse feel trapped, so his instinct is to fight or to escape. Second, the horse is far stronger than you, so he can easily outpull you. Third, and most important for you to understand, is that *it takes two to pull*! If you don't pull, the horse has nothing to pull against and no need to pull. So all you have to do when you feel resistance is to give with your hand or let the rope slide through your fingers until the horse has nothing to pull against. Then you quietly and smoothly try again, *pulling smoothly and quickly releasing* as soon as you feel resistance.

This would appear to differ from some common training methods where the release comes after the animal gives and not while he is resisting. However, this sort of resistance is not a form of disobedience, so it should not be treated as such. Second, at this stage we are training the leader as opposed to the horse. When learning to lead or leading as a beginner, it's safer to give the horse the benefit of the doubt, stop pulling, reorganize, and ask again rather than to keep tugging until he gives. Think of undoing a hard knot or opening a drawer that sticks. As soon as things feel stuck, you stop pulling, loosen things up a bit, and then try again.

> Learning not to use more force when the horse resists is one of the most important skills to develop in working with horses both on the ground and while riding.

Starting and Stopping

The best way to begin learning to lead is on the ground with another person. Take turns being horse and being leader so you understand both points of view. The person taking the role of the horse can either tie the snap end of the rope around her wrist so that she feels how the rope affects her gait, or hold the snap in front of her in both hands as though they were the horse's head, and think about how the rope affects her balance as the horse and leader work together. The leader can try doing some things the wrong way so the horse can find out how it feels when it's wrong. Use the instructions for starting up when you practice, then try them with the actual horse.

Starting Up

1. Stand centered and grounded and facing forward on the left side of the horse's head so that your right shoulder is slightly in front. Without shaking it in the horse's face, gently shake out your whole right arm so that it feels soft and loose.

2. Hold the lead with your right hand about a foot (30 cm) from the halter, with your little finger toward the halter. Hold the excess in your left hand as described previously (figure 8.3*a*).

3. If the horse's attention is not on you, comb the rope toward you until he responds (as described in step 1 of the Moving the Hindquarters instructions in chapter 7).

4. Face forward and look in the direction you want to go.

5. *Without putting pressure on the rope*, let your right arm trail behind you and take a step forward, clucking to the horse at the same time (figure 8.3*b*). If the horse does not begin to move, stay where you are, comb, and gently tug forward on the rope. If you feel any resistance, without moving forward yourself, try another soft tug and cluck. If the horse still does not move, release the pressure and start over.

6. As soon as the horse starts to move forward, allow the rope to go slack. Continuing to pull even lightly will cause tension, and he will not move freely in a relaxed manner.

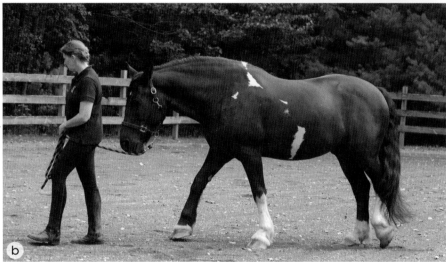

Figure 8.3 As the horse starts forward from the walk, the leader takes up the slack in the rope without putting pressure on it.

Stopping the horse correctly when you're leading is, unfortunately, very counterintuitive, so it needs some practice. When you want the horse to stop, your instinct is to stop yourself; and as the horse passes you, you'll feel the need to get in front of his shoulder and haul on the rope. Actually, from this position you really have no control of the horse if he chooses to break away, since all he has to do is swing his head away from you and use his strength to drag you wherever he wants to go. Furthermore, by blocking his shoulder and pulling, you are actually making it more difficult for him to stop (see chapter 15 for details on how the horse uses his body to stop).

Good Boy!

Until you are more experienced, when praising your horse for following your lead, do not use treats; you want the horse to keep moving, and feeding treats will encourage him to stop for a snack. Instead, praise with your voice and a smile.

Stopping

1. Walk at a normal pace holding the rope and with the horse positioned as previously. Slide your hand up the rope if necessary so that it is about 4 inches (10 cm) from the halter.

2. *Without slowing down*, reach back with your right hand and pull smoothly directly back on the rope while saying "Ho-o-o-o" (see the section Voice Commands in chapter 7). Start with a light pull, increase until you feel resistance, release, and immediately repeat if necessary (figure 8.4).

3. As the horse starts to slow down, slow down with him, but maintain your position ahead of him. When you both come to a stop, you should be in the same position relative to him that you were when you started.

Figure 8.4 Asking the horse to stop.

This sounds very simple, but, because of your natural reflexes, is surprisingly difficult to achieve correctly. Practice it on the ground with another person until you can do it fairly well before starting with the horse.

Turning

Turning is much easier to the left than to the right because you are on the left side of the horse and on the inside of the turn. So you don't have to go as far as the horse, who is on the outside of the turn.

Left, or Inside, Turn

1. Walk in a straight line at a normal pace with the horse positioned correctly.

2. When you are ready to begin the turn, extend your right arm and use the rope to pull the horse's head gently a little away from you (figure 8.5a). Adjust your hand on the rope as necessary so that you can reach. You need to do this because the horse will tend to cut in behind you—taking a shortcut, as it were—and that is not a safe position.

3. As you continue the turn, watch his position out of the corner of your eye and bring him toward you or away from you as needed because you are, in essence, turning your back on him (figure 8.5b). Be careful not to turn so quickly that he is out of range of vision.

4. If he walks slowly, you may need to slow your body to allow him to keep up around the turn. This is better than attempting to drag him around, which would only make him walk more slowly.

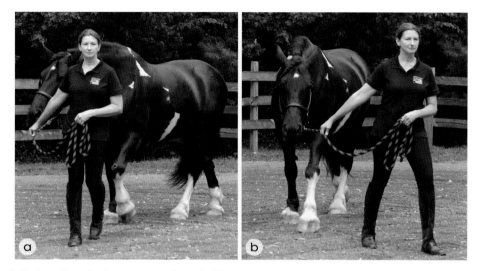

Figure 8.5 Leading the horse through an inside turn.

When you are turning to the right, it can be difficult to stay ahead, especially if the horse is a fast walker and you have short legs. So much so that if you're leading a horse around the ring to the right, you generally move around to his right side so that you are on the inside of the turns. However, if you are just leading the horse around, it's not practical to change sides every time you want to change directions. What you have to do is to get the horse to walk a little more slowly around the right turn while you walk a little faster.

Right, or Outside, Turn

1. Walk in a straight line with the horse positioned correctly.
2. As you approach the turn, check your hand position on the rope, then ask the horse to slow down as in step 2 of the stopping instructions: Without slowing down, reach back with your right hand and pull smoothly directly back on the rope while saying "Ho-o-o-o" (figure 8.6a).

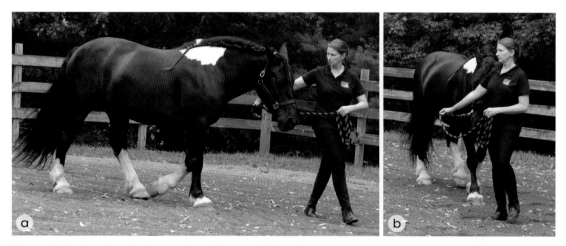

Figure 8.6 Leading the horse through an outside turn.

3. As he slows down, turn and move across in front of his head on the path of the turn you want to make (figure 8.6b).

4. Take longer, and if necessary faster, steps to stay ahead of him. The sharper the turn, the slower he must go and the faster you must walk to maintain your leadership position. Therefore you should practice this on wider turns at first.

5. Keep a close eye on him and use your slow-down signal as necessary but without ever allowing yourself to pull and create resistance. If necessary, stop turning and go straight until you can reposition yourselves.

When you complete the turn, you should still be in the same relative positions.

At this stage, you should not be trying to deal with serious problems with your horse, but it is time to introduce you to some simple methods for dealing with an uncooperative horse. There are two ways a horse can make things difficult. One is when he wants to get ahead of you and take over, and the second is when he doesn't want to come with you or otherwise lags back.

When the Horse Wants to Take Over

Here you can use two skills that you have already learned. What the horse will try to do is get past your shoulder, thus making himself the leader. In this case, the first skill to use is the stopping skill. That is, every time he tries to get ahead of you, you take a long step forward while pulling back on the lead, releasing quickly if he tries to pull and immediately pulling again. In riding this is called an active hand, and you will use it later on when you work on rein skills. Learning it on the ground is an excellent way to start.

If he doesn't respond easily to the stopping treatment, then the next skill to use is the left turn. For this, when he starts to pass you, turn quickly and sharply to the left while pulling his head to the outside so that he can't cut across, just as you did when you started the left turn. If he resists the pull, use the same active hand method, this time releasing quickly when he tries to resist, and then pull smoothly again.

When you turn quickly to the left, you put him behind you, so without using force you reposition yourself as leader. At the same time, keep your first five steps (growing, shaking out, breathing, using soft eyes, and longitudinal centering) and grounding in mind, since they also ask for respect.

Finally, if you are holding a horse that is trying to take over in a way that is really violent, you might have to let him go unless you are very experienced. If you feel that the horse you are holding is going to take over, ask for help. Letting go can be dangerous to the horse and to those nearby, so it is usually a last resort. But if you are at risk of being hurt by holding on, then let go.

This sort of violent takeover is a very rare occurrence, but you should know what to do. Similarly, if you ever have a suspicion that a horse might be frightened in any situation, ask for help ahead of time. Even a horse that is quiet at home can be frightened in a new situation.

Using the Stick for Gentle Persuasion

Virtually everything we do with horses involves moving in one way or another, and their usual response when upset is to move quickly. However, sometimes, for one reason or another, the horse doesn't want to move. Once you're sure that there is nothing really wrong, then you need a way to get him started without starting a fight. Often, when a horse doesn't want to come forward with you when you are leading, all you need to do to get his feet moving is to turn him. As noted previously, the easiest way to turn when leading is to the left. If your horse is sticking and not responding to the requests for movement outlined previously, try starting him off in a left turn rather than straight ahead. By turning, you take him slightly off balance so he is more likely to move his feet. Once he is moving his feet, you can usually redirect him back to the path you

Types of Sticks

Sticks are also called whips, crops, bats, and quirts, among other things. Stick is more of a generic term (figure 8.7). Whip generally refers to a longer, more flexible instrument, often with a lash on the end. Crops and bats are fairly short—around 2 feet (60 cm) or less, with a flat leather loop on the tip and either a knob or a button on the handle end to keep it from slipping out of your hand, and sometimes a loop for your wrist as well. Use wrist loops with caution because if the crop gets caught in something, it's safer to drop it. Quirts are generally thin and flexible. All of these items can hurt quite a lot if you are careless or cruel.

Figure 8.7 Sticks of various shapes and sizes.

originally planned to take. Sometimes it can take a couple of tries, but this method will usually get a sticky horse moving.

After the cluck and the lead rope signals, the other tool for asking a horse to move is the stick. Many, if not most, people think that stick equals punishment. This is not at all true with horses because it's a long way from his head to his tail. The stick is simply an extension of your arm. It should only rarely be used in such a way that it causes pain or even discomfort because that causes tension and resentment. If the horse doesn't respond to a light signal, it nearly always means that something is wrong either with what you are doing or with his perception of it.

When you are working on the ground, the stick should be long enough so that you can comfortably reach the horse's hindquarters from a position near his head, so you will probably use some sort of whip. It should not be so heavy that it is uncomfortable or awkward for you to hold and use, but it should not be so flexible that you can accidentally sting the horse with it. It should have a comfortable handgrip with a knob or button on the end. The stable where you are taking lessons will probably have a variety of whips for you to choose from. Be sure to tell the instructor if the one you are given is hard for you to handle. This is no time to be clumsy.

There are two ways to hold the stick. On the ground, depending on how you are using it, most of the time you will face the direction of the stick so you can see what you are doing. For this work you hold the stick with your thumb pointing toward the lash end of the stick (figure 8.8).

Figure 8.8 Hand position when facing the stick.

However, for some work, especially as the horse becomes more responsive, you will let the stick trail behind you, so your thumb will be wrapped around the handle end. Practice holding and handling the stick in both positions. Also practice changing from one position to the other.

Once you are comfortable with the stick, the next step is to get the horse comfortable with it as well. Even though the stick should not be used abusively, many horses have been abused at some time in their lives and can be very fearful or even angry when confronted with a stick. For this reason you should never *ride* with a stick on a horse you don't know until you have had a chance to test him out on the ground. Also never offer a stick to someone on a horse unless both of you know what you're doing.

The primary objective of the following exercise is to teach you how to work with the stick, not how to train the horse. The horse you are working with should be comfortable with seeing and being touched by the stick and move willingly in response to the stick aid. As with the introduction of the halter, the purpose here is for the horse to be comfortable with you and what you plan to do with the stick.

As with other equipment that you have introduced to the horse, first let him touch it and smell it. Especially with the stick, it is important to approach him carefully.

Introducing the Horse to the Stick

1. Face the horse slightly off to his left so he can see you clearly. Hold the stick down by your side in your right hand, and hold the lead rope in your left (figure 8.9a). Check your seven steps and grounding.

2. Quietly bring the stick, handle end first, up where the horse can see it, holding it where he can reach out and touch it.

3. After he has given it the once-over, gently bring your hand with the stick in it up to his shoulder and lay the back of your hand with the whip in it on his shoulder (figure 8.9b).

4. Stand by his head facing his shoulder. Hold the stick in thumb down position.

5. Holding the stick well away from him, slowly wave it up and down. If he seems comfortable, take a step back toward his hindquarters, waving the stick as you move. He may move forward at this point, which is a natural reaction, so unless he seems frightened as well just pause for a moment and use your voice to ask him to stand.

6. Step back to his shoulder and lay the stick against it, then stroke him with it.

7. Continue stroking him over the rest of his body, going from back and barrel to hindquarters, down his legs and down the lower half of his neck (figure 8.9b).

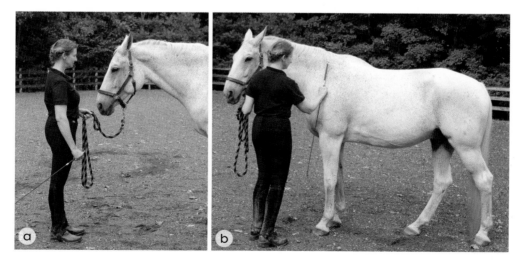

Figure 8.9   Carefully monitor the horse's behavior when introducing him to the stick.

8. Go to his right side and repeat, starting off slowly because some horses are not used to being handled from the right and are more nervous as a result.

9. Finally, stand directly in front of the horse a couple of feet away. Hold the stick with your thumb down and wave it gently up and down to one side, keeping it well away from his face. Watch him carefully so that if he starts to be uncomfortable or raises his head you don't hit him by accident. If he remains calm, quietly bring the stick in a circle up over his head and down the other side.

Once the horse is comfortable with you and the stick, the next step is to get him to respond to it by moving forward. How you position yourself is very important. The horse responds to how you place your center relative to his, so being in the wrong place can confuse him and prevent the response you are looking for. The method of teaching the horse to follow by using the stick that is presented here is derived from Tteam, created by Linda Tellington-Jones.

Using the Stick

1. Position yourself on the horse's left side, facing the direction you want to go and as far forward as you can be while still reaching the horse's hindquarters with the stick. Hold the lead rope in your left hand and the stick, thumb down, in your right hand. Center and ground yourself.

2. Let the horse see and sniff the stick, then bring it back and lay it on his hindquarters very gently so there is no suggestion of tapping. You do *not* want the horse to move off if you just place the stick on his hindquarters. He must learn to wait for the tap, or he might anticipate a request and begin to move off as soon as you start to carry the stick back and before you are ready.

3. Keeping your eyes soft, tap the horse lightly on his hindquarters and at the same time take a small step forward. Watch him for any indication that he heard the tap of the stick. He might flick his ears back or turn his head slightly or contract the muscles in his hindquarters. If he starts to move, praise him and start to walk forward yourself.

    3.A If you can see that he heard the tap but didn't move, that means that he isn't sure what you want. Wait three seconds and then tap the same way, but this time add a cluck, move forward a little more positively, and perhaps comb the lead forward. If he still doesn't move, use the lead to bring his head forward and to the left until he has to take a step, then praise him extravagantly.

    3.B If he did not appear to hear the tap, wait three seconds and then tap slightly harder and wait for any response. You can continue doing this as long as you don't allow yourself to become angry or hit him hard enough to hurt. Once you find the level where you have his attention, stay at that level and continue with step 4.

4. After he either stops on his own or you stop him, start again, using the lightest tap first, then proceed gradually to the level where you get a response. The idea is to use the lightest possible aid rather than jump to the stronger aid immediately. This will help him to learn to respond to the lighter aid.

Practice with him until you feel comfortable using the stick and the horse is responding in a quiet, relaxed manner.

The leading skills that you have learned in this chapter will apply to many situations and can be used with virtually every horse you handle throughout your riding career.

9

Expanding Your Ground Skills

Well, let's see what you've learned about in the way of ground skills so far. You've learned about how to stand and move around the horse and to observe his reactions to you and your activities. You've learned about how to groom him, move him around when he's tied, help with tacking, put on his halter, and lead him.

Notice that I said *learned about*, not *learned* or *know*. You've learned something only when you've done it enough that you don't have any questions about it. You know it when you can do it correctly without having to think about it at all because it has become a reflex.

Now you're ready to learn about three more basic skills, all of which will improve your ability to work with your horse and make you more independent on the ground.

You don't necessarily have to learn the following skills all at once or even in this order, but they are skills you should start working on whenever you feel confident:

1. Leading the horse into the stall and going into the stall to bring him out

2. Cleaning his feet

3. Tacking him up with a bareback pad

Once you're comfortable with leading your horse in the open, the next thing to consider is leading him in slightly more difficult situations. The most common of these is leading him in and out of the stall.

The two kinds of horse stalls are the box stall and the straight, or standing, stall. A box stall, the most common type, is just what the name implies: a big square box, usually about 10 by 10 feet (3 by 3 m) for an average-sized horse. It has at least one large door either sliding or swinging on hinges. A sliding door is usually solid at the bottom but open with protective bars in the upper half so the horse can see out. A hinged door is usually just a half door or perhaps a Dutch door if it opens to the outdoors, often with some sort of removable guard above, especially if the horse is not well mannered. The horse can move around in the stall fairly freely to get to his food and water, and there is plenty of room for him to lie down and stretch out.

The much less common straight, or standing, stall is long and fairly narrow, about 4 feet wide and 8 feet deep (1.2 by 2.4 m). The horse stands with his head facing inward, where his food and water are located. He is kept in the stall either with a halter and tie rope at his head or with a heel rope across the back of the stall or both. Despite the name, horses can and do lie down in a standing stall.

Most newer barns have only box stalls, but standing stalls were more common in the old days. The standing stall is practical for humans because you can fit more horses into the same space, and stall cleaning is easier. If the horse gets out regularly to run around and roll (horses, like dogs, like to roll to scratch their backs), the standing stall is not uncomfortable. Most horses don't sleep fully stretched out—it takes too long to get up if a predator comes along—but some horses like to lie down and stretch out in the warm spring sun or in hot weather.

The occasional horse is difficult to catch in a box stall or has other vices, so keeping him confined in a standing stall might be best for all concerned until the problems are resolved.

Leading the Horse Into the Stall

Leading the horse into a stall sounds as though it should be no problem, but leading a horse in tight places is like maneuvering your car in a parking lot: You can't just think about the front of the car; you have to consider the rest of it as well and calculate the angles correctly. Because some people don't think about this, some horses are afraid to go through narrow places, especially when being led, since they instinctively follow in the leader's track. If the leader turns the corner into the stall too sharply, the horse can hit his hipbone on the edge of the doorway or stall opening, which is very painful. Unfortunately, when a horse is afraid, he tends to want to go faster, so the next time he goes through the door, he cuts the corner and goes faster so it hurts even more. Besides the danger to both individuals, this affects the relationship with the horse and the horse's trust in people.

The most effective and considerate approach is to make a big, wide turn, such as you would make if you were putting your car in a head-in parking space that was a bit narrow. If the stall is on your right, bring the horse over to the left side of the aisle, or about 8 to 10 feet (2.4 to 3m) away from the door or opening, before you begin the turn. This way the horse's body is straight as he starts in (figure 9.1).

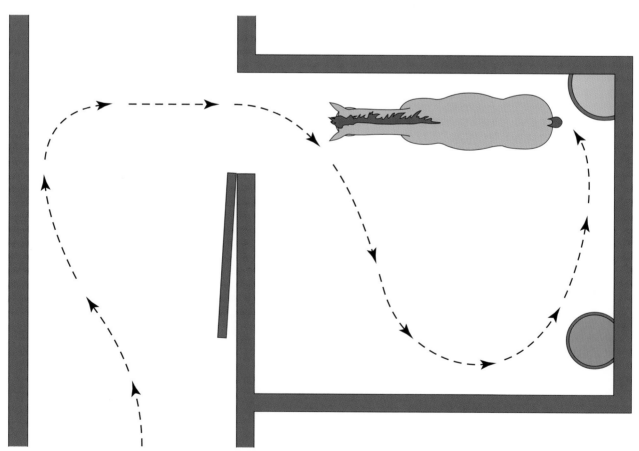

Figure 9.1 Turning pattern for entering the stall.

Horses are usually in a hurry to get back to their own secure environment, where perhaps dinner is waiting, and in his haste the horse himself can be careless. Sometimes, if an experienced person is bringing several horses in from turnout and is in a hurry, she might turn the horse loose outside the stall and let him go in by himself. This is okay once in a while, or with horses that are mature and well trained, but it can cause the horse to try to take over and run into the stall by himself even if his leader doesn't want him to. He might cut the corner or run over the leader in the process.

If the horse shows signs of speeding up or trying to pass you as you approach his stall, ask him to stop for a few seconds, praise him, then start up again. You might need to do this more than once. If you are fairly experienced, you can even turn him around and lead him away for a few steps, stop, then turn around and try again.

When you actually put him in the stall, you should always *lead* him in so that he walks behind you and a little to one side. When you enter a box stall, walk toward the right back corner, then turn the horse around to the left until he is facing out. Entering the standing stall, you can only walk straight in and the horse will not be turned around.

If the horse is already untacked, the final step in a box stall should involve removing the halter and lead rope if that is the custom in your barn, or just the lead rope if halters are left on. Stand close to the door as you do this so you can step out of the stall and be out of the horse's way if he turns quickly to get to his dinner. In a standing stall, if the horse is to be tied, remove the lead rope and attach the tie rope; otherwise continue as in the box stall, walk quietly out of the stall, and fasten the heel rope.

Generally speaking, a beginning rider should not be asked to groom, tack, or untack the horse in the stall. Working in the standing stall is very confining and involves a lot of moving the horse over and walking behind him, which is uncomfortable for most beginners. The same is somewhat true of a horse who is tied in a box stall or who is loose and at liberty to turn around or walk away to eat or drink if he pleases, which is very disconcerting for the novice.

Bringing the Horse Out of the Stall

Entering the stall with a horse is another one of those situations that triggers a sort of claustrophobic feeling ("The horse is so big, and the stall is so small"), so you should certainly have someone experienced assisting you for the first few times until you feel comfortable. As your relationship and comfort around the horse improve over time, you will feel more secure about going into the stall with him.

The stall is the horse's room and is his personal space, especially if he has been living there for some time. Therefore, it is important to extend him the same courtesy that you would if you were entering a person's room. Some horses are very protective of their spaces, so with a horse you don't know it's a good idea to stop a little distance from the door, but within his sight, before proceeding. If he is comfortable with your presence, he will approach you with his ears forward or perhaps, after glancing at you, continue with what he was doing. If he looks angry or aggressive, back away a little and wait. If he doesn't change his attitude, ask for help.

Horse in a Box Stall

If you are already familiar with the horse, start by gathering up the halter and lead if you plan to bring him out. Carry them unobtrusively in one hand with the rope coiled up so you don't trip on it. Before trying to enter the stall or even open the door, you must first speak to him. This is partly to get his attention if he happens to be napping but also to let him know your intentions and to see how he responds. You can cluck or call his name or tap on the door—whatever works—but it is important that you be *sure* that he knows you are there. Watch for some clear indication of this. The horse should turn around or come over to the door to see what's happening. If he is eating or is otherwise occupied with his back turned, he might just lift his head or turn his ears (which means his eyes as well) to see who's there.

If he comes over to the door and you can reach him easily, you can exchange greetings just as you did the first time you were introduced. If his back is turned but there is plenty of room for you to get by, you can enter the stall. As you do so, close the door most of the way so he can't sneak out, but don't latch it. Go directly to his head and greet him. Do *not* touch him on the hindquarters first. If by any chance he was not aware of you or feels threatened by having you in the stall, he might feel trapped and kick. Behavior like this is rare, but as with other animals, horses that have been mistreated might react accordingly when startled.

If there is not room for you to get by his hindquarters, he doesn't move when you cluck, and especially if he shows signs of being irritable, ask for help. He probably wouldn't hurt you, but he might scare you, and that is something you should avoid if at all possible.

If everything goes smoothly, which it probably will, after exchanging greetings put on his halter and lead. The only new problem you might encounter is that he wanted to continue eating and won't bring his head up. Try a cluck first, then cluck again and at the same time nudge (do not kick) his chin with your toe, very gently at first, then a little more firmly, but not enough to really hurt or scare him. Most horses bring their heads up on a regular basis anyway, and when he does, if you move so that you are slightly under his neck with the halter ready to go over his nose, you can probably get it done. This situation can be frustrating for novices because the horse knows that he is more experienced in such matters than you are. Try to be patient but firm, letting him know that you don't plan to give up but also not losing your temper. Determination, not anger, is the way to go. And when you do succeed, shower him with praise, and the next time will be easier for you both.

Now you're ready to bring him out. First make sure that the door is fully open, but block the horse a little with your body until you are ready. Keeping him in correct leading position, lead him straight out until he is almost fully out of the stall before you start to turn him.

Horse in a Standing Stall

Stand somewhat behind the left side of the stall, not directly behind the horse. Begin with the same approach that you use for entering the box stall, carrying the halter and lead with you if the horse is not already wearing one, and you plan to bring him out. It is really important to get the horse's attention because you will have to walk in close to his hindquarters. Once he notices you, if you cluck to him he will probably step over to the right to allow you to enter. If not, add a tap on the side of his hindquarters while still standing off to one side. If he does not respond, do *not* attempt to push him over. Try tapping and clucking once or twice more, then ask for help.

When he has moved over, if there is a heel rope, unfasten it. Drop the heel rope on the far side of the stall out of the way. Some stables have you hook it back up to the ring on the far side, but this makes a loop that the horse can get caught in, so it is better to let it hang as neatly as possible. Walk to the front of the stall, being careful not to push against the horse as you do so. If you need him to move his forehand over more, use the same cluck and tap procedure as before.

If he is not wearing a halter, stand a little under his neck as you put on the halter to discourage him from backing out before you're ready. When his halter and lead are on, turn to face out of the stall, and ask him to back straight out until there is room for both of you to turn (see Getting the Horse to Move Backward in chapter 7).

Once the horse is out on the aisle, you're ready to put him on crossties so he can be groomed and tacked.

Cleaning the Horse's Feet

There is an adage: "No hoof, no horse." This is another way of saying that if the horse's feet are neglected and he goes lame, he is no longer rideable. Most of this is related to shoeing, but daily hoof maintenance should be part of grooming. The tool you will use is called a hoof pick (figure 9.2). The best ones are quite simple, and the business end should not be sharply pointed but should either have a rounded point or be shaped like a slot-headed screwdriver. Some hoof picks have a little brush attached, which is convenient for finishing up.

The part of the hoof that is important to clean is the underside, which consists primarily of the sole and the frog (figure 9.3). The sole is hard and slightly concave; the frog, which acts as a shock absorber, should be fleshy and rounded. The two are separated by shallow grooves called comasures, and the center of the frog has a shallow groove, the cleft, running down it as well. In a neglected foot these grooves can be eaten away, usually by a fungal infection called thrush. Thrush has a bad odor and can make the horse's foot very tender. You should always tell your instructor if you suspect the horse has thrush because it usually requires some sort of regular treatment. Preventing thrush is one of the primary reasons for cleaning the horse's feet regularly. Another is to find any foreign bodies—anything from a small stone to a nail—lodged in the foot. You also would notice any more severe injury and whether the shoe has become loose, shifted out of position, or gone missing.

By now you should be comfortable enough around the horse that working with his feet will not give rise to fear. However, you must consider what is involved for the horse

Figure 9.2 Hoof picks.

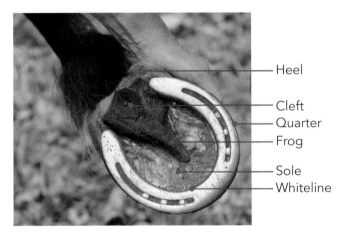

Heel

Cleft

Quarter

Frog

Sole

Whiteline

Figure 9.3 Familiarize yourself with the normal appearance of the hoof so that you can detect signs of illness or injury.

in having his feet worked with. You should work with a horse that is well trained and comfortable with having his feet picked up and handled. You should also have an experienced person with you the first time or two to give you confidence and guide you if necessary. Start the new work after you have spent the usual time grooming and establishing a comfortable relationship.

The first thing to consider is that the horse will have to stand on three feet while you work with the fourth one. So he should be, in horse parlance, standing square. That is, his front and hind feet should each be more or less side by side, and his feet should be underneath his shoulders or hindquarters, not out in front or behind or off to one side. Some horses usually stand square on their own; others don't. If your horse is not standing square, use the instructions in chapter 7 to move him around a little until he is (see figure 7.1). It might take some trial and error to get him in position, but it is good practice for you in understanding how his mechanics work.

Once you have him standing square, the next step is to get him to pick up a foot. The normal procedure is to start with his left front foot. See figure 9.4 for the terms used for the various parts of the horse's legs and feet.

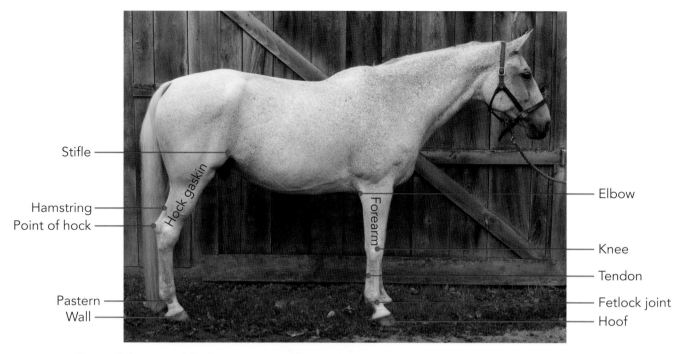

Stifle

Hock gaskin

Hamstring
Point of hock

Forearm

Elbow

Knee

Tendon

Pastern
Wall

Fetlock joint
Hoof

Figure 9.4 Parts of the horse's legs and feet.

Instructions for Cleaning the Horse's Front Feet

1. Stand by the horse's left front foot, facing his tail and holding the hoof pick in your right hand.

2. Slide your left hand down the back to the horse's leg, starting just above his knee. Some horses are taught to pick up their feet in response to a tap or squeeze just below the knee, others just above the fetlock.

3. Using your thumb and fingers, gently squeeze the tendon in the appropriate spot. You can also cluck, and some horses respond well if you give a gentle shove with your shoulder against the upper leg to get him to shift his weight to the other foot. (He has to do this to lift up the foot on this side.)

4. When he starts to pick up his foot, quickly slide your left hand down toward the horse's hoof, and at the same time slide it to the left so that your hand ends up around his hoof with your fingers underneath (figure 9.5a). If you miss and he puts his foot down before you can catch hold of it, just pat him and start over.

5. Step sideways with your left foot so that the horse's knee is resting a little against your thigh. Your knees will be bent somewhat and you will be bending over more or less depending on how high the horse is willing to hold his foot.

6. With your hoof pick, begin at the back of the hoof near the outside edge (figure 9.5b). Pick and scrape carefully on the sole first, then around the frog. The instructor will guide you in how much you should expect to clean, but if the hoof is healthy it's difficult to hurt the horse with the hoof pick. Finish by brushing the loose material off with a little brush if you have one or the edge of your hand.

7. When you are finished, do *not* drop his foot. Instead, move your foot out from under him, then carefully let his hoof slide out of your hand. Some horses find it more comfortable if you gently shake the hoof or move it in a small circle before letting it go. The movement helps him to rediscover his balance and relax.

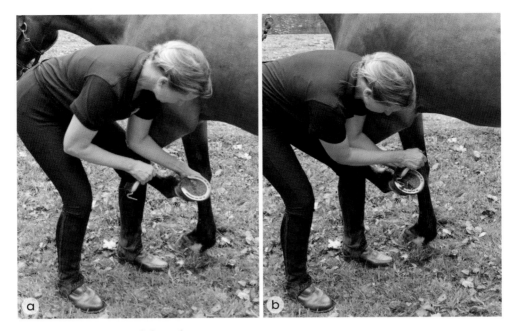

Figure 9.5 Cleaning the left front foot.

Throughout the cleaning process your hand should support the horse's hoof against the pressure of the pick. At no time should you bend his toe downward away from you. Try not to pull his foot out to the side, which novices tend to do because they feel uncomfortable standing so close under the horse.

Occasionally during the hoof-cleaning process something will occur to make the horse want or need to put his foot down. He might lose his balance, or a fly might be bothering him. If he doesn't struggle too much, you can follow the movement with your hands until he becomes comfortable again. However, if he really wants to get away from you, just let his foot go and step out of the way. Try to determine what caused the problem and correct it if possible. If it is fly season, look for flies, especially in places he can't reach easily. Also consider whether you have been holding his foot in a way that makes him uncomfortable or perhaps holding it up too long. Remember that even though you are holding the foot, the horse has to keep his weight off of it, which can be tiring.

Figure 9.6 Cleaning a hind foot.

After you finish the horse's left front foot, repeat the process for his right front foot. Most right-handed people will start out with the right hoof in the right hand but immediately switch hands so that they can use the hoof pick with the right hand. Left-handed people would probably do the same on the horse's left side but would still start with the left front foot first because most horses are accustomed to that routine.

It's probably best to just work with the horse's front feet at first until you get comfortable with the position and technique. Working with the hind feet makes some people nervous, and some horses have more trouble picking up or holding up their hind feet. You would approach the cleaning of the hind feet in the same way as in the front, but you stand well underneath the horse with his leg coming over your thigh and resting on it (figure 9.6).

When cleaning all four feet, you can do the feet on one side before starting on the other, doing the front foot on each side first. You can also just go around the horse counterclockwise. Horses tend to get accustomed to one sequence, so notice or ask what is customary in your barn.

Cleaning feet is usually the last grooming job, so you're ready to tack up.

Tacking Up the Horse With the Bareback Pad and Grounding Strap

Tacking your horse with a pad and grounding strap is fairly simple, especially if you've been watching someone else do it for a while. Start by taking a look at your horse's back. The lowest point should be just behind the base of the withers. This is the strongest place, so it is where your seat bones should rest (figure 9.7). However, you do not sit in the middle of the pad because you need to leave room for your knees to hang in front of you without going off the front of the pad. About three-fifths of the pad should be in front of the low point and the rest behind it. You also need to consider the grain of the horse's hair in putting the pad on so that the hair is not rubbed the wrong way.

Low point

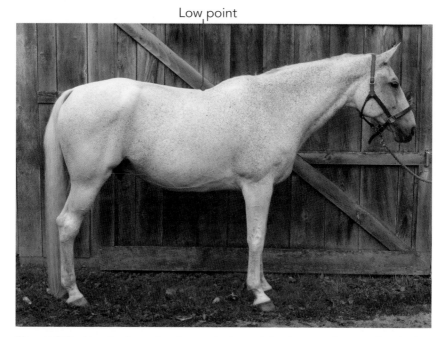

Figure 9.7 Use the lowest point on the horse's back as a reference for placing the bareback pad.

The pad will be held in place either by a surcingle, which goes all the way around the horse and fastens back to itself (figure 9.8) or a girth, which passes under the horse's belly and fastens to billet straps on both sides (figure 9.9).

Since for safety reasons the grounding strap should be attached to the pad, it must be ready to put on as soon as the pad is in place and before the girth or surcingle is completely fastened. Grounding straps can be constructed in a variety of ways (see the appendix at http://tinyurl.com/d8pv7nz for more information on grounding straps). They are based on a western breastplate, and the most comfortable and safest one for the horse uses padded straps that attach to the straps or rings on the upper sides of the pad, and to the girth or surcingle by passing between the horse's front legs. It may or may not open across the top to make it easier to put on. You should familiarize yourself with the grounding strap so that you can put in on correctly without too much fumbling.

Figure 9.8 The grounding strap and bareback pad are secured with a surcingle, which is made up with two 1-inch stirrup leathers and a girth.

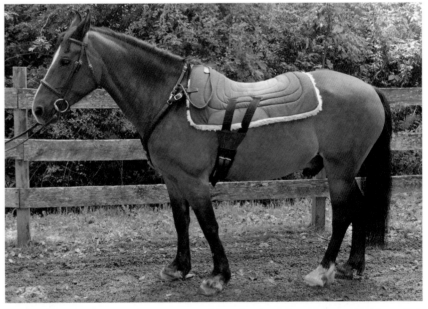

Figure 9.9 The grounding strap and bareback pad are secured with a girth fastened to billet straps.

Putting On the Pad

Every piece of tack has a purpose; the bareback pad has several purposes. First, for the rider, it protects her seat from discomfort if the horse has a prominent backbone. Second, unlike saddles or the horse's bare back, the pad is not slippery, so the rider feels secure. Also, without a pad, a horse leaves hair all over the riding clothes, especially when he is shedding, and sweat marks in hot weather, neither of which is very desirable. But the most important reason for using the pad is that it protects the horse's back from pain caused by pressure from the rider's seat bones, which can be significant if the ride is extended or the rider is tense or bounces. To protect his back, the horse may wear more than one pad.

1. With the horse tied and grooming completed, pick up the pad, holding the center front in your left hand and the center back in your right hand.

2. Standing on his left side near his head, quietly show the horse the pad and allow him time to look and sniff. This is especially important with clothing that might have been worn by another horse.

3. Move to a point by the horse's shoulder and gently rub the pad, following the grain of his hair, down his shoulder and along his back where you can comfortably reach. If he should show signs of fear, don't continue until he relaxes.

4. Still holding the pad with both hands, open it up, lift it up, and place the middle of it over the middle of the horse's withers.

5. Slide the pad back—with the grain of the hair—until the place where your seat will be is over the correct place on the horse's back.

Fastening the Girth or Surcingle

This is where most of the mistakes are made. The area of the horse's barrel where the girth or surcingle passes is quite sensitive. Under the barrel it passes over the horse's sternum, or breastbone, which is cartilaginous in a young horse, so it is very sensitive to pressure. If, as sometimes happens, the girth is tightened more than necessary, it creates pain and tension and sometimes long-lasting fear. Because you'll be putting on the grounding strap in a minute, you will fasten up the surcingle or girth just enough to keep things in place.

Some bareback pads come with an attached surcingle. If this is the case, start from step 2.

1. If using a surcingle, it should have no padding or rings, which can cause discomfort. Starting on the horse's right side, put the surcingle through the girth loop so that the buckle end hangs down. It should hang low enough for you to reach it from the other side under the horse's belly. Lay the top of the surcingle across the horse's back. If using a girth, buckle it to the billet straps on the horse's right side and allow it to hang.

2. Walk around to the horse's left side and stand by his front leg. Put your left hand on his shoulder and with your right hand rub or pat his barrel area on the side, where the surcingle or girth will be fastened. If using a surcingle, take the strap end in your left hand so it doesn't slide around.

3. *Staying by his front leg*, reach under his barrel with your right hand and take the buckle end of the surcingle or girth. Bring it up until it is lightly touching his barrel (figure 9.10).

Figure 9.10 Fastening the girth from a safe position.

4. Fasten the buckle to the strap end of the surcingle or the billet strap just snugly enough so that it is in contact with the horse's barrel, not hanging loose. If there are two buckles, fasten only one.

Putting On the Grounding Strap

Now you are ready for the grounding strap. Be careful not to let the horse drop his head down too low while you are putting it on because he could step on it and scare himself.

1. If the grounding strap opens at the top, undo the fastening and check to make sure you have it facing the right way.
2. Take the right side of the grounding strap in your left hand and pass it around the base of the horse's neck. Reach over the top of the horse's neck with your right hand, take the end of the grounding strap, and fasten it together around the horse's neck. Go to step 4.
3. With a grounding strap that doesn't open, if the horse is crosstied, undo the left crosstie, put the grounding strap carefully over the horse's head as you did with the halter (see chapter 6), do up the left crosstie, undo the right one and slide the grounding strap back, then redo the crosstie. If the horse has only one tie, after putting the grounding strap over his head, undo the tie, slide the grounding strap back, and redo the tie.
4. Attach the grounding strap to the pad on the sides.
5. If there is a snap on the end of the chest strap and a ring on the center of the girth, snap the chest strap to the girth. Make sure it is not twisted.
6. If the chest strap ends in a loop, undo the girth or surcingle and hold it in your right hand while using your left hand to pass the grounding strap chest strap between the horse's front legs. Then pass the girth or surcingle through the chest strap loop and fasten it up as before. Be sure the chest strap is centered between the horse's legs, and check it after tightening the girth.

Tightening the Girth or Surcingle

The girth or surcingle only needs to be tight enough to hold the pad down against the horse's back. It is not possible to make it tight enough to keep the pad from slipping a little off to one side or the other. A very tight girth only makes the horse uncomfortable. An uncomfortable horse is tense and less responsive, and he often has rougher gaits. He also might develop resistance to the girth, not allowing you to tighten or even fasten it easily. This is called being cinchy.

If you happen to be given a horse who is cinchy, even if the practice at the stable is to be unsympathetic, it is still possible to teach the horse that, though others might be rough with him, you will not be. Over time the horse will learn to trust you and stand quietly while you fasten the girth.

Think of doing up your own belt: You want it to be firm enough to hold your trousers up but not so tight that it's painful. And the horse's girth doesn't go around a compressible abdomen but around his rib cage, where there is much less give.

1. Initially the buckle should be fastened just enough so the girth is in light contact with the horse's body. Without unfastening the buckle, pull down firmly on the strap, then pull up, holding the sides of the buckle until the tongue comes out of the hole. If the horse seems tense, try stroking him gently with your palm in the girth area before bringing the girth up against him. If you are familiar with Tteam (the Tellington Touch Every Animal Method developed by Linda Tellington-Jones), use small circles with your fingers to help him to focus and relax.
2. Pull up smoothly and only until you feel firm resistance, then put the buckle tongue in the nearest hole.

3. If there is a second buckle, tighten it in the same way.

4. After the horse has moved around a bit, and before mounting, check the girth by pulling up against one strap, as before. If it comes easily, tighten it up; otherwise leave it as is.

To check the tightness of the girth or surcingle, stand by the horse's left front leg facing slightly to the rear. You should be able to see the horse's head, especially if he isn't tied. Some horses that have been girthed unsympathetically will try to nip when you check the girth. If you keep your left elbow toward him, you can block such an attempt until you have persuaded him that you will be considerate.

Slide your hand under the pad and surcingle at the widest part of the horse's barrel. If it feels very tight, and especially if the horse tenses against your hand, you should probably let it down a notch, even if you have to take it up again later.

When you withdraw your hand, lift it away from the horse's body a little so you don't rub the hair the wrong way. Once you are mounted, you, or someone on the ground if you can't reach the girth, should check the girth again.

You will probably make a few mistakes when tacking up at first, so be sure that your instructor checks your work until you have it figured out. But as long as the horse is comfortable with what you're doing, any mistakes you make are not too serious.

10

The Gentle Riding Aids

The term *aids* is used to describe the various ways you communicate with your horse while riding. As the name implies, their purpose is to *help* the horse to perform the task by showing him what to do and the easiest way to do it.

Usually people think of the aids as the reins and the rider's legs because they are the most obvious, and it is true that they are very important. This topic is covered at length in chapter 18. However, using those aids before your seat is secure is very likely to affect your balance and cause tension, which in turn makes them ineffective. So it's best to wait until your body is ready before learning to use the rein and leg aids.

However, several other aids besides the voice—which was covered in chapter 7—don't create problems in positioning and also are less upsetting to the horse if you make a small mistake. They are used by good riders at all levels, allowing a subtle, almost telepathic, exchange between rider and horse. The communication is less obvious and often less distracting to the horse. You do not have to learn about the aids in the order in which they are presented in this chapter—the order in which you should acquire them depends on your instructor and the lesson setup. However, they are nearly always used in this order, although not necessarily all of them for every circumstance. As you become familiar with the aids you will understand more clearly the logic of the sequence. The aids are intent, eyes, center, seat, weight, and the stick. I'll talk about each aid individually.

> What makes an aid correct is that it makes it as *easy as possible* for the horse to perform the task.

Understanding and Applying Intent

As discussed in chapter 2, intent means having a clear, conscious image of what you want the horse to do, and as far as possible, how you want him to do it. Horses might or might not read your mind; they might simply be aware of small adjustments in your body as you prepare for a new task. It doesn't really make any difference how the communication takes place, but there is no question that the more clearly you understand the task and how to ask for it, the better the results will be.

As you gain experience, when you think of performing a particular task on a familiar horse your body will start preparing for it, which is part of the intent that the horse can read via muscular telepathy. It is also true that if, at some level, you really don't want to perform the task yourself—if you are, for example, afraid of or uncertain about cantering—the intent *not* to canter is the message the horse will receive and probably respond to unless there is some other stimulus to make him canter anyway.

Using Your Eyes

Your eyes are closely allied to intent. If your intention is to turn right, part of the procedure is looking to the right, toward where you plan to go. Your eyes have subtle effects on your body, which help to communicate the message. Using your *soft* eyes (see step 4 in chapter 2) helps in several ways. You are aware of what is happening all around you, so if you are riding with others, it is fairly easy to keep from running or being run into. Second, soft eyes help you to think holistically, which is an important aid to learning and riding better. And since soft eyes are essentially noncontrolling, if the horse doesn't respond as you expected, neither he nor you will be as likely to be aggressive about it.

Moving Your Center

Your center is one of the most subtle and most useful of all the aids. You can use it for working the horse on the ground as well as when riding. Basically *the horse will move away from your center*, so if your center is to the right, it tells the horse to move left.

Movements of the center while mounted have to be very small, since moving your center also affects your weight, which can send mixed signals when used for lateral (turning and moving sideways) work. The center is used in conjunction with intent and eyes to begin virtually any request.

Using Your Center for Transitions

If you wish the horse to change pace forward (for example, to go from a slow to a faster walk), you use your center in conjunction with your weight. That is, you keep your center firmly *behind* the horse's center. We talk more about this in the section Managing Your Weight later in this chapter.

Using Your Center for Turning

Turning is the most valuable function of your center as an aid. It is very clear to the horse, requires almost no effort on your part, and usually reduces and often eliminates your need for any other active aid. It is used in conjunction with your eyes and intent to begin any lateral movement and also to prevent unwanted lateral movement by the horse, such as drifting into the center of the arena.

Before beginning this work, review the section Lateral Centering in chapter 5 and the section Staying Laterally Centered in chapter 6. To use your center as a turning aid, you will use your body in exactly the same way. But instead of keeping your center over the horse's, you will move it very slightly to the side *away* from the direction you want the horse to move or turn.

If you want the horse to move to the right, shift your center *very slightly* to the left. Just as in a game of tag, the horse will instinctively want to go to the right. Since you will be slightly off center, reach down with your right leg a little to keep your weight fairly even. Notice that if you try to move your center too much to the left, your weight will go too much to the left as well,

Don't Rock the Boat—or the Horse

Keeping your center back and still when you want the horse to go faster is counterintuitive—your body wants to rock or lean forward as it would if you were increasing speed on the ground, but this would block and unbalance the horse. It is even more confusing if you are on a horse that is already going fairly fast. If he loses his balance at speed, he will often speed up even more, just as if you are running and trip and end up running faster for a few steps as your legs try to catch up with your body. Unfortunately, this leads some people to believe that using their weight forward is a good way to get the horse to go faster, but since it also makes it harder for him, it leads to more problems for both of you.

and the horse will be forced to go left to keep his balance. When the horse begins to respond to the shifting of your center to the left by moving to the right, immediately move your center to the right until you are even on both seat bones.

When you are comfortable with right turns, start working on left turns. These are somewhat more difficult in terms of moving your center correctly. When you are correct, your right hip will be on a line with or a little to the right of your shoulder. If it persists on staying to the left, it means your body is S-curving and needs to be stretched more.

Practice making small turns with your center until you feel comfortable with it. As with all these gentle aids, don't be discouraged if you don't get perfect results every time. The horse might be distracted, or you might be making small mistakes that confuse him. Especially with centering, trying harder doesn't work. You'll improve with practice and so will he.

Using the Passive Center

The passive center is closely related to intent and is just what it implies. You simply say with your body that you aren't asking for anything. It's a way of saying, "Okay, we're done." Among other things, you can use it with your other gentle aids to say to the horse, while he's walking, "It's okay to stop."

Using Your Seat

When we refer to the seat, it doesn't mean the buttocks muscles themselves. Except for holding you upright, the seat muscles are always relaxed and passive. Contracting muscles, which you do to use them, makes them hard, which in the case of your seat muscles leads to bouncing and discomfort for both horse and rider.

The easiest way to understand how the seat is used is to think of a paint roller. The roller itself is passive; you move it by pushing with the handle, which makes the roller move back and forth against the wall. If you were sitting on the horse bareback, his back would be the wall, your seat would be the roller, your pelvis would be the handle, and the muscles of your upper abdomen (which move the pelvis) would be your hand and arm that push the handle. The motion is transferred through the saddle quite effectively as well.

The objective in using the seat is not to try to *push* the horse. Rather, it acts as a *massage* to relax the horse's back muscles so that they move freely, allowing maximum engagement of the hind legs while still supporting you. The seat assists the horse in moving forward without restraint, and, when used unilaterally, prepares the horse and begins the turn.

You can demonstrate this on the ground. Stand with your feet a little apart, and deliberately tense the muscles in your buttocks and lower back. Put a hand on something to steady yourself. Then see how far you can lift one knee. Now grow, stretch, and shake out so that your lower back is really relaxed and soft, and lift one knee again. Big difference!

Learning to Use Your Seat While on the Ground

1. Place a hand on your abdomen with your thumb at your natural waistline and your palm across your navel area.

2. Grow, then start walking fairly briskly. Feel how the movement of your walk moves your hand forward and backward.

3. Using *only* the muscles of your upper abdomen, *push* your hand forward a little with each step, then allow it to move back.

4. As you walk, first one side rolls, then the other. With your arms by your sides and your elbows bent, start swinging your arms, then let them move in circles, as if pedaling a bicycle backward. This is how your seat works against the horse's back when you're riding him straight.

5. Place your right hand in the front of your right iliac crest (the top part of the large pelvic bone just under your waist on the right side) and continue walking. Feel your hand being moved.

6. Push with the right side of your abdominal muscles only so that your right iliac crest and right hand are pushed forward more than the left.

7. Repeat steps 4 and 5 using your left hand on your left iliac crest.

Notice that when your hand is in the center, your hand is pushed forward on every step, while if your hand is on the side, it is pushed forward only every other step.

Learning to Use Your Seat While on the Horse

1. With the horse walking, repeat the previous exercise that you did on the ground, starting with your hand in the middle and feeling the movement the horse imparts to your pelvis. Then add the extra little push with your abs, which will roll your seat over the horse's back. Notice that both sides of your seat move on each step, so the horse is getting a continuous gentle relaxing rub on both sides.

2. Do the exercise first with one hand, then the other. Now only one side of your seat is giving that little extra roll on just that side of the horse's back.

When you allow your seat to simply follow the horse's movement, as you have done up to now, your seat is passive; it does not tell the horse that you plan to change anything he is currently doing. When you use your abdominal muscles to roll your seat over the horse's back, you are using an active seat.

Using Your Seat to Lengthen the Horse's Stride

Especially if the horse is tense, his stride will sometimes be short and choppy instead of free and relaxed. This can be caused by tension in his back, and frequently a gentle use of the seat aid will help him to loosen up.

1. Grow, breathe, and rock slightly forward and back to help yourself sit lightly and still be grounded on your seat bones.

2. At the walk, place one hand on your center and allow the horse's motion to move your hand forward and back as you did on the ground. The leader should walk freely herself. Both you and she should think about your own backs and how you would like the horse's back to be. If you are holding the reins, they should be loose.

3. Move your hand up so your little finger is on your waistline. Use the muscles under your hand to push your hand forward and back while keeping your lower back, buttock, and thigh muscles soft and relaxed. Think about soft eyes and breathing as well.

The horse should want to drop his head and slow the rhythm of his walk. If he raises his head and becomes more tense, you might be pushing with your seat *muscles* and hurting his back rather than relaxing it.

Using Your Seat for Turning

When you are asking for a turn (say, to the right), using an active right seat, in addition to your other aids, will make the turn easier for a horse that is stiff laterally. The seat aid makes the horse's back more flexible and encourages him to step farther forward with his right hind leg. This helps him to support himself on the turn, thus making the action of turning easier for him.

Managing Your Weight

While it is possible to use your weight laterally to make the horse step sideways—moving your weight to the left to get him to turn to the left—it tends to create a rather clumsy, unbalanced turn. To demonstrate this, while walking on foot in a straight line, move your weight so that it is over your left foot. This will tend to make you go to the left but rather awkwardly. Now, *keeping your weight centered,* try some left turns, and also try moving sideways to the left. You will find that both are much easier when your weight is centered.

The Horse as a Slinky

Getting your horse to collect, or take shorter and higher steps, is not done by compressing his body and trying to pull him together but by making him more flexible so that he bends longitudinally. Think of a spring or Slinky toy. If you squash it together from both ends, it will become shorter but only up to a point. The whole device becomes rigid, and it's impossible to bring the two ends together. If instead you stretch it out slightly until it becomes flexible, you can then bend the two ends around until they meet softly. This is what happens when a horse collects himself. He becomes rounder, not shorter. Muscles are like springs: To work efficiently, they must first be stretched. Then, a rider at a fairly advanced level uses a combination of rein and leg aids, which help the horse to bend (flex) longitudinally, which changes some of the forward motion of the step to a higher step. Think of a marathon walker and a drum major. They are both balanced and flexible and expending the same energy but in different ways.

Generally speaking, your weight should be used as an aid only along the horse's long axis to send him forward. However, it must be used in a very particular way, which does *not* involve your shoulders going forward.

As you discovered when you were learning how to use the grounding strap, the pull on the grounding strap travels through your arms and body and into your relaxed seat in such a way that it grounds you onto your seat bones. How your weight affects the horse depends on where your upper body and center are relative to your seat bones and the horse's center.

When you are sitting, if your center is over your seat bones, which are slightly behind the horse's center, your weight is passive. That is, it does not influence the horse except in his ability to carry your weight. If you pull incorrectly with your hands or allow your hip joints to close, your weight will go onto your crotch bone, and your center—and your weight—will go *forward* of the horse, unbalancing you both. On the other hand, leaning back slightly does not unbalance the horse because of the support of his hind legs, nor will it affect your riding unless you are back so far that your lower back tenses.

So how does the weight work as an aid? It deals primarily with the law of inertia, which says that an object in motion tends to continue at the same speed and direction unless something happens to change it. This is why if you are galloping and the horse stops very suddenly you will continue going forward, at the very least onto his neck and perhaps over his head.

If, however, the inertial force is not as great (that is, if the horse simply slows down without being asked and you want him to keep going), by using your back muscles you can redirect the inertial force from your shoulders into your seat so that instead of your weight going over the horse's neck, it goes into the back of his withers and shoulders. You can feel this by using the grounding strap to represent inertial force pulling you forward (figure 10.1).

Figure 10.1 The grounding strap teaches you to use your weight to send the horse forward.

Watch Your Weight

Over many years of watching jumper classes, I have observed that men, who generally have more weight in their upper bodies, are either very effective or very poor at keeping a horse going forward over fences. It depends entirely on whether they understand how to direct their weight correctly. If, when the horse puts in a short stride or hesitates before the fence, the rider does the right thing and keeps his weight back, the horse nearly always continues over the fence. On the other hand, if the rider does the wrong thing and lets those heavy shoulders fall forward, the horse almost *has* to either stop or fall.

All in all, correct use of your weight is a very useful skill to cultivate.

Inertia Exercise

1. With the horse standing still, check your position, then keep your back erect but otherwise leave your back muscles relaxed. Hold your hands on the grounding strap in normal (correct) position.

2. Pull fairly hard on the grounding strap. Your hip joints will close and your shoulders will fall forward. If a moving horse stops suddenly and you are not prepared, inertia has the same effect on your body.

3. Repeat the pulling exercise, but this time lean very slightly back and use your back muscles to keep your hip joints from closing. Try not to arch or round your back, and do keep your buttock and thigh muscles soft.

4. Feel how your shoulders stay back instead of falling forward. Instead, your seat bones press down and forward into the back of the horse's shoulder blades.

5. If you are correctly prepared when the horse stops suddenly, the inertia will act on your body in this way. With practice you can develop your reflexes to keep you grounded in all but very sudden stops from the faster gaits.

To understand how this works as an aid to influence the horse, try the following method of lifting another person. Standing behind her, place your hands on either side of her back just below her shoulder blades. Bend your knees as much as necessary so that you can push up against her shoulder blades from underneath. If she is small enough and you are strong enough, you can pick her up and hold her firmly and safely.

In the same way, if you keep your seat and your center behind the horse's shoulder blades, if he slows down or hesitates, your weight will push against his shoulder blades . This will help to send him not up but forward (because, unlike your human friend, his spine is level with the horizon). The more weight, the more force is directed into the horse.

Like all the aids we are dealing with in this chapter, the weight aid is not a forcing aid. It simply applies pressure in opposition and direct proportion to the amount of resistance the horse is offering without causing any discomfort.

Using the Stick While Riding

You use the stick to ask the horse for movement. In chapter 8 you learned to introduce the horse to the stick while on the ground. You also learned that the stick is not an instrument for punishment and you should never use it in that way if you're a novice, especially when you are on the horse. One of the wisest maxims I learned as a child was "It's never the horse; it's always the rider." That means that if the horse is not doing what you wanted or expected it isn't because he is mean, or lazy, or stubborn. It simply means that you have not made your desire clear, you are doing something wrong in the way you ask, or you have asked for something that the horse is not prepared for either intellectually or emotionally. That is, either he doesn't understand or can't do what you want or he is afraid to do it. In either case, you have to change your approach, not punish the horse.

When you are warmed up and comfortable, you are ready to try the stick. For riding, you should start with a crop, with a button on the end or a wide knob. Like the whip you used earlier,

No, Thanks!

Be wary of the helpful observer who offers to hand you a stick. A stranger hurrying toward you and your horse waving a stick is a recipe for disaster!

it should feel comfortable and balanced in your hand. You may want to buy your own, but be sure to mark it well, because they do have a way of walking away if left at the barn.

The instructor will hand the stick to you. She should approach the horse from the front on his right side, while holding the stick quietly by her side in her left hand. She will put her right hand on the rein and allow the horse to see and sniff the stick. Then, still holding the rein, she will quietly reach up and hand you the stick in your right hand. You will hold it with your thumb nearest the top and all four fingers curled around it.

Once you have the stick firmly in your hand, put your hand back on the grounding strap, which you hold in your first two fingers, so that you have two fingers around the grounding strap but all four fingers and your thumb around the stick (figure 10.2).

Figure 10.2 Proper position for holding the stick and the grounding strap.

Handling the Stick While on the Horse

1. With the horse standing still, take your right hand with the stick off the grounding strap and turn your head so that you can see what you're doing.

2. Reach back quietly and lay the stick against the side of the horse's hindquarters, trying not to tap. As you reach back, do not tense your buttocks or thighs, and be very conscious of your longitudinal center so that you don't tip forward as you reach back, because your center would then block the horse from going forward. However, just as when you were using the stick on the ground, you do not want the horse to get in the habit of moving off as soon as you bring the stick back. You want him to wait for the tap.

3. Bring your hand and the stick quietly back to the grounding strap and turn your head to face forward.

4. Repeat steps 2 and 3 a few times until you are comfortable, then try without turning your head until after you have placed the stick on his hindquarters. Look to see if it is in more or less the right place. Praise your horse for his patience.

Now you are ready to actually ask the horse to move. Check your position using the seven steps, then put the intent to move into your mind. Use your soft eyes to put your attention forward, and use your weight and center as well to begin the request for movement.

Riding the Horse Straight

You might have noticed that we don't talk about using your stick in your left hand. It is true that there are occasionally times when you do. However, if you observe carefully how horses' feet are placed on the ground when they move, you will see that horses generally place their hind feet slightly to the right of their front feet. This has to do with that natural crookedness we talked about in chapter 6. As a rider, you want to help the horse to be as straight as possible. One of the simpler ways to do this is to use the stick on the right side, which tends to make him move a little sideways away from it.

Follow the same procedure with the stick that you used to get the horse to move forward to a stick command on the ground (see the section titled Using the Stick at the end of chapter 8). Your leader can help if necessary. Her own intent to move will also give the horse the idea. Keep a light feel on the grounding strap so that if he starts forward abruptly you don't lose your balance.

Eliminating the Need for Aggression

The lesson you should learn from this chapter is that at no time are you trying to *make* the horse go, turn, or stop; you are merely asking. Table 10.1 lays out the nonaggressive skills you can apply to get the horse to handle transitions and turns calmly and correctly.

Your goal is to develop your relationship with the horse so that he wants to please you and to develop your communication skills so that he understands what you want. If you are successful in establishing a solid relationship and in learning to communicate clearly, you should never feel the need to become aggressive.

Table 10.1   Applying the Gentle Aids During Transitions and Turns

Always start with the seven steps so that your position is as correct as possible.

Upward transitions

The upward transition is the most natural for the horse and the easiest for him to respond to.

Your intent should be a positive thought that you wish the horse to either increase the pace of the gait he is in or change to a different gait.

Your eyes focus forward to a point you want to reach, which will usually change as you move.

Without creating tension, your weight and center stay behind the horse's. If the horse seems tense or resistant in his back, your seat becomes active on both sides (bilaterally).

Use your voice—a cluck or, if your horse understands, a verbal command such as "walk on."

If you get no response, use the stick. If the horse responds to the stick in some way but not by increasing his pace, do not apply the stick more strongly. Instead, review what you have done, see if you can find a reason he is not responding, and ask for help and advice from your instructor.

Turns

Think about where you want to turn, and plan to start well ahead of time. Think of how far ahead you have to plan if you are making a turn in a car.

Look in the direction you want to turn, but don't focus too far ahead. Two or three strides are usually about right.

Move your center slightly to the side *away* from the turn and slightly back—since turning often causes the horse to slow down—while keeping your weight centered.

Become active with the seat bone on the side *toward* which you want to turn.

Downward transitions

All your quiet aids should become very passive—saying not "you have to stop" but "you may stop now."

Your eyes should be soft, and your breathing should be slow and relaxed.

Your seat movement should be just slightly slower than the horse's movement.

You can use your voice for a very quiet, long "ho-o-o-o-o," which you may repeat as often as necessary as long as it is a suggestion, not a command.

11

Handling the Reins and Preparing to Ride Solo

In this chapter we introduce some of the skills you will need to begin riding on your own without someone on the ground controlling the horse for you. I'm sure you're saying, "Well! Finally!" but trust me, all the preparatory work was worth it. The skills you will need are rein handling and riding the slow trot or jog.

Handling the reins is not the same as *using* the reins; *it's the foundation you will need to use the reins properly.* There is a lot more to using the reins than just pulling on them to make the horse go where you want him to. In the first place, it's his feet that have to move in the desired direction, and the reins aren't attached to his feet! We are accustomed to vehicles such as cars and bicycles where there is a direct connection between the control mechanisms and the wheels, so riding horses requires a major change in thought and attitude.

The reins are, of course, attached to the horse's head, and the horse uses his head for balance. Therefore, when you are connecting to the horse through the reins—known as riding in contact—you are affecting his balance in some way. Ideally, if the horse is doing what you want, you can help him by offering him gentle support to aid him in grounding. At the same time, *he* helps *you* to ground, as you've been learning to do with the grounding strap.

Helping the horse to balance and ground is the most important thing you do with the reins. To do so, you have to be balanced and grounded yourself, which is the main goal of the exercises and techniques presented previously.

To prepare for handling the reins, review Using the Grounding Strap in chapter 5.

> The correct method for picking up and holding the reins in two hands is identical to the way you hold the grounding strap, except for the number of fingers on the reins.

You will use your hands and your entire body to handle the reins in the same way you handle the grounding strap—that is, to center and ground yourself using a soft flexible grasp. Remember that using your hands for maintaining grounding and balancing does not require strength; a very light touch is sufficient in anything except a severe loss of equilibrium.

Before you can learn to use the reins, you have to learn to manage them. This takes some practice because, in the first place, reins are long, *ideally long enough for the horse to be able to fully stretch his head down without pulling you out of the saddle.* Second, the horse frequently stretches his head out and brings it back, so you need to be comfortable with both lengthening and shortening the reins as the horse requires.

For this practice work you won't actually use the reins to affect the horse, so they can be fastened to the side rings of the halter or even to the jaw loop. You should put them on carefully so that there are no twists. They can be made of leather or webbing or nylon, but they should be flexible and comfortable to hold. Some Western rein techniques are slightly different from English, but when the reins are being held in two hands, most things are the same. The descriptions immediately following apply to riding with the reins in both hands. During the learning process, the reins should always have some slack in them so that the horse never feels any pressure.

Picking Up the Reins

English reins are usually two-part reins, joined in the center with a buckle, so when the reins are lying on the horse's neck the buckle is right in front of you.

Western split reins are two separate unconnected reins, but when they are used in two hands they should be knotted, or connected with a slider, which is a small tie or band that keeps the reins together. This is easier and safer because if you make a mistake in adjusting your reins, the rein doesn't fall to the ground. Also, when you ride with unconnected reins in two hands, the tails hang down on either side of the horse's withers, where they can all too easily get caught under the pad or your leg. The knot or slider should be as centered as possible and should be placed far enough back on the rein so that the horse can reach his head down and forward and still leave you sufficient rein in your hands. Sliders and knots are more awkward to grasp than the buckle on an English rein, so when you initially pick up the "buckle," you'll be grasping both reins just below the slider or knot.

Instructions for Picking Up the Reins

You can use either hand to take up the buckle, but we describe the process as starting with the left hand.

1. Pick up the buckle in your left hand with your fingers on top, or grasp both Western reins just below the knot, holding them the same way. Hold the buckle or reins up a little way off the withers and look at the reins carefully, turning them as necessary so there are no twists in the reins.

2. Still holding the buckle or reins up in your left hand, grasp both reins in your right hand with your first two fingers on top, your ring finger between the two reins, and your little finger underneath (outside the reins). Slide your right hand down the reins until you have taken up most of the slack (figure 11.1a).

3. Let go of the buckle and take the left rein in your left hand with your first three fingers on top and your little finger underneath (outside; figure 11.1b).

4. Separate your hands and the reins. Turn the reins as necessary so that the inside (unfinished) side of each rein is against your first three fingers.

5. Spread your hands and carefully flip the buckle or knot end of the reins (called the 'bight') forward so that it lies between the reins and on the right side of the horse's neck under the right rein. The bight will now be lying over your index finger of each hand. Place your thumbs on top of the reins where they lie over your index fingers. *This is where you will actually hold on to the reins.* All your fingers should be in a natural, relaxed curve, *not* a tight fist. The backs of your hands should be approximately parallel to the line of the horse's shoulders, so neither flat nor straight up and down (figure 11.1c).

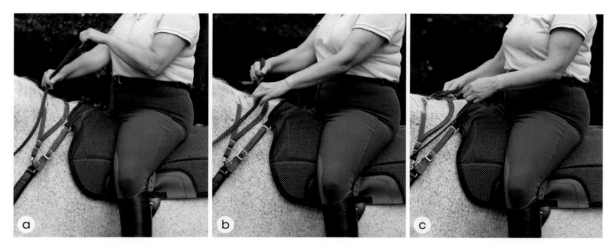

Figure 11.1 Picking up the reins.

Your elbows should hang just in front of your rib cage and should never be allowed to come back farther than the widest part of your ribs, and your upper arm should not go behind the vertical if you are leaning forward. If your elbows are too far back and you try to ground or pull on the reins, you will pull *yourself* forward instead. Now raise or lower your hands as necessary until a line drawn from your elbow to your wrist points to the end of the reins where they attach to sides of the horse's head.

In chapter 5 you learned the importance of your wrist position as it relates to your grounding. This becomes even more important when you start using the reins. An incorrect wrist position prevents you from balancing and grounding against any sort of pressure and is the primary cause of what's known as bad hands, that is, hands that interfere with the horse and so cause him to resist. Here are two exercises to help you to feel and understand this. They require the help of another person.

Holding the Reins: Exercise 1

1. Sit in a grounded seated position with your feet slightly apart and your knees slightly bent but your back vertical. Hold the reins correctly, as described previously. Your helper should be facing you and holding the reins somewhat below your hands, where the horse's mouth would be. You should each have a light, steady pressure on the reins.

2. First, keeping your forearms in place, lift your hands up from the wrist so there is a sharp angle between your wrists and your thumbs (figure 11.2a).

3. Keeping your hands in that position, increase the pressure on the reins until you can feel where the pull is going in your body. Do not allow your body angles to change position—that is, don't bend over or straighten up any more than you are. You should feel the pressure going into the front of your foot and pulling you forward so you lose your grounding.

4. Release the pressure on the reins and find your grounding again. Now change your hand position so that your thumbs are pointing to the other ends of the reins where they enter your helper's hands. Each thumb will point more or less at the end of the opposite rein. Your thumb knuckle and wrist will form an almost straight line, with the thumb itself pointing slightly more downward (figure 11.2b).

5. Now pull again, thinking about pulling *from the underside of your forearm* and not allowing your hand and wrist position to change. You should feel the pressure going into your heels and increasing your grounding.

Figure 11.2 (*a*) Correct and (*b*) incorrect hand position for holding the reins.

This is the stable, solid feeling you want at all times but especially when the horse needs support as well. Although most mature horses can balance well on their own, when you add the rider factor over his forehand, there are times when even the most athletic horse can use a little help (for example, on bad footing where he might stumble or traveling downhill at speed).

Holding the Reins: Exercise 2

1. This is almost the same exercise, but you should be sitting on a chair with wheels, such as an office chair. Your helper will be sitting or kneeling on the ground a little way away.

2. This time, when you hold your hands incorrectly as described in step 2 of exercise 1, the pull will go down your front and onto your crotch bone, and you and the chair will tend to tip forward and not move.

3. However, when you hold your hands correctly as described in step 4 of exercise 1, the pull will go down your back and into your seat bones, and the chair will roll smoothly forward while you stay firmly grounded. If you were on the horse, the incorrect position would block your horse's forward motion, while the correct one would help and encourage it.

Practice picking up your reins and finishing with your hands in correct position, first slowly until you are sure all your moves are correct, then, over time, faster so you can do it quickly in an emergency. For example, you might be walking quietly on the trail with your reins on the buckle when something happened that frightened your horse. If you have an automatic reaction to take up your reins and ground, you have a much better chance of getting both of you back under control.

Lengthening the Reins

Sometimes people think that the horse is being disobedient or trying to get away with something when he asks for more rein, but he usually just needs it for balance or physical comfort—the horse's head is quite heavy, and if he has been carrying it in one position for some time he may just need to relax and stretch for a minute. It is true that if there is a particularly tasty-looking clump of grass on the ground, the horse might be unable to resist temptation. However, because of the strength of the horse's neck, in this situation pulling on both reins is ineffective. Usually, if you pull up on just one rein (the right one tends to work better) at a slight angle across the horse's withers, you will be able to bring his head up. If he is really determined, a tap with a stick on his butt should get him moving again. You should have a firm hold on the pommel or grounding strap so he doesn't unseat you if he moves quickly away from the stick. (Often, when a horse has done something that he knows is naughty he will anticipate a spanking, and react accordingly.)

Lengthening the reins is a skill that you should learn as soon as possible because it is extremely counterintuitive. You are riding along with your reins a little loose, and suddenly your horse stretches his head out and down. You feel the horse pulling on the reins, and perhaps pulling you forward, and your instinct is to grip the reins tightly to control him as well as keep your balance. Usually he does this because he needs to stretch, not because he's trying to be naughty. In fact, this is usually a good sign, showing that he is beginning to relax any tensions he might have. Rather than reward him for this behavior, or at least allowing it, your rein-grabbing reaction might scare him, make him tense up, and instinctively pull against you. Even if he is wearing a severe bit, and you "win," you have only made him uncomfortable for no reason. Keep in mind that for successful riding you want the horse to trust you to make things easier for him, not harder.

So what should you do? When the horse pulls on the reins, simply relax your fingers and let the reins slide through. As noted in the previous discussion on leading a horse, it takes two to pull, and he can pull only if you pull back!

Since resisting the pull is a reflex, try this ground exercise to teach your body to release the rein. Sit on the edge of a chair with your feet back underneath you, as though you were in the saddle. Hold the reins correctly, and have another person hold the other end, lower than your hands. Close your eyes. The other person should tug suddenly and sharply on the reins. Your hands will instinctively clutch them, which will unbalance you. Open your fingers enough to release the reins. Now repeat the exercise several times, releasing as soon as you feel the slightest tug.

After you release, when the horse has stretched as much as he needs and the reins become slack, you can gather them up by shortening, which we discuss in the next section. You can also lengthen the reins without a prompt from the horse if you want to *encourage* the horse to stretch out and relax. Just relax your fingers and slide your hands toward you and toward the buckle or knot until you get the length you want. Then close your fingers again and move your hands forward to their original position, which makes the reins not only longer but looser. You can do one or both reins at a time. You also use this technique if you want to comb the rein, using one hand at a time and keeping a little more pressure on the rein than if you are merely lengthening it (see Moving the Horse's Hindquarters in chapter 7 for details on combing).

Rob Roy's Reins

Many years ago one of my students had a wonderful horse named Rob Roy. Everyone, from the newest beginner to the most advanced rider, rode him. He loved to jump, but he liked to do things his way.

When you ride a jumping course, it is customary to trot a circle at the end of the ring before beginning the jumping. During the circle, Rob Roy would tug at the reins with his head. If the rider let them slip through her hands as much as he needed, he would then bring his head up and continue around the jumps in perfect and quiet style. But if the rider was ignorant and didn't let go, Rob Roy would stick his nose out against the reins and tear around the course as fast as he could, then stop dead at the end as if to say, "Humph. Who needs you?"

Shortening the Reins

Picking up your reins is one way of shortening them in a hurry, but most of the time you use a slightly different technique. Again, it is a skill you will use frequently, because to send a message to the horse often involves increasing the pressure on the reins by pulling. Not much and not hard, but it is a pull, as opposed to the release. To pull without losing your grounding, you have to *shorten* the reins first, so that when you pull your upper arm doesn't go behind the vertical, but without making them *tighter*, until you're ready to communicate.

So when you shorten your reins, what you are actually doing is *moving your hands down the reins* toward the horse's mouth, and in order to do so you stretch out your arms.

Instructions for Shortening the Reins

You will shorten one rein at a time starting with the left rein. Begin by holding your reins and hands correctly as described previously. (Reverse the directions if you want to shorten the right rein first.)

1. Turn your hands from the semivertical position to an almost horizontal position with your knuckles on top.

2. Keeping your right middle and ring fingers lightly curled around the right rein, use your index finger to grasp the bight of the left rein from the top, close to your left thumb (figure 11.3*a*).

3. Keeping hold of the left rein with your right hand, slide your left hand down the rein toward the horse's head as far as is comfortable (figure 11.3*b*). Do not lean forward or extend your arm stiffly. Let go of the left rein with your right fingers.

4. To shorten the right rein as well, which you would normally do, bring your right hand *forward* until it is beside your left hand, with both hands horizontal.

5. Open the first finger on your left hand and take the bight of the right rein. Pull the rein through your right fingers until the reins are even.

6. Release the right rein from your left hand and turn both hands to the semi-vertical position (figure 11.3*c*).

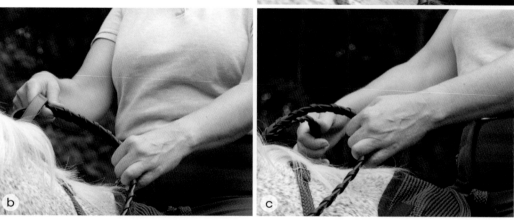

Figure 11.3   Shortening the reins.

To practice shortening the reins, after the previous steps lengthen the reins as described and repeat the shortening and lengthening several times. The shortened, extended-arm position is the position from which you pull the reins, which we discuss in a later chapter.

Sometimes you want to shorten your reins because they have become too loose, perhaps because the horse stretched out his neck, pulling the reins through your hands, and then returned his head to its original position. In that case it is not necessary to extend your arms. Merely hold your hands and arms in their normal position while you shorten the reins as above until you have the amount of contact you want.

If the reins are long enough to be comfortable when the horse puts his head down, as they should be, when he is carrying his head up the bight might be quite long. It's possible that the end of it can get caught around your foot or stirrup, which could be dangerous. The solution is fairly simple and uses the same technique as shortening.

To loop the extra rein, bring your hands together horizontally as before, then pass the bight in your right hand around your left index and middle fingers, making a loop (figure 11.4*a*). Make the loop fairly large at first, then adjust it by pulling it through your left hand as you separate your hands (figure 11.4*b*).

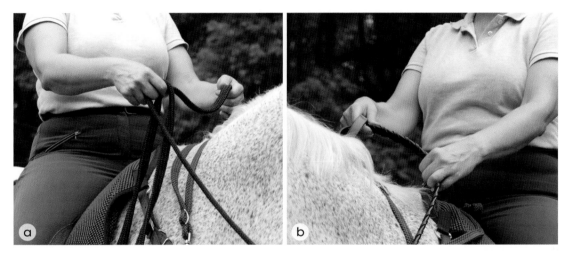

Figure 11.4 Looping the excess reins.

Looping and holding the reins in this way is the same as bridging the reins, which allows you to quickly take the reins in one hand. Taking the loop in just one hand is called a half bridge. If you let go with your right hand and hold your left hand horizontally, you can pull on one rein or the other by rotating your hand from side to side using your wrist as a pivot (figure 11.5). The half bridge is also the way you use the stick on the horse's hindquarters without interfering with the reins.

Figure 11.5 The half-bridge.

If you want to be able to use either hand by itself, you would make a full bridge as follows. After you have placed the bight of the rein in your left hand, you keep hold of it with your right hand and pick up the bight end of the left rein in the first two fingers of your right hand, and slide your hands apart (figure 11.6).

Figure 11.6   The full bridge.

Managing Western Split Reins With One Hand

One-hand riding and neck reining developed as a way for the rider to multitask. A rider must be able to direct the horse with one hand—using neck reining (described in chapter 15)—while roping with the other. For this type of rein handling, the grounding exercises and most of the techniques described previously still apply with some slight modifications, so you should be sure to read those as well.

In most cases you will be riding only single handed if you are using a curb bit, which is normally used primarily for more advanced riding. Curb bits operate on leverage and often have long shanks to increase the leverage. The leverage action can be severe if not used properly, so curbs are generally used with a loose rein and very little contact on the horse's mouth. This requires both knowledge and confidence, so although you should be aware of this method, you would not use single-hand riding and curb bits in these early exercises.

Unattached split reins are used for one-hand riding because, unlike joined reins, when held in one hand they lie flat and smoothly together. When lying on the horse's neck or withers, split reins cross over each other in the center, with the tails hanging down over each shoulder.

If holding split reins with one hand, you can use either your right or your left hand. To hold them in your right hand, pick up the reins at the crossover point with your left hand. Grasp the reins loosely with your right hand, *fingers underneath, thumb on top*. If you want to keep the reins separated, you can put your index finger between the reins (figure 11.7).

Using your left hand, draw the reins through your right hand until most, but not all, of the slack is out. The tails of the reins should drape down the shoulder on the same side as your rein hand. To hold the reins in the left hand, perform the same sequence using the opposite hand.

Your rein hand should be in front of the pommel, elbow down and relaxed, thumb on top and pointing toward the horse's nose with a straight line from your elbow to his mouth, regardless of the drape in the reins. Notice that your hand and wrist position is the same as described earlier. Only the reins are reversed, with the bight coming out from under your little finger instead of between your thumb and forefinger.

If you need to hold the reins in two hands without knotting them, unattached split reins are usually held in a bridge with the end of each

Figure 11.7   Holding split reins in the left hand.

rein held in the opposite hand, separated by your fingers from the main rein, like the full bridge described in the English section (figure 11.8). The bridge keeps both reins in both hands so that if you have to let go with one hand, you haven't dropped that rein to the ground. You should be careful that the tails don't get caught under the saddle or pad, as they tend to do when held in this manner.

Shorten split reins by dropping the tails, then pulling on one or both tails with the other hand. Lengthen them by sliding your hands together, then drawing them apart again, allowing the tails to slide through your hands until they are 12 inches (30 cm) apart again.

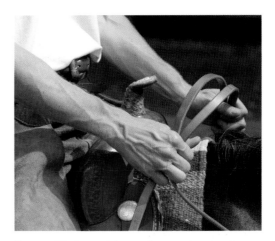

Figure 11.8 Holding split reins in a bridge.

Using the Grounding Strap and Stick With the Reins

The grounding strap is not just for beginners. There will be times throughout your riding career when you will want to use it, especially if you ride and train young or spoiled horses. The instructions are for holding the reins in two hands.

Put in the simplest terms, you hold the grounding strap in your first two fingers, your rein in your first three fingers, and the stick in all four fingers. This allows you to hold each one separately without dropping any one of them (figure 11.9). You can put both hands on the grounding strap or take either one off as needed and still have the grounding strap for support.

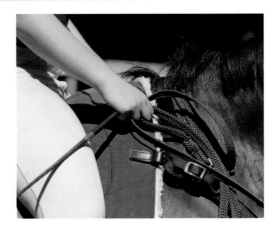

Figure 11.9 Holding the grounding strap, stick, and reins.

Instructions for Using the Grounding Strap and Stick With the Reins

To use the stick, you will have to let go of the grounding strap with that hand and put that rein into the other hand for a moment. The stick is usually carried in the right hand, so the procedure is as follows.

1. Remove your right hand with the rein and stick from the grounding strap and, with your hands horizontal, bring it close to your left hand, as though you were going to shorten it.
2. Reach out with your left forefinger and take hold of the bight of the right rein.
3. Let go of the rein with your right hand, keeping hold of the stick.
4. Use the stick as described in chapter 8.
5. Take the right rein back into your right hand and replace it on the grounding strap.

Incorporate these skills into your lesson so that you can pick up and adjust your reins without disturbing your or the horse's balance. Then when the time comes you will find using the reins as aids comparatively easy to learn.

The Sitting Trot or Jog

Up to now, if you have been following the program, you have always had someone nearby who was guiding and controlling the horse so that you could focus on developing balance and grounding. The next step is to ride by yourself in a confined space large enough for the horse to move around in comfortably but not so large that he is able to do anything that you aren't ready to deal with.

You still won't be using the reins, but you will use your gentle aids to help to guide him and keep him going. You can use your emergency dismount in case something comes up that makes you uncomfortable. But you still need one more skill: to be comfortable at a slow trot. To practice your skills, you have to keep the horse moving. If you get a little too enthusiastic with your stick, he will probably break into a trot, so you should be prepared.

In English riding the gait you will work at is called a slow trot, and you will learn to sit to it. In Western riding the same gait is called a jog, and sitting it is the way it is usually done. There are several ways to ride the trot, all of which you will be learning later on in the book, but I have found that this is the easiest way to start.

Notice that in English riding it is called sitting trot, not bouncing trot. This is an important difference because if your seat leaves the horse's back and then comes down again, it can be quite painful for him, especially if prolonged. Try this little exercise to give you an idea of how sitting feels to the horse compared to bouncing.

Sitting Versus Bouncing Exercise

Hold your forearm out and pretend it's the horse's back, moving up and down. Make a fist with your other hand and place it on the middle of your forearm. Just let it lie there of its own weight while you move your arm up and down. You can move your arm faster or up and down more, but as long as your hand lies steady on your arm so it follows the movement, there is no discomfort.

Now continue the movement of your forearm, but hold your fist still so it doesn't follow the movement. Instead, it will bang against your arm, which is annoying and eventually uncomfortable. You can imagine what the weight of a full-grown adult bouncing on the horse's back would feel like!

Preparatory Ground Work

If you have access to a small trampoline, you can get a really good feeling for riding the trot. Keep in mind that the gaits are already programmed in your body. The bounce of the trampoline, while not essential, gives excellent feedback, similar to what you will get from the horse. You will need something to hold on to while you're on the trampoline to help you ground. A piece of rope tied to a heavy chair leg will work.

Whether you are on the ground or the trampoline, begin with the seven steps. Then start walking in place, feeling the rhythm and how your body moves and interacts with the floor or the trampoline. Try to put your feet down very softly, which means keeping all your joints, starting with your spine, very loose.

After a few minutes, begin to jog slowly in place, trying to keep the same soft, flexible feeling throughout your body, and hitting the ground as softly as you can. Notice that even though you aren't going high or fast, the jog is still much bouncier than the walk. This is true of the horse's gait as well. Jog for a while, then walk a few steps, then jog again. Think about how your body moves differently at the different gaits.

Riding at the Slow Trot (Jog)

You are still using your leader and will need her for this task so that she can control the horse's speed and gait while you are learning to sit. Begin the exercise after you are well settled on the horse. You might find it helpful if an experienced rider demonstrates sitting the trot first so you get an idea of how it should look. Notice how she uses the grounding strap and how her seat doesn't leave the horse's back at all.

Prepare for the trot by using the seven steps and the grounding strap to get relaxed and grounded. Growing and shaking out are particularly important steps as you prepare for the trot. The additional bounce must be absorbed by your inner thighs and buttocks, which must be very soft and relaxed, and by your lumbar spine, the flexible part of your back at your waist, between your rib cage and your pelvis (figure 11.10). The shake-out will help to loosen up the muscles, and growing will stretch and loosen the spine. You will also need a slightly stronger feel on the grounding strap to counteract the bigger movement, so practice taking that stronger feel without creating any tension in the areas of your body that contact the horse.

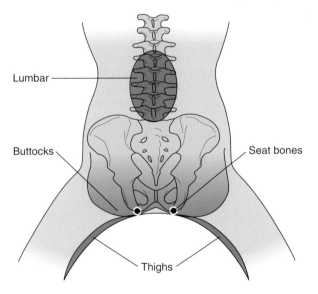

Figure 11.10   Areas that absorb shock during the trot.

Having the horse walk over rails on the ground, if available, or down a slight grade will make his walk a bit springier and prepare you for the new movement.

When you're ready, the leader can ask the horse to trot. If she starts jogging slowly herself, keeping her body grounded and landing softly, the horse will tend to copy her, making the gait smoother for you. As the horse starts to trot, allow your body to sway back a little (figure 11.11); leaning very slightly back during the trot makes it easier to sit. Then think about breathing, maintaining soft eyes, and your following seat. Use your grounding strap to keep you down on

Figure 11.11 The slow trot.

the horse's back, but don't pull on it so hard that you make yourself tense, which would defeat the purpose.

The first time you attempt this, the leader should trot the horse for only a few steps, just to give you the feeling. After that, if things go well, the trots can get longer but should be confined to straight lines at first so you don't have to deal with lateral centering. You can continue to trot each time as long as you are sitting comfortably, but if you start to lose the feeling and can't regain it right away, have the leader bring the horse back to the walk, reground, and start again.

Once you are comfortable on the straightaway, try some gentle turns. Even though the horse is going only a little faster, the livelier movement tends to make staying in the center more difficult. Practice at the walk, making a tight turn and using a strong lift and weight shift to keep you centered (see Following the Motion in chapter 5 and Maintaining Lateral Balance During Right Turns in chapter 6). This will be less effort at the trot because the horse will lift you up. Keep the turns fairly brief at first, beginning with left turns as you did at the walk. Once you have the knack, try some longer turns. Also work on sharper turns, since you will be riding by yourself in a fairly small space.

Finally, try an emergency dismount from the trot. The leader should start you at a slow jog that you can sit to easily, then speed up the trot just enough so that sitting becomes more difficult, at which point you should dismount. By now you should be well versed in turning, facing forward, and landing softly and safely with toes relaxed and knees and ankles bent. You will find it much easier to get your right leg over because the motion of the trot will be lifting you up. The leader should stay well in front of the horse so you don't bump into her.

What might surprise you is how quickly the horse stops as he feels your center coming forward in front of him. I used to bet my students that they couldn't get to the ground before the horse had stopped. I usually won.

A Taste of Freedom

Now that you are prepared to handle just about anything a quiet horse might do in a confined space, you should feel very confident about being turned loose. The space should be small enough that the horse isn't tempted to go too fast if you make a mistake, but not so small that he can't move easily in a straight line for a few strides. It should be square or rectangular if possible so that you aren't constantly turning and having to think about your lateral centering, as is the case with a round area.

The first time you are turned loose should be in the last 20 minutes of your lesson so you are well settled on your horse and have had a chance to review any skills if you feel the need. Even though you will not have anyone on the ground controlling the horse, you will not have to use the reins to be safe. As noted in chapter 2, what keeps you safe is the horse's trust in you and *his desire to keep you safe*. And, unlike a car or bicycle, he will not self-destruct if not controlled at all times. What you will discover when you are turned loose is that, far from trying to gallop away, the horse will most likely go over to the entrance to his space and stop. When you ask him to move, he will walk in a little circle and stop again. Frustrating, but hardly life threatening. However, if you are quietly persistent and can stay centered and grounded, after a while the circle will become larger and you can begin to use your gentle aids and get a response.

Now you can use your free time to work on all your skills, both in terms of position and using your gentle aids to ask the horse to go, turn, and stop. If you feel that things are starting to get out of control, dismount and regroup, then remount and continue.

This exercise is particularly helpful for riders whose previous experience involved trying to control the horse before they were ready. The insecurities resulting from an inevitable failure make the rider very tense, especially with rein aids. A few lessons without reins on a quiet horse can work miracles for confidence.

12

Introduction to Riding in the Saddle

For some time now you have been riding on a bareback pad, while your body learned to adjust correctly to being up on the horse's back. At some point, depending on many factors, your instructor will feel you are ready for the saddle. It could come sooner or later than it appears in the book, and you can always go back to the bareback pad at any time, either to fix something that wasn't quite right or just for fun. For example, both sitting the trot and emergency dismounts are easier to learn and practice bareback.

At my New England stable, everyone rode bareback during the winter months, partly because it is much warmer because of the warmth from the horse and because you can wear heavier clothes on your legs and feet. More important, most riders felt that they returned to the saddle in the spring with a position that was more secure and correct than before. But now it's time to talk about the saddle.

A modern English saddle consists of a framework, called a tree, which comes in various sizes to fit various horse shapes, with padded panels on the underside to make it comfortable for the horse. On top of the tree is a shaped seat and side flaps, also in various sizes and shapes to fit the rider, and on each side, stirrups hang on adjustable, beltlike straps called stirrup leathers. The stirrup leathers hang on steel stirrup bars, which are fastened directly to the tree. The whole thing is fastened down to the horse's back with a girth, but it is the tree and the horse's withers that keep the saddle from turning sideways (figure 12.1).

Western saddles are similar in construction except that the padding of the panels is replaced by separate, thick pads. The stirrup leathers, called fenders, instead of being beltlike, are wide to protect the rider's legs from chafing. Western saddles also have a horn, a raised handlelike object on the front of the saddle originally intended to hold a rope (figure 12.2). Rather than a girth, which is usually made of leather and has two moderate-sized buckles on each end, the Western saddle uses a cinch, which is made of thick string, leather, or nylon, and has a large loop or buckle that fastens with a strap and a special knot.

But to get back to the stirrups, they hang loose and swing from the saddle, and beginners have problems keeping their feet in them. The way to keep your feet in the stirrups is neither difficult nor complicated. If your legs hang down without tension, their weight resting on the stirrups is enough to keep your feet in them without any other effort. And *this* is why you've been spending all this time learning to be comfortable on the horse with soft, relaxed—and therefore heavy—legs.

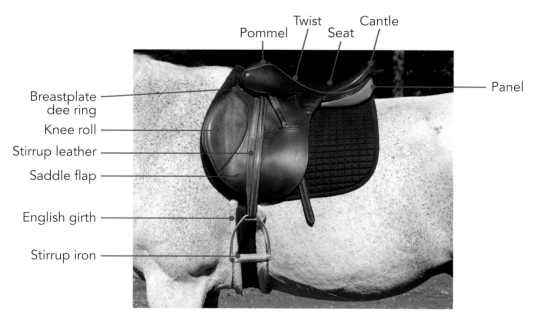

Pommel Twist Seat Cantle

Breastplate dee ring

Knee roll

Stirrup leather

Saddle flap

English girth

Stirrup iron

Panel

Figure 12.1   The English saddle.

Seat Seat rise Horn

Cantle

Rear rigging dee

Skirt

Fender

Swell

Seat jockey

Front rigging dee

Latigo strap

Stirrup

Western cinch

Figure 12.2   The Western saddle.

Preparing For Saddle Work

Stirrups present a problem to beginners. Initial fear-based tension draws the legs up, making it difficult to keep the feet in the stirrups. Once that tension is overcome, gravity takes over and the feet stay in the stirrups without effort. This is why you've been spending all this time on the bareback pad learning to be comfortable on the horse, with soft, relaxed, heavy legs.

When you start riding with stirrups, your legs should still be soft and long, but your feet will be in a different position and you need to do some preparatory work *while you're still on the bareback pad*.

The exercise is called fixed leg, as opposed to the loose leg you have had up to now. Many riders associate fixed leg with gripping, which is very tiring and, as you know, very undesirable in terms of comfort and function of the horse and rider. We try to avoid that by working back and forth between loose and fixed leg so that you maintain the maximum amount of softness.

We start by finding out where you will place your feet. The stirrups are commonly used several ways, each of which are called by several different names. I use the term *full seat* to refer to *sitting* on the saddle, as opposed to *standing* in the stirrups, for which I use the term *half seat*. When the saddle is placed on the horse's back correctly, the lowest point is in the saddle's center. As a result of gravity, that is where your seat bones will rest, with your center over them. However, the center of the saddle is located several inches behind where the stirrup hangs, where your bubbling spring (illustrated in figure 2.2) sits on the back bar of the stirrup (figure 12.3).

So in full seat, your center, while it will be over your seat—which is your base when you sit—will be behind your bubbling spring, your base when you stand. When you are sitting, your feet will have a tendency to go even more forward, especially if you push on them. Why do you care?

Figure 12.3 Center of the saddle relative to the bubbling spring.

Because if you need to stand up, the farther out in front of you your feet are, the harder it is to stand up. If they are too far forward, standing might not be possible. Think of getting up out of a chair: The first thing you do is pull your feet back underneath you.

This brings us back to the fixed leg. It's how you learn to keep your feet in the best place with minimal tension.

Finding the Fixed Leg

While sitting on your horse on the bareback pad, with your leg loose, swing your foot back until the back of your heel is directly under the side seam of your pants. Move only your foot and lower leg; don't lift your knee up. Practice that a few times while looking down over your shoulder so you begin to know how it feels when your foot is under you. In between, shake your leg out and make it loose again.

Placing your heel under your side pants seam brings your foot back about where it should be when you are in full seat in the saddle. The optimal location depends somewhat on the discipline and thus the saddle you will be riding in. Make sure your lower leg is still hanging as loosely as possible. Unless your legs are quite short, or the horse is either very large or very wide, looking from the front, your shin should be about vertical—neither wrapped around the horse's barrel nor sticking out to the side.

The next thing to do is to position your foot as if it were in a stirrup. The stirrup holds up the front of your foot, while the back of it falls down of its own weight, more or less, depending on your and the horse's conformation and your flexibility. Some people's heels naturally go down more easily than others, but as long as you aren't tense, whatever you get is all right.

To get the feeling of this position without stirrups, stretch your legs out in front of you so that your knees are straight and you can see your whole leg. Slowly move your toes in a circle, up and out and down and in. You'll see that when your toes are up and out the farthest, your ankle is the most flexed. Relative to your toe, your heel is 'down' as far as it will go. Now look at your shin and calf (be sure your knee is not bent). Also notice that although your toe is rotated outward, your shin and knee are not.

Shake your legs out to release any tension, bend your knee, and take a fixed leg position with your toes straight ahead (figure 12.4*a*). Rotate your toes as before and watch your lower leg carefully. You will see that when you rotate your toe all the way out with your knee bent, your foot will be pointing out and your lower leg rotates outward as well. This has to do with the way your knee joint is constructed and is something you want to avoid. It is known as riding on the backs of your legs and it creates a weak, tense leg position (figure 12.4*b*). Therefore, when rotating your toe outward and upward, you have to consciously think about not letting your shin turn out (figure 12.4*c*). With practice this will become easy. You'll feel some pull in the front of your shin and in the tendon on the back of your heel, but you shouldn't feel it anywhere else.

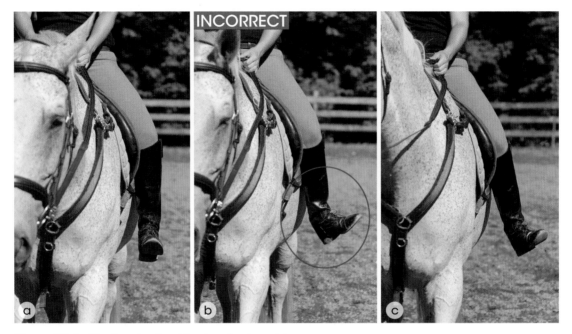

Figure 12.4   Finding the fixed-leg bareback position.

Practice the fixed leg on bareback over several lessons, alternating frequently between loose leg and fixed leg. Since fixed leg creates a little more tension, and your leg's instinct is to be tense, you have to make sure you loosen it up each time until you can keep the tension to a minimum and release it easily.

Adjusting the Stirrups and Saddle

The first step, once you are in the arena but before mounting, is to pull down the stirrups. When leading, English stirrups are always slid up the leathers so they can't swing and get caught on something, scaring the horse and perhaps damaging the saddle. (Western stirrups are much heavier and the straps are stiffer, so this is rarely a problem.) Begin by pulling the stirrup leather out from where it has been tucked through the stirrup, and quietly pull each stirrup down.

You won't know exactly how you should adjust your stirrups, that is, how long they should be. But a rule that will make it possible for you to mount and to keep your feet in the stirrups once you are on is to make them the length of your arm.

English Stirrups

To adjust the stirrups on an English saddle while on the ground, start on the left side and place the fingertips of one hand on the stirrup bar where the buckle is. With the other hand, lift up the stirrup and hold it up to your armpit. It should be about an inch away from your body. (figure 12.5).

Figure 12.5 Adjusting the stirrups on the English saddle.

Adjust it as necessary by letting go of the stirrup and pulling on the loose end of the stirrup leather until the buckle comes away from the bar, then shorten or lengthen it as needed. When you are finished, pull the buckle back up to the bar by pulling down on the undersection of the stirrup leather until you hear the buckle click against the bar.

The next step is to adjust the other stirrup. The most important part of that is to be sure they are even. You can't trust that the last person left them even or even that the leathers match, and you can't tell by looking at both of them from the front because the horse might be standing crooked or the saddle might not be centered on his back. But there is a sure way, which is to measure the distance from the bottom of the saddle flap to the top of the stirrup. If it's a very short distance, hold your fingers against the leather and see how many fingers fit in the space (figure 12.6a). If it's longer, take the stirrup and flip it upside down, then see where the bottom of the stirrup is relative to the bottom of the flap (figure 12.6b).

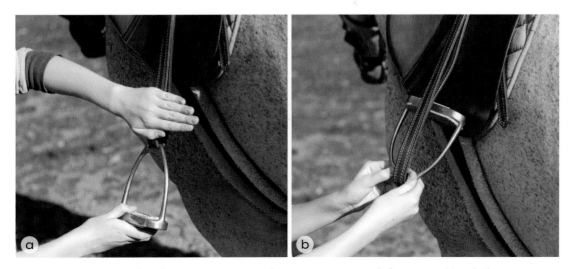

Figure 12.6 Ensure that the stirrups are even by measuring (a) with fingers or (b) with the stirrup.

Then go around to the other stirrup and adjust it so that it matches as closely as possible. Many riders ride with uneven stirrups without realizing it. If one stirrup has to be a little shorter because the holes, or the leathers themselves are uneven, make it the left one, since most people tend to sit too much to the left, if anything. Having the shorter stirrup on that side encourages you to sit more to the right, which helps level you out.

Western Stirrups

To adjust the stirrups on a Western saddle, start on the left side and place the fingertips up under the top skirt where the fender goes under and hold the stirrup up to your armpit. It should just touch your body (figure 12.7).

Figure 12.7 Adjusting the stirrups on the Western saddle.

Adjust as necessary by unbuckling the stirrup gather strap and shifting the stirrup buckle up or down. Some Western saddles use a Blevins-style buckle with a slide to keep the adjustment in place. Others use a single- or double-pronged buckle.

The fender on a Western saddle is attached through the tree to the stirrup adjustment underneath. Once it is adjusted, you'll need to pull the fender up for shorter stirrups or down for longer stirrups so that the stirrup hangs correctly and you can reattach the stirrup gather strap (figure 12.8). The gather strap prevents the stirrup leather from bunching up under the ankle and prevents the stirrup from flipping up through the fender.

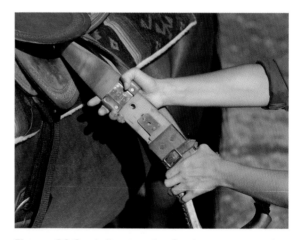

Figure 12.8 Adjusting the fender to ensure that the stirrups hang correctly.

Checking the Girth or Cinch Before Mounting

Either you or the helper will check the girth or cinch one last time before mounting. A major error is to tighten the girth or cinch very tightly in an effort to keep the saddle from turning during mounting. Since it is the horse's conformation (his body shape, specifically his withers) that keeps the saddle in place, the girth needs to be only tight enough to hold the saddle snugly down. In fact, it is quite possible to mount a horse with good withers from a mounting block and ride on level ground with no girth at all! Tightening the girth (detailed in chapter 9) to the point where it makes the horse tense is unnecessary and potentially dangerous.

With an English saddle, you adjust the girth at least once more from the saddle. Western saddles are difficult to adjust when mounted, so it is good practice to lead the horse around for a few minutes at the walk and the jog to allow his muscles to relax before making a final adjustment on the ground. You may also dismount after 10 to 15 minutes and adjust the cinch if the saddle feels loose. Either practice is preferable to trying to forcibly tighten the girth before the horse is ready.

Mounting the Saddled Horse

The first thing that's different about riding in the saddle is the way you mount, and mounting more easily is one of the advantages of using stirrups. Even if you're mounting from the ground, you always have a step up. I am only average height, but I can mount virtually any saddled horse from the ground unassisted. Of course, I've had a lot of practice, and it is more a matter of technique than strength.

If you have ridden before, let me start by saying that I don't teach the classic method of mounting from the front—that is, starting by standing by the horse's shoulder, facing the rear. I don't teach it for several reasons. First, it is extremely difficult to do correctly; second, it severely unbalances the horse; and third, because of the second reason, many horses dislike and fear being mounted in this way and can even react quite dangerously.

The reason that the classic method of mounting is taught is that the occasional horse will kick at the rider during the mounting process. I believe that if the horse is that uncomfortable about being mounted and ridden, I wouldn't want anyone to try riding him at all until I had resolved his fear and trust issues. Otherwise this horse is an accident looking for a place to happen! And if you mount such a horse from the front because you think he might kick you, he might try to bite you instead!

Recall that when we talked about mounting bareback, we emphasized the importance of staying centered at all times. The same is of course true when mounting in the saddle. You should also begin by mounting using a mounting block, which is easier. In fact, although you should be able to mount from the ground if necessary, no matter how well you mount you are still putting a fair amount of lateral strain on the horse as you pull yourself up from one side.

It is much kinder to the horse to use a block or a leg up whenever available.

Centering Saves the Day

Being centered while mounting once saved me from what could have been a nasty fall. I was asked to exercise someone's horse, about whom I knew very little. He was brought out to me to mount. The mounting block was in a paved courtyard. He seemed reasonably quiet as I prepared to mount, but as soon as I stood up in the stirrup he took off at a gallop across the courtyard. Because I had a firm grip on his mane and the saddle and was centered over my stirrup, I was able to kick free and dismount. Luckily, as usually happens, he stopped as soon as he felt me coming down ahead of him. I'm not sure who was more scared: me, the horse, or the groom who had brought him out!

The method presented here works equally well for all disciplines because it requires a minimum of rotation. Centering is easier, and it is easier to keep the saddle balanced and place your hands correctly.

During all phases of the mounting process, someone should be holding the horse for you until both your balance and your rein skills are adequate if the horse should move away. Since you will probably be somewhat awkward at first, your helper should hold the horse on the far side with one hand while pulling down on that stirrup with the other, to both stabilize the saddle and help the horse to balance (figure 12.9).

Figure 12.9 Make sure the horse and saddle are secure before beginning the mounting process.

The horse should stand at the mounting block with the left stirrup near the left side of the block so that when you are in mounting position, the stirrup will be in a convenient place. If the block is small, it should be placed so that you are standing near the cantle of the saddle.

As you did with the bareback mount, practice each step a couple of times before moving on, going back to the beginning each time to get the sequence patterned into your reflexes.

Using the Mounting Block

1. Give your horse an encouraging pat and quietly step up onto the block. Stand about opposite the cantle but where you can reach the pommel comfortably with your hands. Face the horse's head.

2. Go through the seven steps and grounding. As you did before the bareback mount, stroke the horse first on his shoulders, then behind the saddle on his loins and croup.

3. If you are using the reins, pick them up as described in chapter 10 but only as far as holding them in your right hand, somewhat shortened, but not tight. If you are not using reins yet, go to step 4.

4. Place your right hand, with or without reins, on the right side of the pommel with the heel of your hand resting on the flap and your fingers tucked under the pommel (figure 12.10a).

5. With your left hand, reach down and hold the stirrup, turning the outside of it toward your toe (figure 12.10*b*). Insert your left foot so that your bubbling spring is resting on the back of the stirrup.

6. Take a firm hold of the mane in your left hand. You may not be able to do it at first, but your goal is to do most of the pulling with your left hand, which is on the mane, rather than with your right, which is on the saddle and might cause it to turn. As you go up, you move your right hand so that you can push down with it on the right side of the saddle, which stabilizes it.

7. Using your hands to help you as before, push off with your right foot and go up until you are standing in the left stirrup with your left knee straight and your right leg hanging beside it. Do *not* try to put your right leg over the saddle yet. You will be facing slightly forward, leaning slightly over the saddle to stay centered over the horse (figure 12.10*c*).

8. Keeping your balance, bend your right knee and bring it up over the cantle and down on the horse's right side, rotating your upper body as you do so. Gently let your weight come down on the saddle (figure 12.10*d*). If this is your first time in the saddle, you will not be using the stirrups. Once you are settled, quietly lift your left foot, take it out of

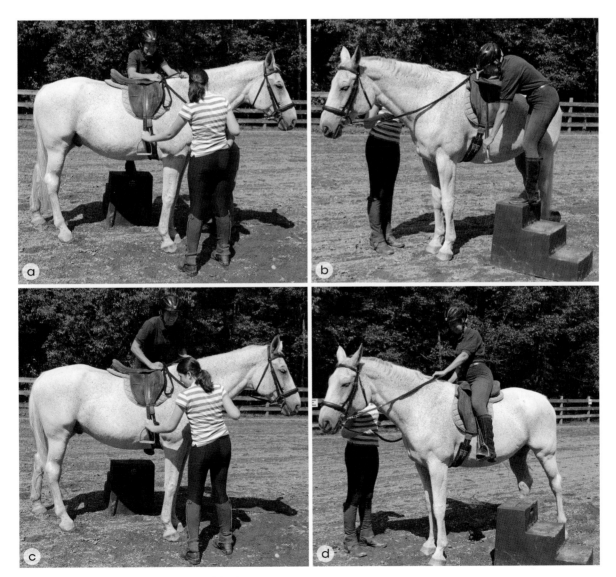

Figure 12.10   Using the mounting block.

the stirrup, then let it fall again. If you will be using the stirrups, use your right toe to find the stirrup and work your foot into it until your bubbling spring is settled on the back bar of the stirrup. You can get assistance from your helper with the right stirrup at first, but try not to use your hand on the stirrup leather unless the stirrup is badly twisted. Occasionally something happens to upset the horse during mounting, and you want to be able to pick up your stirrups and still have your hands available either for holding on or for using the reins.

Later on, when you are more secure, you should learn to put your right foot into the stirrup *before* you sit down. The occasional horse with a sensitive back needs time to adjust before he can take your whole weight, so you may remain standing in your stirrups for a few minutes until he warms up.

Tightening the Girth While Mounted in the English Saddle

Immediately after mounting, you should check and, if necessary, tighten the girth. When you sit on the saddle, the padding both on and under the saddle compresses a little, and some horses who tense up against the girth before mounting will relax once you're on.

A ground person should help you with this at first, but you can learn the motions and soon be able to do it for yourself. Eventually you can even do it when the horse is moving.

Tightening the Girth From the Saddle

1. Lift your left foot and knee and bring them up and forward so that they are in front of the saddle flap. If you're using the stirrups, leave your foot in the stirrup and carry it with you (figure 12.11).

2. Place both reins in your right hand and keep it on or near the pommel.

3. Note: *A ground person should perform this step until you are comfortable on the saddle.* With your left hand, lift the saddle flap up by sliding your hand underneath it from the front. Slip your fingers under the front billet strap only and pull up. *Never pull up on both billet straps at once when you are mounted, since that could undo the girth completely.* If it comes up easily and the buckle tongue disengages, pull the strap up until it feels snug, then use your index finger to guide the tongue into the nearest hole. Repeat with the back billet strap. If the straps offer resistance and feel tight, leave them alone and check again later, usually after about 10 minutes, when the horse has warmed up.

4. Let the flap down again and bring your leg back to its original position.

Figure 12.11 Leg and hand position for tightening the girth from the saddle.

The next task is to dismount and remount at least once more to go through the sequence again. Try to mount a couple of times in each lesson for a while to develop your skill. However, don't mount more than three times in a row because the constant lateral pull is tiring for the horse.

Dismounting From the Saddled Horse

As with the mount, the dismount I teach is not the one that many modern instructors use. The one that is usually taught begins with you removing both feet from the stirrups so that there is no danger of getting hung up in one. However, if you are centered and balanced during the dismount, as you were during the mount, this should never be a problem. The common method is really an emergency dismount and is entirely appropriate if the horse is moving. However, if he is standing still, the extra effort you must use to get your right leg clear of the cantle results in throwing your weight abruptly and strongly forward over the horse's forehand. This unbalances the horse severely and can cause him to move suddenly or even buck. Alternatively, rather than a foot getting caught in the stirrup, your right leg can get caught on the cantle, making the dismount a real struggle and dangerous if the horse gets upset.

The dismount I learned years ago is the safest and the easiest for the horse and the rider. It's pretty much the mount in reverse. Later on, when you're at ease in the saddle, you'll work on the emergency dismount, probably at the slow trot, which is easier for both you and the horse.

Safe and Easy Dismount From the Saddle

1. With the horse standing still, let your reins out as necessary so that you can maintain control and still find a comfortable handhold on the saddle with your right hand, while your left hand holds the mane on the withers just in front of the saddle (figure 12.12a). You can put both reins in one hand if you prefer.

2. Stand up in both stirrups, using your hands for balance, then remove your *right foot only* from the stirrup.

3. Stay grounded on your left foot and *keep your center over the horse's center* as you bend your right knee and carefully bring your right leg over the cantle and the horse's back (figure 12.12b). Allow your right leg to drop and hang beside your left leg. Ground and center, making sure your feet are relaxed.

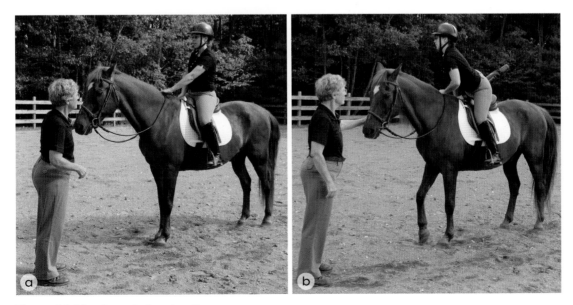

Figure 12.12 Completing the dismount.

(continued)

4. Lean on your hands and your hips and take your left foot out of the stirrup (figure 12.12c). Wiggle your toes to relax your feet and ankles for the landing.

5. Roll on your hip to face forward as you allow yourself to slide down toward the ground, so that your clothing doesn't catch or, in the case of belt buckles, damage the saddle (figure 12.12d). Keep hold with your hands as long as possible and land on the balls of your feet with your knees slightly bent. Keep one hand on the rein as you move to the horse's head (figure 12.12e).

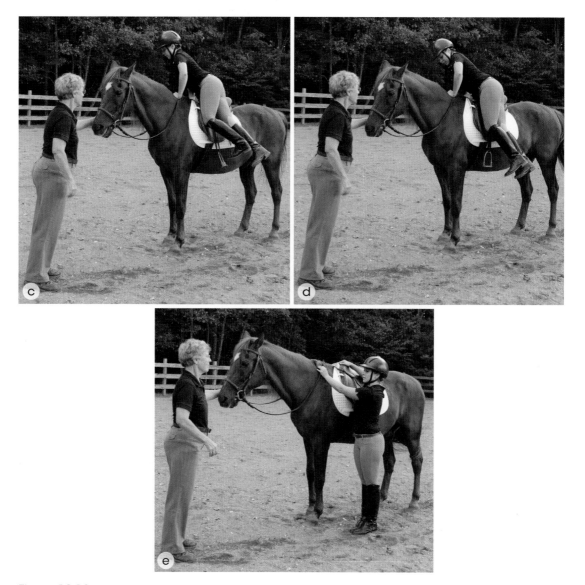

Figure 12.12 *(continued)* Completing the dismount.

Getting Comfortable in the Saddle

The saddle, in order to be comfortable, has to fit you reasonably well. Once you are pretty sure you will continue riding, you should purchase your own saddle. It's a fairly big investment, but a good saddle will last indefinitely with reasonable care. Ask your instructor for guidance.

Saddles also need to fit the horse. But for normal riding, unless either the horse or the saddle is a very unusual shape, the use of pads and padding will take care of any discrepancy. Some newer saddles are self-adjusting to the horse's back. It has been my experience that a saddle that doesn't fit the rider, and interferes with her balance, causes far more problems for the horse than one that fits the rider, but not the horse. And of course, in competition professional riders usually use their own saddle on whatever horse they happen to be riding.

So, what should you look for? First, looking at it from the ground, the saddle should sit level on the horse, tipped neither forward nor back. This is sometimes hard to see, since the pommel and cantle aren't always the same height, but the lowest part of the seat should be in the center of the saddle (figure 12.13).

Figure 12.13 Properly placed and balanced saddles.

Once you have remounted, the first step is to do the knees-up exercise, which puts you squarely on your seat bones so that you can ground on them. This exercise is described using an English saddle. You will have to adapt your leg position for the Western saddle.

Knees-Up Exercise

Holding the pommel, lift your feet up and forward until your knees are level with the top of the saddle, then quietly let your feet rest in front of the saddle flaps on the horse's shoulders. Do this one leg at a time, and be sure the horse is being held and doesn't seem bothered. (It's rare, but some horses have been kicked aggressively on the shoulders to make them turn.) Once you're settled, think about how you are centered on your seat bones. Finally, bring your legs down slowly, one at a time, *only as far as you can without losing the connection to the saddle in your seat bones*. Your legs might not hang down as far as they will later on when your muscles are more adjusted, but that's all right.

When I had my stable with a large lesson program, once a student was ready to start in the saddle, she was assigned her own saddle that she always used, no matter what horse she rode. This is unlike the usual practice where the saddle is assigned to the horse. Each of my horses did have his own personal equipment, which included any special padding so that the saddle sat on him correctly. I followed this practice for over 20 years and never had a sore-backed horse from a poor saddle fit. At the same time, the students found it easy to develop a correct position.

Keeping your connection in your seat bones, go through the seven steps with your feet out of the stirrups to complete your centering and grounding. *The saddle should feel comfortable under your seat* (figure 12.14). If it makes you sore, it will inevitably cause tension. Some saddles are wider across the seat than others so that your legs are forced apart or, conversely, your seat bones rest on the tree instead of the saddle seat. You should have about a hand's breadth of space behind your buttocks; if you have much more than that, the saddle is too large and will not help you to stay centered on the horse as it should. If there is less room behind you and especially if you feel any pressure *under* your crotch bone, the saddle is too small. There will be some pressure against the *front* of your crotch bone as the horse moves and your body follows the movement, but this is normal and not uncomfortable. All of your weight should be on your seat bones.

Figure 12.14   A saddle that fits the rider well is comfortable and helps the rider develop a correct position. The whip held by the rider on the right shows the proper alignment of her center and foot.

Your First Ride in the Saddle

Before you try to use the stirrups, you should spend some time just getting used to the feeling of being on the saddle. Your horse should still be wearing a grounding strap, but you will probably find it easier at first in full seat to hold the pommel of the saddle instead. Tuck the first two fingers of each hand under the pommel a little to each side. Unless you are using a hand for something else, it's best to hold lightly with both hands to help keep you sitting squarely. Later on you can go back to the grounding strap, reins, and stick.

Once you are mounted on the English saddle, your stirrups should be crossed in front of you so that they are out of the way (figure 12.15) and don't bang against your ankles. The instructor or helper will do this for you. The stirrup buckle needs to be pulled down away from the bar about 6 inches (15 cm), then the stirrup leather is carefully folded up and forward so that the stirrup lies on the horse's opposite shoulder.

When mounted on the Western saddle, just take your feet out of the stirrups. Because they are longer than for English riding and are mounted differently they won't be in the way.

Now you are ready to start. What is different about riding in a saddle without stirrups, as opposed to a bareback pad, is that horses' backs are sort of gable (Λ) shaped, which gives you quite a lot of lateral stability. In addition, most pads have a texture that tends to keep you from slipping.

Saddles, by contrast, have a rounded convex curve on top, and the leather can be quite slippery. As a

Figure 12.15 Stirrups crossed in front of the rider.

result, lateral centering is much more of a problem. The stirrups, of course, will help with this, but it's important not to lose your upper-body centering skills. You will also find that while losing your lateral center is easier in the saddle, regaining it is also easier.

Avoid trotting until you've had a chance to practice some emergency dismounts. Because of the slippery factor, you will be much more inclined to grip if the horse trots unexpectedly and thus you are liable to bounce, which is uncomfortable and scary for both of you.

If possible, you should either have a leader or work in a small, confined, preferably rectangular space so that you don't have to think about control, and most of your work can be on the straight. Begin with straight lines and smooth short curves, feeling your following seat and your lateral centering. Someone should walk behind you for a little while and make sure that you are centered and the saddle stays level and centered on turns.

Going from the knees-up position and then back to normal position will help you to feel grounded on your seat while loosening up your legs. Riding to music for a while is another way to enjoy a practice period while your body finds its comfort zone. The goal is to practice everything that you were doing on the bareback pad (except trotting) until you start to feel just as secure in the saddle without stirrups before moving on.

Finish with a dismount using the stirrups, followed by one more mount and dismount to refresh your memory. Loosen the girth if you won't be unsaddling right away. In an English saddle, without touching the buckles, slide each stirrup up the *back* side of the leather as far as it will go, then tuck the leather through the stirrup. Take your horse back to his well-earned rest and reward.

From Bareback to Saddle and Back Again

My practice with new students, even if experienced, was to start them on the bareback pad so that we could work on all the same things you have been working on. Some of my students were not sure they could deal with bareback, but they soon found that it was easy and helpful in overcoming some of their faults.

After they were comfortable, the day came when they went back to the saddle. More often than not, the reaction on the first day, especially if they were given stirrups as well, was "Boy, this is *much* harder than bareback!" But they soon found their comfort zone again and happily switched back and forth between both methods as needed to improve their skills.

13

Saddling Up and Starting With the Stirrups

Putting on the saddle is very similar to putting on the bareback pad. In fact, with the Western saddle, you begin with the pad exactly as you did for bareback but without the surcingle. An English saddle goes on the same way unless it has the pad attached, then it goes on together.

The difference between putting on the pad and putting on the saddle is that the saddle has that rigid tree. If it is not placed correctly on the horse, it can cause serious damage over time. Saddles, especially Western saddles, are also heavy. If the saddle is not put on with care, it can hurt or frighten the horse.

Take a careful look at the horse's back and shoulder in the withers area (figure 13.1). Place your hand on the shoulder near the top, then slide it back and you will feel how it goes inward. This is where the tree points should sit. If the horse has good saddle conformation, in addition to his withers keeping the saddle from slipping to the side, his shoulders in front of that little hollow will keep the saddle from sliding forward, and the spring of his ribs behind it will keep it from sliding back. Not all horses have perfect conformation, and some will need to wear a breastplate to keep the saddle from sliding back or a crupper to keep it from sliding forward (figure 13.2).

Figure 13.1 The body of a horse with good conformation helps keep the saddle in place.

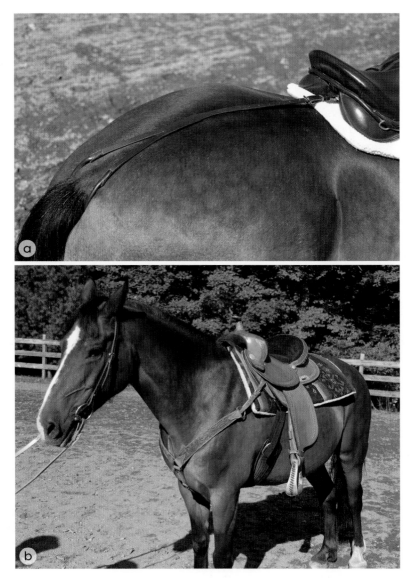

Figure 13.2 If the *(a)* crupper is used regularly, the portion going under the dock (base of tail) should be about twice as thick. The *(b)* breastplate fits above the horse's shoulder point, preventing the saddle from sliding back.

You must prepare the saddle for putting it on so that the horse doesn't get hit by flying stirrups or girths. If you are using an English saddle, the stirrups should be up. The girth might already be attached on the right side; if so, you should fold it back over the top of the saddle. If the girth is not attached, you can either lay it over the top and tuck it through the stirrups or lay it aside until you are ready for it. For the Western saddle, you should bring the right stirrup and the cinch up and hook them over the horn.

Putting On the Saddle

If it is separate, begin by putting on the pad, as described in chapter 9. Place it somewhat farther forward than you want it because you will be sliding it and the saddle back into place together.

As you did with the pad, allow the horse to look at the saddle and sniff it. If he seems unsure, gently rub it against his shoulder.

Now you're ready to put the saddle on. It must go on gently and smoothly, not crash down on the horse. To do this, you must lift the saddle up *above* his withers. This can be difficult if you are small or the saddle is heavy, so you might want to practice swinging it up onto a fence or something similar. It is particularly necessary to practice with Western saddles because they tend to be more awkward to handle than English ones.

To swing the saddle up, hold the pommel firmly with your left hand and the cantle with your right. Stand by the horse's withers facing his tail and turn your arms and shoulders away from the horse so that you are holding the saddle behind your right hip. Swing the saddle forward

Figure 13.3 Positioning the saddle.

and back a time or two to build up momentum, then swing it strongly up into the air above the horse's back. Let it down gently onto his withers and slide it back until you feel the tree drop into place behind his shoulder (figure 13.3).

The next step is to fasten the girth or cinch. If it's an English saddle and the girth is already fastened on the off (right) side, you can fasten it up just as you did for the bareback pad (see Fastening the Girth or Surcingle in chapter 9). If it is not fastened, because it is adjustable on both sides you proceed a little differently.

Once the saddle is on, you will be doing virtually all the adjusting on the near (left) side, so you want to leave plenty of room for adjustment. The best way to do that is to fasten the girth on the near side first, putting it at or near the bottom holes in the billet (girth) straps. Then walk around to the off side and buckle it up so that it is snug but not tight. If it still seems too loose after you have taken it all the way up on the off side, return to the near side and take it up more. You might need to check with your instructor about the tightness at this stage.

You will be using your grounding strap with the saddle, so put it on next as you did with the bareback pad, making the girth snug but not tight when you are through. Depending on the style of the grounding strap, it may attach to the breastplate dee rings, or to the billet straps. Your instructor will guide you. Later you will adjust the girth one or more times, again as you did with the pad.

Billet Straps on the English Saddle

English saddles generally have three billet straps, and most people think that you are supposed to use the front and back ones. However, if you look at the way the buckles on the girth are placed, you will see that they are quite close together, so if you use the front and back billet straps, you are putting a strain on the girth. And using the back strap rather than the middle one does not hold the saddle on any more securely. Therefore, you should use the front and middle straps for most horses and saddles. What you should *not* do is use the two back straps. The front strap is attached to the saddle separately from the other two so that if one of the two front straps breaks, the other will hold. The second and third straps are attached together, so if either broke you would have no girth at all.

Unless the Western saddle is new, the cinch is usually left attached on the off side. Unhook it from the horn and check to make sure it is hanging straight with nothing caught up in it. Then reach under the horse's belly to pick it up as you did when fastening the bareback pad.

Cinches fasten with a latigo strap that is already attached to the saddle, using a special flat knot. Make sure the strap has no twists in it, then insert it through the cinch ring from inside to outside (figure 13.4a). Take it back through the saddle ring from outside to inside (figure 13.4b). Depending on the length of the latigo strap, you might need to make this loop between the saddle and girth twice. If the cinch has a buckle end, the buckle tongue should line up with one of the latigo holes on the final wrap of your girth loop. Finish this portion of the wrap by taking the end of the latigo from the outside to the inside of the saddle ring, pulling the end out from behind the ring down and to the left toward the shoulder, then bring the end of the strap around the whole strap from back to front, just below the saddle ring (figure 13.4c). Finally, bring the end through the saddle ring from inside to outside, this time pulling up and to the left toward the shoulder (figure 13.4d), and tuck it through itself where it crosses, just below the ring (figure 13.4e). The balance of the latigo strap can be left to hang down if it isn't too long (figure 13.4f) or threaded through a tie strap holder, usually a ring or slotted piece of leather attached to the left side of the saddle in front of the swell. *Never rely solely on the buckle of a Western cinch.* The latigo strap should always be fastened as described.

Tighten the cinch by loosening or undoing the final knot and then pulling down on the underneath section of the latigo and up on the outer section simultaneously until you have the desired degree of tightness. Then pull the slack through the ring and tighten the knot.

Tightening the cinch is very easy to do because you are using a pulley effect, which doubles your strength. As a result, many people make the cinch much tighter than it needs to be or should be. As has been said, what keeps the saddle from turning should be the horse's withers. In addition, once you are riding with stirrups, your lateral centering on the stirrups can have a big effect, either positive or negative, depending on whether your centering is good or not. If the horse has flat withers, the best solution in addition to good lateral centering is a properly chosen, fitted, and adjusted breastplate. Trying to manage with an overtightened cinch or girth alone will only result in a tense, uncomfortable horse who will inevitably become either unsound or dangerous.

Western saddles may have a single rigging (single cinch fitting) or double rigging (with or without a back or flank cinch). The rear cinch was developed to keep the saddle stable when roping cattle, when a forward pull on the horn could cause the saddle to tip dangerously forward. The flank cinch is usually connected by a buckle. The area on the horse's barrel where it lies is quite sensitive, so the flank cinch should be left somewhat loose. However, it should rest no more than an inch away from the horse's body so that there is no risk of his getting a foot through it. You should be able to easily slip your fingers with your hand flat between the horse and the flank cinch. There should also be a keeper strap between the front and rear cinches to keep the rear cinch from slipping back and catching the horse in the flank, possibly causing him to buck violently. If this keeper is not attached, don't ride with the rear cinch. When using a double-rigged saddle, always tighten the front cinch first, then the rear. When undoing the cinches, undo the rear cinch first, then the front.

Starting With the Stirrups

Even if you are comfortable controlling your horse by yourself, you will learn to use the stirrups more quickly if you have a hand leader so that you can focus entirely on position for this work. Being on a longe line is not a good option in the beginning because it involves constant circling, so constant lateral centering. You should begin work mostly on straight lines.

Once you're comfortable in the saddle, you're ready for the stirrups and the various ways to use them. Put simply, when you ride in a saddle, you either sit, with loose or fixed legs or your feet in the stirrups, or you stand up in the stirrups. As stated earlier, in this book sitting is called full seat and standing is called half seat. However, it isn't quite as simple as that. There are actually three types of full seat, three of half seat, and one in between, called the three-quarter seat.

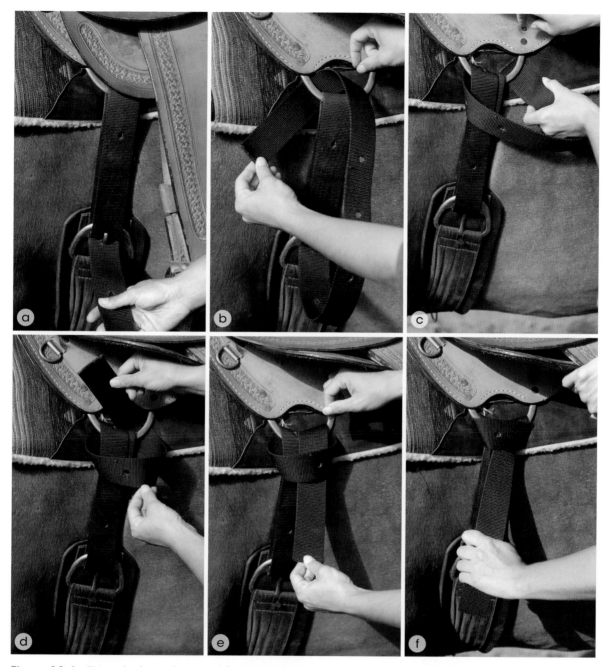

Figure 13.4 Tying the latigo knot and fastening the cinch.

In this chapter we discuss the three full seats:

- Full-seat ∩ position (read as n position)
- Full-seat ∧ position (read as A position)
- Full-seat forward position

I cover the half-seat positions and the three-quarter seat position in chapter 14.

The ∩ and ∧ positions have to do with your legs and feet, and the shape they make when you sit on the horse. It's easiest to learn about them on the ground first.

Finding the ∩ and ⋀ Positions on the Ground

1. Stand with your feet a little more than shoulder-width apart. Use the seven steps to get centered and well grounded. Your feet should be flat on the ground. Your feet and knees should be pointing straight ahead.

2. Slightly bend and spread your knees until your shins are almost vertical viewed from the front. Adjust your hip angle (more forward or more straight up) until you feel centered. Imagine that there is a horse between your knees. Your calves will lie close to the horse's sides and your inner thighs from one knee to the other will form a soft curve. Your legs are now in ∩ position.

3. Staying grounded and keeping your feet flat, bend your knees by pushing them down and forward so that your ankles bend as well (figure 13.5a). Straighten and bend several times, bending only as far as is comfortable. Think about how far you can bend and how it feels as you hold the position. Notice that your weight is on the *outside* edges of your feet.

4. From the bent position, without changing anything else, roll your feet inward so that your weight is on the *inside* edges of your feet. The outside edges will come slightly off the ground. Notice that your shins are no longer vertical and your knees are close together (figure 13.5b). Step apart with your feet until your knees are the same distance apart that they were before. Your lower leg now forms an almost straight line from your foot toward your crotch, and your base (the distance between your feet) is much wider. Your legs are now in ⋀ position.

5. Straighten and bend your legs again. Notice how much more freely your knees and ankles move than they did in ∩ position.

6. Go back and forth between the two positions a few times so that you understand how they feel.

a   b

Figure 13.5 Finding the (*a*) ∩ position and the (*b*) ⋀ position.

When you are on the horse and want to change from ∩ to ∧ position, you will need to move your foot out to the side. Your tendency will be to push against the stirrup only, which would move your toe out and cause some unwanted leg rotation, which we talked about earlier.

While you're still on the ground, take your ∧ position but with your feet a little closer together. Keeping your weight on the inside edge of your foot, push *just* your heel out to the side so you make yourself a little pigeon toed. Move your heel in and out a couple of times while you watch what your leg is doing. You'll see that the movement comes all the way from your hip joint, so when your heel moves out, the outside of your hip comes a little forward and your knee turns inward. All of this helps you maintain a correct leg position.

It's also useful to know that if you have trouble with this on the horse or your instructor tells you that your knees are turned out, it is a sign of tension in your lower back muscles that control the hip joint and you need to correct it by releasing from there, not by trying to squeeze your knees in. Refer back to the section called Breathing Away Body Tension in chapter 5. These two positions, the ∧ position and the ∩ position, each have a separate purpose. When your legs are in ∩ position, your lower leg is close to the horse's barrel, which is important for giving leg aids. Also, your inner thigh is soft, allowing you to sit deeper and follow the horse's movements with your seat while helping him to relax his back and move more freely and softly. The ∩ position is used almost entirely for full-seat work.

The ∧ position is used mostly in half-seat work. When your legs are in ∧ position, your knee and ankle joints have the maximum flexibility essential for absorbing the movement of the gaits when you are standing in the stirrups, especially at speed or over rough terrain. For full-seat work, the purpose of ∧ position is to widen your base of support, which is important for lateral stability, especially in unexpectedly difficult situations.

Simply by changing your foot position, you can alternate between ∧ and ∩ positions with little thought or effort and without disturbing your upper-body position at all.

You'll work on your foot position on the horse but not use the stirrups immediately. After mounting, cross your stirrups. If you pull the buckles down before mounting, it's fairly easy to cross them yourself and a useful skill to have. If you are riding Western, just drop your stirrups. Ride for 5 or 10 minutes until you feel grounded. You will need a ground person to help adjust your stirrups at least the first time, even if you are experienced.

∩ Position

To assume the ∩ position, shake out your legs, including your thighs as far as you are able. Uncross your stirrups and use the Knees-Up Exercise you learned in chapter 12 to find correct placement on your seat bones. Finish with your legs in loose-leg position.

Swing your lower legs back and forth gently to make sure they are loose. Let your leg fall where it feels comfortable, then take the fixed-leg position (see Preparing for Saddle Work in chapter 12). If you and the horse are a perfect fit, your knee will come down to just above the horse's lateral midline, your shin will hang vertically, and your calf will lie in light contact with his barrel. Longer or shorter legs and taller, shorter, wider, or narrower horses will all change the fit somewhat, but the important thing is to stay on your seat bones and adjust your leg position accordingly.

Checking the Stirrups

The ground person should now check your stirrup length against your fixed-leg position. The bottom of the stirrup should hang about a half inch (a little more than 1 cm) above the ball of your foot. She should adjust the stirrups as necessary and pull the buckles up into place.

When the stirrups are adjusted, take your fixed-leg position again. The ground person will lift up your leg for you and place it in the stirrup. Your goal is to be completely passive so that when she lets go of your leg, your foot falls down onto the stirrup *of its own weight*, without any effort on your part.

Does Leg Length Matter?

There is a fallacy that to be an effective rider you have to have relatively long and preferably strong legs. Actually, because the human calf and the horse's barrel are both convex, like)(, they contact each other over a very short space. And because the muscles they affect cover most of the horse's side below the saddle flap, the actual point where the leg contacts the horse is not significant. And, as we explain further in chapter 18, leg *strength* has no part in creating movement.

This fallacy arose because many short-legged people have relatively large upper bodies, especially men with their heavy shoulders, which gives them a very high center of gravity. This in turn means that it is difficult for them to stay centered, especially longitudinally, which unbalances the horse and makes him seemingly unwilling to go forward, leading some people to conclude that such riders require stronger leg aids. Not true.

Many short-legged people with more favorable proportions are excellent horsemen, and even those with difficult proportions can become excellent horsemen as well if they are willing to spend the time developing their longitudinal balance. (See appendix at http://tinyurl.com/d8pv7nz.)

She will first take hold of your lower leg and, without moving it forward, back, or sideways, lift your foot straight up a few inches and let it fall. Your instinct will be to lift your leg yourself, and she should correct you if you do so. She should lift and drop your leg several times until you have released all the tension.

Then she should take the stirrup, turn the outside of it toward your toe, lift your foot, slide the stirrup over your toe until the back bar (the back half inch of a Western stirrup) is under your bubbling-spring point (at the very back of the ball of your foot,) and drop your foot onto the stirrup. Your bubbling-spring point should rest on the back bar.

> In order for your center to be in the correct place relative to your feet, the stirrup leather *must* hang vertically when your foot is in correct position with your heel under your trouser seam.

If there is any major variation, see the appendix at http://tinyurl.com/d8pv7nz for options on saddle fits.

Settling In

Do *not* push down on your feet in an effort to put more pressure on the stirrups. In the first place, the weight of your leg is more than sufficient to keep your foot from sliding around on the stirrup. As we said earlier, when you are sitting, your center is behind your bubbling spring on the stirrup, so pushing on your feet will move them forward, which reduces your lateral stability and makes changing from full to half seat much more difficult. However, sometimes your feet will sneak forward anyway, so to avoid this, think about having a fixed leg; that is, think to keep your knee bent, your foot back, and your toe slightly raised. This takes some practice at first, but since your body wants to feel centered and grounded, you'll soon find that you notice when you lose the position, and can correct it. A little tip: If you can see your toe when you're sitting erect, your foot is too far forward.

Very rarely, you might be put in a saddle where your feet end up behind your center so that your feet go back rather than forward when you press on them. Generally speaking, you probably just need a saddle with a larger seat, or the saddle might be tilted forward.

Now go through the first five steps so that you are centered and grounded over your seat bones. You should be in ∩ position, so your feet should be flat on the stirrups, pointing straight ahead with the weight slightly on the outside edge, and your thighs should lie softly against the saddle. If the conformation of the horse makes your knee come away from the saddle a little, that's all right as long as your knee isn't *turned* out.

Begin to walk. Think mostly about your following seat at first, and try to feel it in your feet as well. That is, if you allow your legs to hang of their own weight, the pressure on the stirrups stays constant as does the pressure on your seat bones as the two move up and down together. Don't do any sharp turns yet. When you do begin turns, try to use the same centering motion in your upper body to move your center as you did without stirrups. You will be using your stirrups for lateral balance as well, but you don't want to become entirely dependent on them. If you should accidentally lose a stirrup or it should break, you will need the upper-body centering reflex to stay on.

Probably at least 80 percent of your riding, if you ride English, or 95 percent if you ride Western will be in full-seat ∩ position, so it is very important to get it right. Except for having your feet in the stirrups, you should feel exactly the same as you did on the bareback pad and just as secure. Practice at the walk, checking little details first on the straight, then in turns and transitions, until staying centered and grounded is easy and you are beginning to correct automatically when you lose it.

∧ Position

When you are secure in full-seat ∩ position, you should start trying the full-seat ∧ position. The ∧ position will prepare you for half-seat work, but when you're in full seat its primary purpose is to give you greater lateral support.

To prepare for the ∧ position, start on the ground standing with your feet fairly close together. Sway your upper body to one side, as would happen if your horse suddenly moved the other way. You'll find that if you move your shoulders more than a little bit, you lose your balance. Now place your feet in ∧ position as if you were on the horse (see Finding the ∩ and ∧ Positions on the Ground). You'll find that with your feet far apart you can move your upper body a long way without losing your balance.

With your knees and ankles bent as you did earlier, move your center from side to side by straightening first one leg and then the other. Notice how you *push* and *straighten* your leg at the same time so that your center—and your weight—moves over the other foot. If you push just on one foot, without straightening, your center will stay over that foot, which is not what you want.

Checking Foot Position Once You Are Mounted

On the horse, take up your fixed-leg position (see Finding the Fixed Leg in chapter 12) with your toe rotated out and up so your ankle is flexed and your heel down. Be careful to keep your shin from rotating. Your feet and lower leg will be farther away from the horse's body than they were in ∩ position.

Have the ground person place your feet in the stirrups as she did when you were working on the ∩ position. Now your ankle is flexed, but your calves are pointing straight ahead. It is possible to rotate your toe out farther with your knee bent, but that will cause the shin rotation that you want to avoid. The soles of your feet are tilted outward so that your weight is toward the inside edge of your foot and your foot rests against the inside stirrup post (figure 13.6).

To keep this position, you have to exert constant pressure on the inside edge of your foot. To keep your toes from turning out, this will include the heel area as well as where your foot rests on the stirrup. Press

Figure 13.6 Correct ∧ position.

on the inside edge of the ball of your foot on the inside corner of your stirrup, then push the inside of your heel out as well, as you did during the ground work (See Finding the ∧ position on the ground).

Since your center is *behind* your foot, with the pressure your foot will have a tendency to go forward as well as out. Use the same technique to bring and keep it back as you did in the ∩ position. This will take quite a lot of practice in the beginning. Once you know what you are doing, you can practice it at home or at work while sitting on a chair.

Settling In

Practice going from ∧ to ∩ position at the standstill without moving anything else or letting your feet slip forward. That is, from the ∧ position, allow your foot to fall inward until your calf is close to the horse and your foot is flat with the weight a little toward the outer edge. Then push your whole foot outward so that your ankle is flexed but your foot, shin, and knee are pointing straight ahead and your heel is still back under your trouser seam. Depending on your and the horse's conformation, your calf might come away from his side, but that's all right. For the most part it is your intent and center that tell your horse to keep going, not constant leg pressure, which would be impossible to maintain for long periods, anyway. (We talk about leg aids in chapter 18.)

Once you start moving around, after finding your following seat as you did in the ∩ position and getting the feeling of keeping even pressure on both feet on the straight, start trying some turns. Now you'll use your feet to help you center just as you did on the ground. As the horse turns to the left, first think to move your center to the left in your upper body, then push on your right foot and straighten your right knee, which will add a lot of power to the move. Your body should stay perpendicular to the horse's body, just as it does when you center without the help of stirrups. This is especially important when you and the horse make turns at high speed and he leans into the turn. Practice both left and right turns, keeping even weight on both feet all the time.

You should find it easier to center correctly to the right when you are using the stirrups than without them. When you feel you have the knack of using your stirrups to center, try shorter and faster turns to gradually speed up your reflexes. Also try with your eyes closed so that your body learns to feel and react without conscious thought. Once you have this skill thoroughly fixed in your muscle memory, it will be very difficult to be caught unawares and fall if the horse spins or spooks sideways.

Full-Seat Forward Position

This position has two functions. It is the down part of posting (covered in chapter 16) and, if done correctly, allows the body a momentary rest in each stride so that a capable rider can post for as long as the horse can trot. It helps to prepare you for posting, as well.

It is also useful if you are going slowly—at the walk or jog—in full seat and your horse approaches a small obstacle that he might hop over. If you take the full-seat forward position when you are far enough away not to unbalance the horse, you will be better prepared to stay centered and balanced and deal with a small bounce.

Finding Full Seat Forward

Start from full-seat ∧ position.

1. Keeping your spine straight and your face level, bend forward from the hip as though you were preparing to get up out of a chair. Look for the degree of bend that feels as though you could stand up in the stirrups.

2. Take the grounding strap in your fingers as usual, *then place your hands, knuckles down, on the horse's withers for balance.*

3. Without allowing your seat bones to leave the saddle, try to shift most of your weight from your seat to your stirrups. If you are centered over your bubbling spring, this will be very easy and your feet will not move forward or back at all. It is the same thing you do when you are preparing to stand up from a seated position in a chair

4. If you are successful, try it again with your arms folded and perhaps with your eyes closed.

The goal is to be forward without being ahead of either your base or the horse's center (figure 13.7).

Figure 13.7   Full-seat forward position.

Sitting the Trot in the Saddle

Sitting the trot in the saddle is almost the same as on a bareback pad. The big difference is that the saddle is flat and slippery, making lateral centering more difficult at first.

You should work at the walk until you are really comfortable, centered, and relaxed both with and without stirrups.

It is probably best to start without stirrups and with a loose, not fixed, leg (figure 13.8a). Use your hand on the pommel to ground you, and so that you can lean slightly back without tension. Start with short distances on the straight. Then go to easy turns and finally to fixed leg (figure 13.8b). Once you are secure with that, dropping your feet onto the stirrups should not present a problem. You might find that rather than just holding the pommel, holding it with your outside hand only and placing the fingers of your inside hand under the side of the cantle just behind your seat bones give you more stability while you are learning (figure 13.8c).

Figure 13.8 Sitting the trot in the saddle *(a)* with loose leg, *(b)* with fixed leg, and *(c)* with stirrups and holding the cantle with the inside hand.

If you are patient and spend the time necessary to develop a secure, relaxed, and correct full-seat position at the walk and slow trot, the skills that you build on this foundation will come much more easily. And if it isn't easy, it isn't correct.

14

Half-Seat Positions and Preparing for Faster Gaits

Most experienced riders associate trotting with posting (see chapter 16). Traditionally, posting is the first method of trotting that is taught to beginners, even before sitting trot. I moved away from this method because I realized that to post correctly you must first be able to both sit and stand during the trot and remain secure and balanced. Learning posting before perfecting sitting and standing skills might cause you to never learn posting correctly. This is hard on both you and the horse. Since trotting is the most-used gait after walking, especially on long rides, riding becomes much harder than it needs to be.

When you are able to ride in the stirrups in full seat, without tension in your inner thighs, you are ready to start half seat, that is, standing in your stirrups. Freedom from thigh tension shows that you can maintain your lateral centering, which is important as you raise your center of gravity, working with no weight on your seat and your center over your stirrups instead of over the center of the saddle.

Half seat is used to distribute your weight over the horse's back in a way that makes the faster gaits easier for both of you. When you sit, your weight presses primarily over the center of the saddle, which of course is padded. But sitting all the time in one spot can be tiring for you and the horse. (A western saddle distributes your weight over a larger area, so this is less of a problem.) When your weight is on the stirrups, it is distributed, via the tree, over a much larger area of the horse's back. Also, when you are sitting, your back and seat alone can't absorb as much shock as your knees, ankles, and hip joints do when you are standing. Imagine going off a ski jump sitting down!

Working From the Hip Joint

Up until now you have been riding with your upper body vertical so that your center is always directly over your seat bones, which form your base when sitting. When you ride in half seat, you will stand with your center over your bubbling spring, which is resting on the back bar of the stirrups. The stirrups hang from the stirrup bar of the saddle, which is several inches in front of the deepest part of the saddle seat. Therefore, to put your center over your feet and not risk getting ahead of the horse, you have to lean forward. Let's talk a little more about that.

To keep your upper body steady and still flexible as the horse moves, your torso must stay firm and connected. The tendency when you lean forward is to round your back and to arch it when you lean back; the former tends to make your back too loose, and the latter makes it too tight.

What you must teach your body to do is to work from the hip joint only, without changing your spine. This is called opening and closing your hip joint.

Hip Joint Exercise 1

Standing squarely, bend forward as far as you comfortably can, allowing your back to round. Notice how your rounded back feels and also how your hip joints are closed (figure 14.1a). Now straighten, arching your back as you do so. When you are vertical again, keep your back arched and notice how it feels (figure 14.1b). Keeping your back arched, cross your hands behind your back as high up as you can, which locks your spine in one position (figure 14.1c). Now bend forward, then straighten up. *To do so with your back locked, you have to close (lean forward) and open (straighten up) from your hip joints only* (figure 14.1d). Repeat this several times. Also try this sitting in a chair. Don't try to go too far forward—just enough to feel your seat bones tipping up.

Figure 14.1 Lean forward by (a) rounding your back and straighten by (b) arching your back. Then, locking the back, lean forward by (c) closing your hips and straighten by (d) opening your hips.

Obviously, you don't want to ride with your back locked. So grow, using your arms, until your back is straight and relaxed. Place your hands behind your back again, palms out, but this time put one hand at shoulder blade level and the other at waist level so that you can feel any movement forward or back in those areas. Again, open and close your hip joints several times, making sure that your spine stays still and only your hip joints move. Now hold your arms out in front of you more or less as you would if holding the reins, with your upper arms hanging slightly in front of your shoulders and your forearms pointing toward an imaginary bit. Open and close as before, keeping the upper arm position by letting your hands go forward as your center moves forward over your feet (figure 14.2a), and back as your center comes back over your seat bones (figure 14.2b). If you find that you tend to pull your arms back when you are in a forward position, it is an indication that your center is in front of your base.

Figure 14.2   Practicing the proper hip joint, spine, and arm positions required for riding.

Hip Joint Exercise 2

When you are in half seat, your seat is not available as a base. Let's find out how the body deals with that.

Stand upright with your feet a few inches away from a wall, your legs straight, and your buttocks against the wall. Hold your arms straight out in front of you. You should have about the same amount of pressure on your bubbling springs as you do on your heels, and you should feel balanced and grounded. *Without allowing your buttocks to press more against the wall,* close your hip angle as before (figure 14.3a). You will find that you can't close very far before you start to feel insecure and unbalanced. That's because your center quickly goes in front of your bubbling spring points. If you keep going, you'll have to take a step to move one bubbling spring forward or fall down.

Stand up straight in front of the wall again, but this time stand with your feet—and your buttocks—6 to 8 inches (15-20 cm) away. Close your hip angle again, trying to stay centered over your bubbling spring (figure 14.3b). What happens is that your buttocks bump the wall! This tells you that to stay balanced when you bend over, your buttocks must go back as your shoulders come forward.

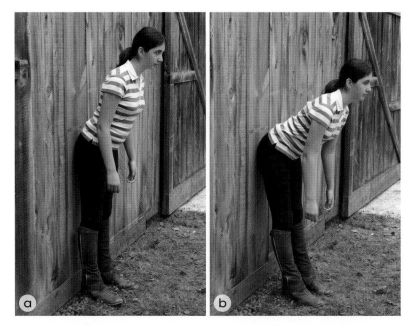

Figure 14.3 *(a)* Unbalanced and *(b)* balanced position with a closed hip angle.

Hip Joint Exercise 3

Now a slightly different exercise. Stand away from the wall with your legs straight. Close your hip angle as much as you can and still feel comfortably balanced. Your arms should be hanging straight down (figure 14.4*a*). Rock back and forth from your heels to your bubbling springs. Then, without changing anything else, push your knees forward and allow your body to fold up as you do so (figure 14.4*b*). You'll find that the more bent your knees are, the more comfortable you feel about leaning forward. That's because having your knees in front of your center makes you more secure. Compare the relative positions of your knees and center.

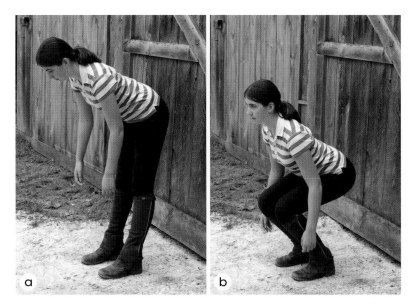

Figure 14.4 Feeling the difference between bending with *(a)* straight legs and *(b)* bent knees.

Barefooting

In the past few years barefoot walking and barefoot running have gained attention. This method of moving involves putting your forefoot, specifically your bubbling spring, on the ground first. There are several reasons for doing this. One is that you can ground immediately rather than at the end of the stride. Another is that your upper-leg joints receive little or no shock each step, promoting healthy joints. Because it encourages greater muscle awareness and good balance, barefoot walking techniques might well improve your ability to work in half seat.

If you are riding race horses or jumping (chapter 20), you need shorter stirrups in order to have a more closed hip angle. However, a shorter stirrup raises your center of gravity, so disciplines that don't require a very forward position prefer to use a longer stirrup. The longer stirrup can present a problem if the horse does something that causes your upper body to go forward because it goes ahead of your base, from which it can be difficult to recover. Saddles in those disciplines have deep seats and high pommels or swells, which can save you providing you don't get tossed up at the same time. But in every discipline the stirrup hangs somewhat in front of the deepest part of the seat, so you do need to lean at least a little bit forward in order to stand up.

Staying Grounded in Half Seat

Riding in half seat, even though you are on your feet, is quite different from walking on the ground. When you walk, you put your heels down first, taking weight on your heels, then transfer weight onto the foot. Only at the end of the step do you put your full weight momentarily on the bubbling spring. When riding in half seat, all the weight is on the bubbling spring all the time.

When you begin riding with your weight on the stirrups, you might feel insecure partly because your body is accustomed to grounding onto your heel as well as the bubbling spring, and partly because, although the stirrups are fixed laterally, they are free to swing forward and back. This is necessary for enabling you to keep your feet underneath you when going uphill and downhill and jumping, which we talk more about in chapter 19. Your body finds this disconcerting at first, and your feet and leg joints tense up, making it difficult to stay grounded. This is one of the reasons people lose their stirrups.

Following are two preparatory exercises.

Half-Seat Preparatory Exercise 1

Stand on the bottom step of a flight of stairs. Use the handrails to aid your balance. Stand in your stocking feet so that you can feel your bubbling spring clearly. Before you start, use your hand to find the bubbling spring again (see figure 2.2). It's slightly *behind* the ball of your foot, and when you're standing on the right spot, you feel the most secure.

Run through the seven steps, then stand with your bubbling spring on the step, holding the handrails and moving your feet around until you're sure you've found it. Keeping your toes and ankles relaxed, allow your heels to drop, which they will do naturally, since there is nothing to hold them up. Bend your knees and close your hip angle slightly at first. Keep your face vertical. Now think about grounding by releasing tension from the ground up and from the top down.

Try the following movements:

1. Wiggle your toes to help your feet relax.
2. Roll your feet from inside to outside to find the most comfortable position.
3. Gently shake out up and down your legs.
4. Run through your body mentally to find tensions, then breathe or shake them out.

Once you are secure on the step, you're ready for the second exercise.

Half-Seat Preparatory Exercise 2

Instead of standing on a fixed step, stand on something that will roll forward and back—ideally, a round pole 3 to 4 inches (8-10 cm) in diameter, strong enough to take your weight. Heavy plastic or wood usually works well and is easy to find. You will need something to hold on to with your hands. It can be a fence, another person, or, if you are riding at a stable that has jumping, another pole on jump standards at a convenient height. The ground should be smooth and level so that the ground pole can roll fairly easily.

Take the same position that you took on the step. If possible, someone should stabilize the pole so it doesn't roll while you get used to the different shape under your foot. Then experiment with your longitudinal center, *moving it forward by bringing your shoulders forward and back by pushing your hips back.* Notice how, if your center gets behind the pole, the pole will roll forward. This is the same as having your stirrups—and your feet—go out in front of you. You can get the same effect by *pushing* down on your heels, which pushes your center back. Getting ahead of the pole will move it backward so that your feet go out behind you. This is less common than the other way but can occur if you start to fall forward over the horse's head, and contributes to the usually inevitable conclusion of falling off.

Once you understand how it works, practice getting a little ahead or behind your stirrups and then recentering yourself. If you can train your body to do this as a reflex, it will make your seat that much more secure.

Heels Down

Heels down is something we hear a lot about. Certainly in equitation classes, which are judged partly on position, if your heels are up it's considered a major fault. From a judging and also a practical standpoint, what makes it wrong is that having your heels up is an indication of tension in your thighs and seat. Standing on the ground, if you squeeze your thighs and buttocks, your heels will start to lift; when you release the tension, they will drop down again. Put more simply, if nothing interferes, the weight of your legs and gravity will keep your heels down without any further effort on your part. How far they go down has to do with your personal conformation, but as long as there is no tension, wherever your heels go is correct for you.

Using the Grounding Strap in Half Seat

In the early part of this book you learned how to hold the grounding strap so that it grounded you onto your seat bones. It has to do with hand position and allowing the pull to flow through your body without tension (see chapter 5). You might find it helpful to use an exercise to help you ground on your feet before you try standing on the stirrups.

Grounding Exercise

Using a rope that you can hold comfortably, place it around something like the leg of a heavy chair or the bottom of a fence post. Use the seven steps to ground yourself, then hold the rope as you would hold a grounding strap (think wrist position). Gradually take pressure on it while maintaining your grounding. Notice how you have to use your low back and buttock muscles to keep yourself upright without getting tense. Try various degrees of pressure to represent various amounts of thrust. Also try bending and straightening your knees and opening and closing your hip angle to feel how these affect your grounding. You should find that if you use your whole body correctly, you can take quite a strong hold without getting stiff or tense. You simply feel more securely grounded.

Now you're ready to put everything together and try it out on the horse. There are four seats for which your weight is on your stirrups rather than your seat:

1. Three-quarter seat position
2. Half-seat open position
3. Half-seat closed position
4. Half-seat centered position

Three-Quarter Seat Position

Three-quarter seat is, just as it sounds, a position halfway between half seat and full seat. We include it with half-seat work because your weight is on the stirrups. Three-quarter seat has two main purposes. First, it is a learning device to prepare you for half seat. Second, it is a way to take your weight off the horse's back without having to actually stand up, which is useful, for example, if the horse is uncomfortable with your full weight on his back before he is warmed up. Because of the nature of the gait, half seat at the walk is awkward and difficult, but because you don't need the greater shock absorption that half seat affords, three-quarter seat is a practical option.

After warming up so that you are sitting correctly with your feet solidly on the stirrups, you are ready to try three-quarter seat. Your feet should be in ∧ position. Begin at the standstill so that you don't have to deal with following the horse's motion before you have found your balance on the stirrups. The first part of this exercise is very similar to full-seat forward position, but your weight will be in a different place.

With your eyes closed and your arms dangling at your sides, slowly close your hip angle as though you were preparing to get up out of a chair. When you feel you are at the correct angle, see if you can put all your weight onto your feet but *without* actually lifting your buttocks off the saddle. The seat of your pants will be just touching the saddle, but your seat bones will not (figure 14.5). Your arms should be hanging totally relaxed. If there is any tension in them, it means you aren't yet balanced.

Many riders find that they have to lean farther forward than they thought in order to shift their weight onto their feet, so practice a few times while keeping your eyes closed, which forces you to feel what's happening. When you can find the three-quarter seat position easily, put your arms in rein-holding position, open your eyes, and go from full seat to three-quarter seat and back a few more times, making sure that your arms stay relaxed. As you lean forward, lift your chin slightly so that your face stays vertical.

Figure 14.5 Three-quarter seat position.

Finding the Open Position

Now you're ready to work at the walk. You'll be riding in a slightly open position. That means that rather than try to stay perfectly balanced, you'll open your hip angle just a tiny bit, using a light pressure on your grounding strap for balance as you practiced on the ground. You should feel that if you let go of the grounding strap, you would sit down again, but not hard. The purpose of the open position is to keep your whole torso slightly behind the horse's center at all times. You are less likely to fall forward and cause the horse to lose his balance, and the horse will keep going more willingly with your center firmly behind his. Practicing the open position in three-quarter seat also helps prepare you for open half-seat work.

Practicing the Three-Quarter Seat at the Walk

In full-seat ∧ position, pick up your reins, stick, and grounding strap and ask your horse to walk, or have the leader start him walking (figure 14.6). When he is walking steadily, take up your three-quarter seat on the long side of the arena. As you reach the corner, take full-seat ∩ position around the end, then repeat, moving your feet to ∧ position, then shifting to three-quarter seat. Remember to keep your seat touching the saddle but not resting on it. You should have a light steady pull on the grounding strap. Allow yourself to ground onto the stirrups. Review the seven steps in your mind, especially soft eyes, breathing, and following seat or stirrups.

Figure 14.6 Three-quarter seat at the walk.

When you feel comfortable on the straight in three-quarter seat, continue around the corner. Feel how you can use your outside leg to move your center slightly to the inside without pushing yourself higher off the saddle— your seat should always be touching the saddle. You should feel equal pressure on both feet throughout the exercise.

Use these tips to help your grounding:

- Don't curl your toes (an instinctive move to try to hang on to the stirrups as though they were a tree branch).

- Wiggle your toes to relax your feet and ankles.

- Be sure your feet stay in ∧ position. The weight should be toward the inside edge of your foot, which should rest against the inside post of the stirrup.

- Pretend you have wide, flexible feet like a duck.

Work on three-quarter seat as long as necessary until grounding on the stirrups is easy and comfortable. Practicing the ground exercises at home between lessons will speed up the process. *Only when you have perfected three-quarter seat at the walk should you try half seat and the trot.*

Half-Seat Open Position

We begin with open position just as we did for three-quarter seat and for the same reasons as described in the section Finding the Open Position. Since you will need to be higher off the saddle, take up your stirrups one or two holes at first. As you work with the half seat, experiment with stirrup length until you find the most comfortable one. Don't forget that different-shaped horses can affect stirrup length, so if you are on a new horse and don't feel comfortable in half seat, start by changing your stirrup length. Basically, thinner horses call for a shorter stirrup, and wider horses call for a longer one.

Adjust your grounding strap or use the mane so that you can modify your hip angle as much as necessary. Start at the standstill as you did with three-quarter seat to allow your body to get used to the higher position. Begin with three-quarter seat, then slowly *bring your hips up and forward* just until your seat is clear of the saddle by an inch or two. *Allow your shoulders to go back* at the same time so that your center stays over your bubbling spring (figure 14.7).

Try to keep your lower leg in place, pushing your knee forward so that it stays well in front of your center.

As with the three-quarter seat, you should have a light pull on the grounding strap so that if you let go you would sit down gently. Practice going from three quarter to half seat

Figure 14.7 Half-seat open position.

and back, keeping an even pressure on the grounding strap and letting the pull go through your body into the stirrups. You might have to adjust your hands on the grounding strap each time. Try leaning a little too far back and pulling hard on the grounding strap. Notice the tension that creates—you have to adjust your hip angle to stay almost centered and use the grounding strap primarily for balance.

When you feel secure and grounded in half seat at the standstill, return to full seat and take up the walk. Think about your following seat and stirrups, then go into three-quarter seat, still walking. Go through the seven steps, paying particular attention to grounding. As you approach the long side of the arena, ask, or have your leader ask your horse to trot. When you feel him start, move up into half seat, leaning slightly more forward to stay centered. Shorten your hold on the grounding strap as needed. Your elbows should hang slightly in front of your shoulders (figure 14.8).

The first few times, just trot on the straight and come to the walk before the corner. When you feel ready, try trotting around the short side. Since the horse is going faster,

Figure 14.8 Half-seat open at the trot.

the thrust throwing you to the outside will be greater. Again, don't push yourself up as you use your outside stirrup to keep you centered, and keep the stirrup pressure even.

As long as you feel reasonably secure and comfortable, you can keep trotting in half-seat position until you feel tired. If you can recover from small errors, it is all right to keep going. But if you get really disorganized, stop and regroup. Use the same checklist for your grounding as you used for three-quarter seat (see the section titled Practicing the Three-Quarter Seat at the Walk earlier in this chapter). It is particularly important to have very soft, flexible ankles and knees and the lightest feel on the neck strap that you can have and still feel secure.

Half-Seat Closed Position

Once you are able to stay behind your horse's center in open position fairly consistently so that it feels easy and you don't tire quickly, you can start working on closed position as well. Closed position is used for learning posting, riding uphill, and jumping, so it is an especially important skill for disciplines that involve jumping.

You still must keep your center behind the horse's center for the same reasons. In closed position you do so not by leaning slightly back but by pressing against the horse's neck with your hands, pushing your hips back. This is harder for the horse to balance against, but since the pressure is steady, most horses can adapt to it quite easily. The exception is a horse that carries his weight too much on his forehand, quite common in young horses still learning to adjust to the rider's weight. It can also be the result of the horse's conformation—the way he is built. A horse with a croup higher than his withers is an example of this.

Closed-Hip Exercise

To get the feeling of holding yourself back with a closed hip angle, stand in front of a window sill, heavy table, or heavy chair. Take a closed position with knees bent and your back at about a 45-degree angle. Place the heels of your hands on the chair and push firmly, allowing the force of the push to go through your body onto your feet (figure 14.9). *To do this, you must push forward and downward with your knees as you push back with your hands.* If there is someone whom you feel comfortable allowing to do this, have her try to push you forward by pushing on your buttocks from behind.

Figure 14.9 Learning the direction of the thrust for half-seat closed position.

In the closed position, you will be leaning more forward, so your hips will have to go back more (see Hip Joint Exercise 3). That will require a shorter stirrup. As you did with the open position, experiment until you find the optimal length. Disciplines that use a long stirrup, such as dressage and Western, would be able to do only a very modified version of closed position, but it still is valuable as a preparation for posting.

After warming up, start with three-quarter seat at the standstill. The difference between being on the ground and being on the horse is mostly in your hand position. On the horse you will press on his neck with a straight wrist and closed fists, which would have been too uncomfortable against a hard surface (figure 14.10). Since at some point you will be using the reins, it is important that your wrists be in correct position all the time.

Figure 14.10 Proper hand and wrist position for the half-seat closed on the horse.

Figure 14.11 Half-seat closed position at the standstill.

Go to half-seat closed at the standstill (figure 14.11). Be sure your knees don't slide back. Keep your face vertical—nod your head up and down to loosen your neck if necessary.

When you're ready, go to the trotting closed position just as you did in open position, starting in closed three-quarter seat at the walk. Think about your longitudinal centering; you shouldn't have any feeling that you might fall forward. Practice some downward transitions, making sure that you don't coast forward as the horse slows down.

When you are comfortable in both open and closed positions, practice going back and forth between them until you feel secure and centered all the time. Once you have achieved this, the half-seat centered position—that is, being balanced in half seat without help from your hands—will occur by itself when the horse is going forward easily on his own. Then things start to be really fun!

15

Bits, Bridling, and Introduction to Using the Reins

Bridling and simple rein aids can be introduced either before or after beginning saddle work. You might learn to bridle fairly early in your ground education, depending on the horses you ride, your comfort level and ground skills, and the practice at your barn. The only criteria for starting the rein aids are that your seat must be secure and centered and you must be independent of your hands for balance at least at the walk. That is, you should be able to maintain a light, even, steady contact on the grounding strap with both hands on the straight and during gentle turns and transitions.

When we talk about bridles, we name them by the type of bit, so a bridle with a snaffle bit would be spoken of simply as a snaffle, as in "My horse has a light mouth and usually goes in a snaffle." But "I'm in a terrible hurry. Would you mind putting on his bridle for me?"

Bits are devices usually made of smooth metal and sometimes covered in rubber. What they all have in common is that they go into the horse's mouth up near the corners. However, they do not rest on his teeth because the horse has no teeth between his incisors (or canines, in the case of male horses) in the front and his molars in the back. He has just an area of gum called the bars inside each corner of the mouth (figure 15.1). You sometimes read that the horse "took the bit in his teeth" and ran away or some such thing. Unless the bridle was very poorly fitted, this is not possible and in any case would be extremely uncomfortable for the horse.

The two basic types of bit are the snaffle and the curb. Other bits, such as Kimberwicks and pelhams, combine the two, but if you understand the two basics you can figure out the others. Hackamores and similar devices have no mouthpiece. Figure 15.2 illustrates various bits and devices.

Snaffle bits are the most commonly used bit in English riding but are also used by Western riders. The English snaffle has a single rein ring on either side that attaches directly to the mouthpiece and has no chain or strap under the horse's chin; the Western version may or may not have a shank to which the rein is attached, and as well as a curb chain (see below). The English and shankless Western snaffles act on the corners of the horse's mouth and are the easiest for the horse to ground against, helping him to lengthen and round his body. When used for turning, the pull on the rein to the side applies pressure on the opposite side of the horse's face, encouraging him to turn toward the rein.

Curb bits are most commonly used in Western riding but are also used in English disciplines. The curb has a single rein ring on either side that is attached at the end of a shank, which is in turn attached to the mouthpiece. It has a chain or strap under the horse's chin. It acts on the horse's bars, chin, and poll to create lowering of the head and flexion and therefore helps him to collect himself. When used for turning by Western riders, curb bits are most often used with a neck rein effect.

The double or full bridle uses both bits so that an advanced rider can help the horse to lengthen and round and then collect as needed. It is used primarily in dressage. Hackamores and other devices that have no mouthpiece work on the horse's nose and sometimes his poll and chin, depending on such things as shanks and curb chains.

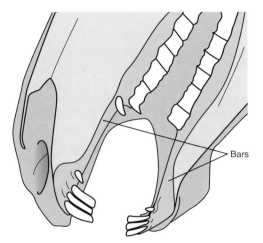

Figure 15.1 Horse's teeth and bars.

Figure 15.2 *(a)* Mild hackamore, *(b)* English snaffle, and *(c)* Western snaffle.

There is a perception that all of these devices work by causing pain. *That is often true but should not be*. Any of these devices can be very mild and humane or very severe. A really good Western horseman can ride a horse in a spade bit, which is among the most severe of bits, and have the horse comfortable, balanced, and happy. A really bad rider can make a horse miserable with the mildest possible device.

> As one of my trainers used to say, "It's not what's in the horse's mouth; it's who's on the other end of the reins."

Mouthpieces that are comfortable for the horse, and padded nosepieces, curb chains, and short shanks are very mild. The narrower and sharper the points of contact, and the longer the shank (which increases leverage), the more pain can be caused. But, as you will understand more clearly as you advance, causing pain does not necessarily create obedience, and it certainly doesn't ensure cooperation. In teaching I have found that using devices that *cannot* cause discomfort, so that force doesn't work, result in the rider's learning to use her aids correctly—that is, in a way that makes it easiest for the horse to do the task.

Putting On the Bridle

As with any new procedure that you haven't done with a particular horse, you should start with the same sort of introduction. It's important that he feel comfortable both with you and with the bridle.

Before starting to put on the bridle, unfasten the throat latch and the noseband or noseband section of a caveson, depending on the type of bridle. You can hold the caveson noseband in your right hand with the crown piece if it gets in your way. If there is a curb chain or strap, undo it as well unless it is very loose.

The process of putting on the bridle is similar to putting on a halter with the crown piece fastened, as described in chapter 6. In this case, though, you must also manage the reins, the brow band or ear loops, and the bit.

Standing just behind the horse's head, put the reins around the horse's neck first so that neither you nor he steps on them during bridling. The reins also give you a little something to control the horse with, between the time that you remove the halter and the bridle is on. English and joined Western reins should be placed on the horse's neck just a few inches behind his poll (figure 15.3). Unattached Western split reins can be placed closer to the withers, or if the horse is trained to ground tie—that is, to stand still if the reins are dropped on the ground—the reins can be allowed to hang down.

Many horses are ridden in some sort of hackamore or other bitless bridle, which makes bridling easier. If this is the case, you can put the bridle on almost exactly the way you did the halter, but read all the following instructions first for dealing with brow bands and such.

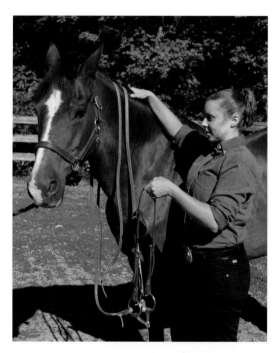

Figure 15.3 Placement of the Western split reins on the horse's neck.

Placing the Bit and Fastening the Bridle

Putting the bit in the horse's mouth can be difficult (not that the horse will try to bite you, of course, but it's rather awkward). What you will do is hold the bit up against the horse's teeth. When he opens his teeth, slip the bit in. The trick is in finding the place where his teeth meet so that when he opens them, the bit will go in. Here's how you do it.

1. Standing behind the horse's head as you did for haltering, hold the bridle by the crown piece with your right hand, and hold the bit across your left palm (figure 15.4a).

2. When you're ready to insert the bit, you might need to encourage the horse to open his mouth. You can do this either by inserting your left thumb in the upper-left corner of his mouth or a couple of your left fingers in the upper-right corner of his mouth where the bars are. Depending on which method you use, the thumb should be curled around the front left side of the bit, or the fingers around the back right, with the unused digits flattened out so they don't get in the way.

3. Bring the bit up by lifting the crown piece, and slide it under the horse's upper lip.

4. Slide the bit down the horse's top teeth until you feel the place where his top and bottom teeth meet—and where his mouth opens. Flatten your hand and push your palm upward gently, which encourages him to open his mouth while keeping your fingers out of the way (figure 15.4b).

5. Use the crown piece to hold the bit gently but firmly in place until his mouth opens. Many horses will open their mouths without further effort on your part.

6. If he doesn't open his mouth, insert your thumb or fingers into his bars and gently pry his mouth open a little.

7. Do *not* try to force the bit past the horse's teeth. Just continue to lift gently while encouraging him to open his mouth more. Once the bit is between his teeth, remove your hand from the bit. Since the bit feels uncomfortable against his teeth, he will work his mouth and tongue until the bit rests on his bars where it belongs. If there is a curb chain or strap, guide it with your fingers to be sure it doesn't accidentally get into his mouth as you lift up the bit.

8. Put the crown piece over his ears one at a time as you did with the halter. If the bridle has a brow band, be sure it goes below the base of the ears as you put them through the crown piece. If you are using a Western one- or two-ear bridle, lift the crown piece, gently fold his ear lengthwise with your fingers, and insert it through the ear loop (figure 15.4c).

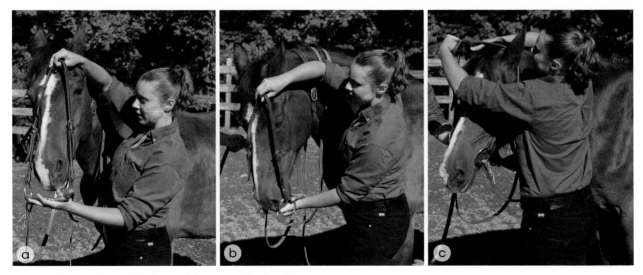

Figure 15.4 Placing the bit and fastening the bridle.

9. Fasten the throat latch across the cheek, not up in his throttle, and the caveson snugly but not too tightly. You should be able to slip two fingers under it comfortably.

10. Finish by tucking any loose ends of straps through the keepers (the little leather loops next to the buckles) and the runners (loops that slide on the straps). Tuck only the very tip end of the strap under the runner. The tip of the strap is tapered so it is thinner than the rest. If you force the runner up the strap, it stretches and will no longer hold.

If you will leave the horse in his stall for a few minutes, you can put the reins of an English bridle underneath the stirrup leathers (figure 15.5*a*) or over the horn of a Western saddle if they aren't so long he could step on them. For a longer period you can twist them up securely around his neck, then slip the throat latch *between* (not around) them and fasten it (figure 15.5*b*). You should never leave the horse even briefly with the reins lying on his neck because he will very likely put his head down and the rein will slide to the ground where he will step on it and probably break the bridle. Neither of you will be happy.

Figure 15.5 Placement of the reins (*a*) under the leathers and (*b*) twisted around the horse's neck.

Using Hand Effects and Rein Effects to Communicate

If at all possible, begin your communication work with the reins using a very mild bitless bridle, or even attach reins to the halter. In this way you won't hurt the horse accidentally and you won't be able to force yielding through pain, which would teach you bad habits. If you use the reins correctly (and use good judgment about the tasks you attempt), you do not need any sort of forcing mechanism for communication work. You might find it helpful to review chapter 8 on leading the horse and communicating with him through contact and pressure.

> The most important thing to understand about using the reins—and the bit—is that they *cannot* control the horse. Unlike the handlebars of a bicycle or the steering wheel of a car, the reins are not connected to the horse's "wheels"—that is, his feet.

The reins are connected to the horse's head, and the horse uses his head for balance. The reins can be used in such a way that they *help* the horse to balance, and thus to center and ground, so that the horse's body connects the reins to his feet. When you use the rein aids correctly, they change his balance slightly but still allow him to move his feet to rebalance. This is the way you can use the reins to ask for changes in direction or speed with his feet.

The reins can also be used in such a way that they *interfere* with his balance. This causes tension and disconnects the reins from his feet, causing resistance as the horse struggles to regain his balance. It is important to realize that horses have an extreme fear of losing their balance and falling because the horse that falls down is the one that gets taken by the predator.

The goal in using the reins for communication is to use them in such a way that the horse moves his feet in the direction and speed that you want and feels comfortable doing so. To accomplish this goal, you want to keep his feet connected to his head through his body—in other words, help him to stay centered and grounded. If he gets too stiff, you lose the connection. If he gets too floppy (known as going behind the bit), you also lose the connection in a different way. In any case, if you aren't getting the result you expected or wanted, it's up to you to change what you are doing to make it easier for the horse.

At this point you should be secure enough in your own grounding that, while you aren't ready yet to help the horse to ground, you can begin to learn how to use the reins to communicate with him in ways that won't create resistance.

You started developing rein skills when you were learning to lead, and now we'll talk about how you can apply these skills to ask the horse for simple turns and transitions. You also learned some important rein-handling skills in chapter 11. You will use all of these skills in combination with the gentle aids that you learned in chapter 10. *Keep in mind throughout, that you are training yourself, not learning to train the horse.*

Use of the reins is divided into two parts: hand effects, which is *how* you pull the rein, and rein effects, which is the *direction* in which you pull the rein. The hand effect you will learn in this chapter is the active hand; the rein effects covered here are the leading rein (typically used for English riding) and the neck rein (typically used for Western riding) and the direct rein of opposition for all disciplines. Whether you ride English or Western, reading about all the methods described in this chapter will improve your understanding of how the horse responds.

Active Hand

You should have learned quite a lot about hand effects when you were learning how to lead. The active hand is a combination of pulling (applying pressure on the rein) and releasing (letting go so that the pressure stops). You will often read that you should never pull on the horse's mouth, but that is an oversimplification because to use the reins at all you must apply some pressure. The real rule is that *you must never pull when the horse is pulling.* You can't outpull him anyway, and pulling is simply the horse's way of telling you that he is unable to respond at that particular moment. And of course, you should never pull sharply or yank on the reins in a way that could cause pain. Far from creating obedience, causing pain is more likely to result in panicky, dangerous behavior.

To learn to pull and release the reins, practice with another person. Sit in a chair with your partner sitting below you on the ground playing horse. She holds the bit ends of the reins in her hands, and you hold the rider end. Start with your hands in normal riding position (see Picking Up the Reins in chapter 11).

To pull correctly, you always begin by shortening your reins without making them any tighter; that is, you extend your arms as you shorten the reins. Then check your hand and wrist position (see Shortening the Reins in chapter 11). Both these actions are essential to maintaining your grounding as you pull. If you lose your grounding, your arms will become tense, and the horse will respond with tension and resistance.

Pulling Exercise

For this exercise, the person holding the bit end should offer light resistance but still give to your pull and follow it with her hands and arms. In other words, she should try to mimic a horse giving to the rein.

Begin by using only one rein at a time. Imagine a line that runs from your elbow to the bit, and pull along that line so that your hand comes up as it comes back and stays in the same vertical plane. Start with your arms fairly extended but not stiff, lifting your wrist and bending your elbow as you pull (figure 15.6). Stop pulling when your elbow reaches your rib cage so you don't start to tip forward. If you need to pull more, shorten the rein again and continue as before.

Figure 15.6 Practicing the line of pull for the active hand.

Practice pulling with one hand, then the other, and finally with both until you can stay grounded, hold your hand and wrist correctly, and pull along the elbow-to-bit line fairly consistently. Your helper should give you feedback on how it feels. It should be similar to a person holding her hand to help her balance—that is, neither so strong that it pulls her off balance nor so weak that it gives no support. Your partner should also offer various amounts of resistance while still giving to your pull. The less resistance she offers, the lighter your pull should be, but still steady to offer support.

Releasing Exercise

Once you have the pulling down pat, the next step is for your partner to, without warning, lock her fingers and elbows so that she no longer gives to the pull. Again, start with one rein at a time. Your goal is to feel the overt resistance and immediately release. To release, you stop pulling and push your hand forward toward the bit until the rein becomes loose. If the "horse" continues to pull, allow the rein to slide through your fingers as well. *The rule about releasing is that it isn't complete until there is no pressure on the rein at all.* This is why it is important that reins be long enough so that if the horse needs to put his head all the way down and forward to stretch or to balance—which happens frequently in young horses especially—the rider can release as much as necessary without losing her position or grounding.

A release is always followed immediately by a *smooth* reestablishing of contact, shortening the reins as much as necessary, and a repeat of the pull until you meet resistance again, or until you achieve the result you were looking for. Frequently the horse's resistance is the result of what he is doing with his feet. For example, if he needs to swing his right front leg forward, he needs a little freedom to do so. Therefore, he would resist, the rider would release, and the horse would take the step. Then, as the foot hit the ground and started to swing back, the horse would be able to give again.

One way to think about using the reins is to think about undoing a hard knot in a shoelace or opening a drawer that tends to stick. You can pull as long as it comes easily, but when it starts to stick, if you keep pulling, it just gets more stuck. You have to loosen it up again in some way before you can undo or open it, and you might have to do this several times before you achieve the result you want.

Combing the rein in the same way that you used combing the lead rope (see chapter 7) is often very effective with a horse that tends to immediately resist any sort of steady pull (virtually always the result of a previous bad experience). You can also combine combing with an active hand, combing until you feel resistance, then releasing. Try these on the ground and have your ground person tell you how she feels.

Introduction to the Leading Rein
(English or Western Snaffle)

When you are leading the horse forward on the ground, the direction of pull on the lead should always be forward—that is, ahead of the contact point on the horse's halter or bridle (figure 15.7). This causes the least resistance, especially when turning. It tends to stretch and open up the horse's body, making it easier for him to respond.

When you are mounted, it is not possible to pull the rein forward relative to the horse's head. There will always be some opposition, since some of the direction of pull will be toward the rear in opposition to the direction the horse is moving rather than forward. However, if the direction of pull is upward, at an angle of 45 degrees or more with the bit, it restricts the horse's front leg movement the least, so it interferes with his balance the least. Therefore, it results in the least resistance (figure 15.8). (Besides using his head and neck, the horse uses his front legs for balance, much as you would use your hands.)

One of the results of holding the reins at this angle is that you are using your hands in a very obvious way, which bothers some people who have been told that their hands should always be low and quiet. When you are more experienced, have more tools to use, and are riding a horse that has the knowledge and skills as well, that is the way you will ride. But both of you must be ready. The first time I saw the leading rein being used was at a clinic with the then-Portuguese Olympic coach Nuño Oliveira, who was considered one of the finest horsemen in the world.

Figure 15.7 Line of pull for leading the horse forward on the ground.

He was on a horse that had been giving his owner a lot of trouble. Sr. Oliveira started with his hands in normal position, but within seconds he had both hands in leading rein position up near the horse's ears. As we stared in surprise, he said firmly, "First you must show the horse what to do."

Steering is best practiced with the horse alone in a fairly confined space so that you are not concerned with his getting into trouble by getting too close to another horse or going too fast.

Begin the rein exercise when going to the right, since yielding on the right side is easier for most horses. You do not need a leader.

After both of you are warmed up and moving freely on loose reins, shorten the right rein, reaching forward and up with your right hand until the rein is at a 45-degree angle with the bit, but don't use any pressure yet. Do not allow your center to move forward or any tension to start in your lower back, seat, or legs. Adjust the reins if necessary to allow for the length of your arms and the horse's neck. Now start by asking for a right turn as you did before, in chapter 6, using your intent, eyes, active seat, and lateral center.

As your horse starts to respond, begin using your right hand actively, smoothly establishing contact and then pressure on the rein by lifting your hand up along

Figure 15.8 Line for pull for the leading rein when mounted.

the 45-degree line. The pull on the rein pulls the bit ring on the opposite side against the horse's cheek so he tends to move his head toward the pull. It is okay to bring your hand higher but not more to the rear than 45 degrees, since the latter is more likely to cause resistance. Remember to keep your wrist higher than your fingers. Gradually put enough pressure on the rein so that the horse responds in some manner, either by starting to turn, resisting, or yielding in his neck only, not with his feet as well.

If he turns, follow his head to the side with your hand, maintain the same degree of pressure, praise with your voice, and after a step or two ease the rein pressure and recenter yourself. Both reins should then be loose enough so that there is no pressure or contact as the horse's head moves with the gait.

If he resists at any point, immediately release by moving your hand toward the bit until the rein goes slack, then smoothly apply pressure again.

> When the horse resists, your release of the reins should be very quick and make the rein *very* loose. Always re-apply pressure slowly, and make the rein only *moderately* tight.

If the horse yields to the rein with his head and neck but doesn't turn (move his feet in a new direction), *keep the rein pressure steady*; do not release. Lower your hand and move it out to the side so that the rein is parallel to his track and your hand is directly behind his head (figure 15.9). This creates some opposition so that the horse finds it easier to ground his feet and turn.

Figure 15.9 Helping the horse to reground during a turn. Use a lowered hand and firmer rein contact, so that the horse takes the rein to maintain his balance.

Applying the rein aid is one of the skills that many people have trouble with. So let's review it step by step.

Using the Leading Rein for a Simple Right Turn

1. Starting centered and grounded, shorten your right rein, moving your hand forward as you do so that you aren't pulling yet.
2. Use your gentle aids—intent, eyes, center, weight, and active right seat (chapter 10)—to prepare your horse for the turn.
3. Keeping the rein slightly loose, raise your right hand up until the rein is at a 45-degree angle with the bit.
4. Pull smoothly upward at the same angle.
5. As the horse moves his head to the side, move your hand to the side as well.
6. If the horse resists (pulls against you), release along the same line, then repeat.
7. If the horse turns his head but not his feet, lower your hand and keep the pull steady and more toward the rear.
8. If the horse slows down or tries to stop, without increasing the pull, move your center back and use your voice or the stick to ask him to keep going.
9. When the horse turns, lower and release the rein, center yourself, and praise him.

After you have worked on right turns, try turning left as well. If the horse is very resistant to right turns, work on left turns first.

Introduction to Neck Reining (Western Curb)

Begin the lesson by warming up as usual on a loose rein, using a somewhat confined space. When you are both loosened up and ready to work, you should be riding right hand around because right turns are generally easier for most horses.

Neck reining (called the indirect rein in English riding) is mainly used with a Western curb. As the name implies, the rein pressure is primarily against the horse's neck (figure 15.10). The reason for this has to do with riding with both reins in one hand.

When you are learning, as with the leading rein, your hand is carried up and forward, so that the rein is applied against the upper third of the horse's neck so as not to create any opposition. The curb is more restrictive than a snaffle, so the pull on the rein needs to be very light. A well-trained Western horse, will respond to the lightest of touches on his neck by an

Figure 15.10 Using the reins to apply pressure on the horse's neck.

experienced rider. Western curb reins are both carried in one hand, of course, but as you carry your hand to one side or the other, the rein not against his neck becomes looser.

Your gentle aids, particularly your center and weight, are very important As your rein hand comes against the horse's neck, your tendency will be to lean in that direction, which could confuse the horse as well as make it more difficult for him to move his front legs in the desired direction. Instead, think to keep your center slightly to the opposite side of the turn, and turn your shoulders to bring the reins across.

To get it clear in your mind, let's go through it step by step. Be sure you warm up before starting.

Using the Neck Rein for a Simple Right Turn

1. Center and ground, then shorten your reins and bring your rein hand forward so that it is above the center line of the horse's neck, about one-third of the way from his poll, with the reins *slightly* loose. If the reins are too loose, you will have to move your hand too much in order to make contact, which will affect your centering.

2. Use your gentle aids—intent, eyes, center, weight, and active right seat (chapter 10) to prepare the horse for the turn.

3. Lift your hand and move it to the right, bringing the rein up against his neck. You should feel a light pressure on the rein, with the left rein snug and the right rein a little loose.

4. If the horse turns, follow him with a light pressure for a few steps, then release and praise.

5. If the horse shows discomfort by raising his head or opening his mouth, release the pressure and start again, trying to use less pressure and applying it more smoothly.

6. If you get no response at all, check your other aids, release and try again.

Slowing or Stopping Using Direct Reins of Opposition (English or Western Snaffle)

You will use both hands for this use of direct reins of opposition, which is to ask the horse to slow down or stop. Direct refers to the direction of the pull, parallel to the line of the horse's movement. Opposition means against the horse's movement (that is, back) as opposed to the 45-degree upward movement of the leading rein.

You learned in chapter 10 that, as prey animals who need to be able to leave in a hurry if a predator attacks, horses find upward transitions, such as from walk to gallop, far easier than downward transitions, such as gallop to walk. While the horse has the ability to make a sudden stop—sometimes more sudden than his rider is prepared for—it is not something he has to do very often in the normal course of his life. Having a rider on his back also adds to the difficulty. Cold weather also plays a part. A rider who expects prompt downward transitions from a cold horse usually ends up angry and frustrated, as does the horse.

The key when asking the horse to slow or stop is to learn to keep even pressure on both reins as you pull so that the horse can ground evenly. You should pull along the line of elbow to bit, or slightly above it, rather than below it. If the horse makes one rein tighter, you ease or release it; if he makes it looser, you take up the slack. (It's a bit counterintuitive at first.) Generally the horse will have one rein that he tends to pull on more and one he pulls on less. Sometimes he will swap sides in the middle of the transition if it is difficult for him.

Handling the Reins of Opposition Exercise

As you did while learning the active hand, have a partner act as the horse while you practice handling the reins of opposition. During this ground exercise your helper should keep an even pull on both reins at first and feed back to you if she thinks you are pulling too much or too little or not evenly. Once you feel comfortable with that, then she should make the pull unequal between the two reins, pull hard as though she were resisting, or give too much so you lose the connection. In each case you try to adapt as quickly and smoothly as possible while maintaining your centering and grounding.

Finally, you should walk together with the helper in front of you. Start without the reins. You must walk in step so that your movements coordinate as they would on the horse. Try to be very loose while following and gradually let your arms start to swing. If you are in step with your feet, your arms should swing together as well.

When you are moving together fairly well, take up the reins, with the helper holding the reins one in each hand and you behind her holding them in a light connection. Your goal is to allow your bodies to move together and allow your arms to follow the movement of her arms through the reins as she walks (figure 15.11). The movement will be much greater than the movement of the horse's head, but the exercise will help you to find the feeling of being passive and noninterfering with the reins.

Bending your elbows so that your arms stay flexible and following, gradually

Figure 15.11 Learning to handle the direct reins of opposition.

increase the pressure on the reins while continuing to follow the movement. Stay grounded and keep the rein pressure even on both sides, releasing or taking as necessary. Your helper should find that slowing down or stopping just feels like the obvious thing to do.

Allowing the Horse to Slow or Stop

When you are ready to use this method while you are mounted on the horse, remind yourself that you cannot stop him; he must stop himself. Your job is to make it easy for him.

1. Warm up at the walk until you are grounded and your following seat is moving smoothly. This will help to keep the horse's back relaxed so that he can use his "rear brakes" (hind legs) effectively

2. When the horse is walking freely and you feel centered and grounded, start using your intent. Your intent should be to *allow* the horse to stop, that is, to say to the horse, "You don't have to keep going; it's okay to slow down and stop now." Remember to breathe, keep a soft following seat and let your center come slightly back but not so much that your seat is driving the horse forward again.

3. Shorten both reins and smoothly apply a little pressure on both reins. Remember to keep a little lift in the pull so that you pull along the line of elbow to bit, which is very important in keeping your grounding (figure 15.12). Gradually increase the pressure as you did when turning until the horse slows down, or resists by pulling back, or rolls his chin in toward his chest without slowing down.

Figure 15.12 Using a passive body and a very light rein signal makes it easy for the horse to stop.

If he resists, release the rein or reins he is pulling against and ask again. If he rolls his chin in, hold the pressure, shortening your reins if necessary, and lower your hands until he grounds and starts to respond with his feet. If he slows down, *maintain the same pressure until just before he stops, then release smoothly*. The release allows him to use his "front brakes," that is, to reach out with his front legs to complete the downward transition.

The other possible response you might get, especially if he is wearing a strong bit, is to throw his head up in the air, which is a sign of fear and discomfort. If this happens, release all pressure and begin again using a much lighter aid and watching carefully for any signs of fear. This is why starting with the mildest of control devices is the best way to go.

The big difference between the slowing (stopping) exercise and the turning exercise is that the horse is quite likely to respond differently to each of the two reins. Think more about how each rein feels than whether or not you're getting the stop or the slowing down. Much of the time you will find that you keep a steady feel on one rein while you use the other rein actively. Just as when you were working on the ground, when you get it right the horse will stop because that is the easiest thing for him to do. (When you're learning, avoid situations where the horse really wants to keep going, such as other horses going into the barn.)

Stopping Using Direct Reins of Opposition (Western Curb)

When riding single handed, the Western method of using direct reins is almost the same as the English method described in the previous section, except that you use the two reins together instead of separately. This means that it might be a little more difficult to stop the horse straight because, as we said, the horse tends to respond slightly differently to the two reins, which affects his grounding. However, your concern at this point is to get a relaxed transition. Making it straight is something you can work with later on.

Whatever your discipline, if your horse is wearing a severe bit, it is easy to pull too hard and create tension, making it more difficult for the horse to stop. Stopping quickly is not achieved correctly by using greater force but by gradually developing the horse's strength, ability, and understanding through careful training and a lot of praise.

Learning to use simple rein aids might give you the illusion that you can now control the horse in most circumstances. The way people get into trouble is by putting the horse into situations where *he can't control himself* (that is, overfacing him so that he becomes frightened and insecure). Use good judgment when you are trying something that you have not done with that particular horse before so that you *both* feel secure and you don't lose his trust. If you are consistent about this, in time the horse will come to trust you even in new and scary situations.

Perfect Posting

Posting the trot, or rising to the trot, was invented by English postboys, men who rode one horse of each pair that pulled the mail coaches centuries ago. The horses usually trotted continuously and fairly fast for an hour or more between stations. Standing the whole time was too tiring, and sitting a fast trot in any comfort was difficult if not impossible. Probably the first discovery was that if you stood for a while, then sat for a step, it rested you and you could go on a lot longer. Eventually the postboys found that sitting one step and standing the next was even easier and hardly tiring at all. And posting was born.

Like a lot of riding, posting is a matter of how your body responds to the motion—in this case the thrust of the trot. Each time the horse takes a step forward, the thrust throws you back. To put it another way, when the horse trots, he bounces you up *and back* with each step.

To keep from bouncing all around when you are trotting in full or half seat, which would be uncomfortable for both you and the horse, you must resist every backward-throwing thrust. It's rather like running up a slight slope. If you do this for an extended time, you get tired.

When you post, you *resist one push* by bringing your hips forward and up, then *give in* to the next thrust and allow your hips to come back and down. So the down movement of the post is a little rest period for your whole body. This little rest period makes correct posting almost effortless for long periods.

Posting is primarily associated with English riding, since Western horses are more likely to be ridden at a jog in full seat than in a full-fledged trot. However, many Western riders and instructors recommend posting for any prolonged trotting, since it is much easier on the horse and rider. This, of course, is one of the big reasons for learning to post correctly.

Posting gives novice riders far more problems than it should. To begin with, we practice posting every day.

> Each time we sit down or stand up from a sitting position, we are executing half of a post.

In addition, the horse's motion does most of the work, so a capable rider can post on a horse as long as the horse can trot.

Why does it give most beginners so much trouble? One problem is that beginners are often asked to post before they are secure and relaxed in the saddle, both sitting and standing —all the stuff you've been working on up to this point. This is why we haven't talked about posting until now.

The other problem is that our perception of what our bodies do when we stand up or sit down is skewed. We think that we lean forward when we stand up and lean back when we sit down, so beginners learning to post lean forward as they go up and lean back as they go down, and they swing back and forth all over the horse!

Let's first find out what our bodies really do when we stand up or sit down, keeping in mind that we must be able to do so and remain centered and grounded.

Centering While Posting Exercise 1

You can use a straight chair or an office chair, but this exercise is best done using a moderately high stool or something similar so that your legs are a little straighter, as they would be if you were in the saddle with your feet in the stirrups. Start from a seated position.

1. Prepare to stand up. The first thing you'll probably do is to bring your feet more or less back underneath you. Next, you'll lean forward as far as you need to to get your center over your feet—or rather, your bubbling spring—because you absolutely won't be able to stand up unless you do. Since you're probably leaning fairly far forward, your hip angle will be pretty closed, especially if the chair is low.

2. Let your arms dangle down loosely, and try not to use them for balance. Now start standing up very slowly, and notice what your body is doing from the hips up. It gradually straightens up until, when you're all the way up, your torso is vertical. So, you started out leaning forward, and *as you stood up, you leaned back* until you were up straight. (figure 16.1 *a-c*)

Figure 16.1 Practicing the changes in body angle required for posting.

3. Without moving away from the chair, and still leaving your arms dangling, very slowly sit down. Bend your knees and reach back with your seat bones until they are over the chair. To do this and still stay centered, *to sit down, you have to lean forward* from the hip (figure 16.1*d* and *e*). Only after your seat bones are securely on the chair and you plan to remain there can you lean back so that your center is over them (figure 16.1*f*).

Figure 16.1 *(continued)* Practicing the changes in body angle required for posting.

So, do the following to stay centered and grounded while posting: Starting from a full-seat forward position—which, if you remember, is the down position of the posting trot—you lean *back* as you stand up and lean *forward* as you sit down. Practice this several times so that you have a clear mental picture of what you are doing.

Now let's look at the posting movement slightly differently. Instead of thinking about going up and down, notice that when you go up and down your hips are moving forward and back. So think about moving your hips forward (which will bring them up) and back (which will bring them down).

The reason for thinking this way instead of *up, down* is that when you are on the trotting horse, *his movement pushes you up*, as you will have discovered if he trotted fast when you were trying to sit. While posting you need to go up only as far as his movement sends you, no more. However, if you are thinking to go up, you will try to push yourself up and you will go up too high. This will make you stay up too long, and your timing will be off. Thinking *forward, back* is not a complete solution, but it often helps.

One thing about posting is not natural and will need some practice. Normally, as you stand up, you straighten your knees until your legs are completely straight. You wouldn't want that on a moving horse, though, since you need the bent knees and ankles to absorb shock, and your bent knees also help your longitudinal balance. So you have to teach yourself to straighten only from the knees up, and only as far as you need to while staying centered.

Centering While Posting Exercise 2

You need something like a fairly large, heavy box, but you can use an ordinary chair if necessary. If you have a box, put your toes and knees against the box. That's the position they would be in if you were on the horse with your feet in the stirrups in correct position. If you're using a chair, rest your knees against the side of the seat and place your toes directly under the front of your knees.

Since you aren't sitting down, your upper body should be fairly erect and centered over your bubbling spring. Dangle your arms. This would be the up position of the post. To go down, keep your toes and knees in place and your center over your feet, then push your hips back (and down) until you're more or less in a sitting position but still centered over your feet (full seat forward). Practice bringing your hips forward and up and then back and down while keeping your toes and knees in place, staying centered over your bubbling spring, and keeping your arms free of tension (figure 16.2).

The toe–knee position will feel strange at first, so it's important to keep practicing it until it starts to feel comfortable. Keep your toes open and relaxed—they will tend to tense up until you can stay really centered. I know I keep repeating the word *centered*, but that's what good posting is all about!

Figure 16.2   Learning to maintain a steady lower leg position for posting.

Finding Posting Rhythm on the Bareback Pad

If possible, begin learning to post by watching an experienced rider at the posting trot. When done correctly, the posting appears effortless and the rider's lower leg does not move relative to the horse. The still leg shows that the rider's center is constantly over her bubbling spring and does not move either forward or back, which is one of the more common errors in posting.

The first thing to learn is to feel the timing of the post and how you respond to the horse pushing you up. This is most easily done on the bareback pad, or possibly on a saddle without stirrups, and with a cover to make it less slippery. You should have a hand leader for the initial trot work.

Starting at the standstill, fix your leg with your knee up a little higher than normal. Unless the horse is trotting, there is no motion to lift you, so you must use your hands to help you go up for this part of the exercise. To be able to do this, place your hands firmly on the front of the withers, knuckles down, wherever they feel comfortable. Close your hip angle, pushing your hips back a little on the horse's back so that your center is over your feet.

Begin to walk. Since the walk has four beats and the trot only two, you want to think in two, so count 1-2, 3-4 to the horse's rhythm. Keeping your toes and your eyes up, use your hands and abdominal muscles to start to lift yourself up and forward on 1-2 and down and back on 3-4. You don't actually have to go up more than a tiny bit; just try to feel the timing. Try not to grip with your thighs to lift yourself because that would tend to lock your hips, making it harder for you to stay centered.

When you are feeling the timing pretty well, you're ready to try the trot. It's easier to post if the trot is a little faster than you would do for sitting work because it will tend to bounce you up a little more. Start in the full-seat forward position with your hands holding the grounding strap, but press your knuckles on the horse's withers or neck. Slide back a little on the pad so that your center is not ahead of the horse's as you lean forward. Experiment with your knee position—higher or lower—to see what seems to give the most support. Try to keep your leg firmly fixed by keeping your toes up and spread out, not curled up.

Use your seven steps as necessary to be as centered and grounded as possible. Have the leader start the horse trotting slowly at first so that the horse is not bouncing you up very much. Now the rhythm is 1, 2. When you are feeling the rhythm, ask the leader to have the horse trot a little faster, and use the additional bounce to see if you can start moving your hips forward and up and then back and down (figure 16.3). You will press somewhat harder on your hands, but the pressure should not *change* as you move your hips back and forth. If it does, it means you're moving your center back and forth rather than opening and closing your hip joint. Do only a few steps at a time, then walk and rest. Normal posting with stirrups is easy; all you're trying to do here is get a feel for how the horse's movement affects you.

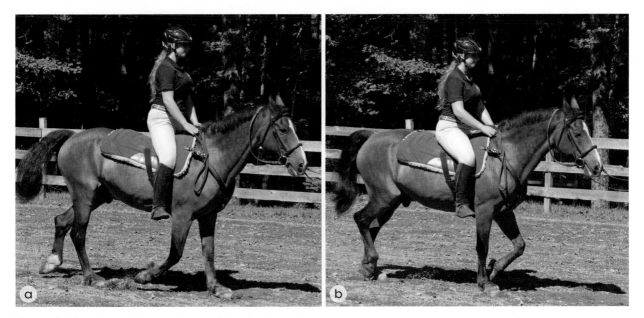

Figure 16.3 Up and down phases of bareback posting.

Posting in the Stirrups

Different disciplines ride with stirrups of different lengths, which affect posting. With a longer stirrup your leg is straighter, which means you can't lean very far forward without losing your balance, nor can you go up very high. With a shorter stirrup your hips are farther back on the saddle, so you have to lean farther forward to get up, but you get more longitudinal support. You can also go up higher. Shorter stirrups are easier on a horse that is thin or has a big, bouncy trot;

longer stirrups are easier on a wide horse or a horse with a smooth trot. There are other reasons for stirrups of various lengths, depending on the discipline.

In a Western saddle you can't lean very far forward without running into the horn. The same is true of a dressage saddle with a deep seat and high pommel. Both disciplines are ridden with a fairly long stirrup. Your center must be over your bubbling spring, so it's important that the stirrup not hang too far forward; the farther forward the stirrup hangs, the farther forward you have to lean to be centered over it (figure 16.4). If the stirrup is long or the pommel is high, it is impossible to post in balance.

Once you're back in the saddle or have your stirrups back, after warming up start working in half-seat open position to get grounded and comfortable on the stirrups. Next, with your horse standing still, start posting, very slowly at first. Your hands should be holding the grounding strap but pressing down lightly with your knuckles on the withers or lower neck for balance (figure 16.5). Begin with your body in full-seat forward and feet in ∧ position, then bring your hips up and forward until you are in half-seat open or slightly closed position.

Figure 16.4 The stirrup length and placement determine the amount of lean required to be centered.

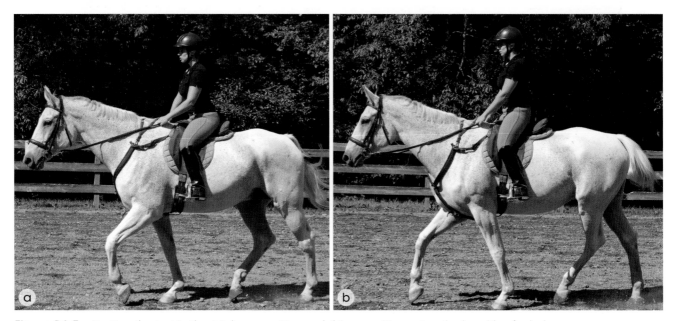

Figure 16.5 Posting the trot in the *(a)* down position and *(b)* up position using the knuckles for balance.

Focus on keeping your knee pressed forward as you did in the box exercise and your center over your feet so that your stirrups don't move forward and back at all. They may move toward and away from the horse's sides as you put more or less pressure on the inner edges of your feet each time you sit and stand. Avoid the tendency to curl your toes, which might occur as your body tries to adjust to the changes in position. It might help to have the instructor hold your lower leg in place while you find the correct moves to keep you in balance. You can also try with your arms folded or hanging down to make sure you are in good balance. Closing your eyes is another good test.

Next, work at the walk to check your timing and centering on a moving horse with your feet in the stirrups. Take up three-quarter seat at the walk and think about your following seat and feet. As your outside seat and foot drop, think *down*; as your inside seat and foot drop, think *up*. When you feel ready, move into the trot in half-seat closed position, with a light pressure with your knuckles on the horse's withers area, wherever you feel comfortable and balanced.

Again, pay attention to your following seat and feet. As you feel your outside seat and foot dropping, allow your hips to go back and down until your seat bones touch the saddle, then come immediately forward and up. Regain your balance if necessary, then repeat. Continue in this pattern, doing only one posting stride at a time, until you can maintain your center and balance through one stride. Then try two or more, always returning to the half seat if you lose your centering. Rest fairly frequently and go through the seven steps to relieve any tensions you might have developed.

When the rhythm feels steady, which will probably take a lesson or two, you might notice that you are hitting the saddle a little hard or double bouncing as you connect. This occurs because holding your body in forward position uses the buttock and low back muscles, making them a little tense. You need to add a little rest-and-relaxation movement, the final action that makes long-term posting possible and both you and the horse more comfortable.

Chair Exercise—The Rest

Sitting in an ordinary straight or office chair, lean forward in full-seat forward position and hold the position for a little while. Notice there is a slight tension in your lumbar spine and seat. Deliberately let that area of your back get rounded so your buttocks roll underneath you and become soft.

Now tighten your back a little, raise your chest, and, using your feet for support, start to go up just a little. Then down and release the tension again. Be sure you don't release the tension too soon, or you will bang on the horse's back. Your seat bones should be fully on the saddle before you release. The rest is just for a second, but that's all you need. When you are back on the horse again, add the little rest movement to each sequence.

Understanding Diagonals

The trot is a two-beat gait in which each diagonal pair of legs moves together: The left hind leg and right foreleg leave the ground and return to it at the same time. While that diagonal pair is in the air, the other diagonal pair—right hind and left fore—will be on the ground and vice versa. You will always be posting on one diagonal or the other—that is, going up and down with one or the other pair of the horse's legs.

If you have been watching classes with riders posting, you will sometimes hear the instructor say to a student, "You're on the wrong diagonal!" What does she mean, and why does it matter? On a turn, the horse's inside hind leg is important for his balance, so you want to interfere with its function as little as possible. Therefore, when you are working in an arena or riding circles, *you want to be off his back when his inside hind leg is in the air*, making it easier for him to place it wherever he needs to. And since his inside hind and outside front legs work together, you move up as that pair of legs comes forward. The diagonals are called left and right after the *front* leg of each pair, because it's easier for the rider to see the front leg and know whether or not she is on the correct, outside (front leg) diagonal (figure 16.6).

Figure 16.6 Posting on the correct (right) diagonal. The rider is in the up position while the horse's outside front leg is in the air.

There is another way to determine your diagonal as soon as you start posting, without looking—something normally achieved only by more advanced riders but really quite easy if you are conscious of your following seat. When you started posting with stirrups, you started by thinking about your following seat and tried to think *down* when your outside seat dropped and *up* when your inside seat dropped.

Here's what's happening: When you are sitting, each time the horse lifts his hind foot to bring it forward, your seat on that side drops, so you know that when your left seat drops, the horse's left hind leg is in the air. Therefore, to start out on the correct diagonal, be aware of your following seat first at the walk, which will make it easier to find as you start to trot. Then in the trot as you feel your outside seat drop, which should be the down part of the post, you know to go up on the next step in order to be on the correct diagonal. It probably will take a little practice to get the timing right, but once your body learns, it becomes automatic.

If you ride mostly on trails, it is important to be aware of your diagonals, since they don't feel any different, and not to post on the same one all the time because that would develop the horse's muscles unevenly. Depending on how long you trot at a stretch, you could take a different diagonal each time you trotted, or change diagonals on a time schedule such as every five minutes, or simply choose a landmark to change at now and then.

Sometimes you find a horse that has a weakness or discomfort that bothers him more on one diagonal than the other. To stay comfortable, he might take an irregular step to throw the rider to his easier diagonal. If you had a horse that kept pushing you to the same diagonal, you would want to have the veterinarian check to see what the problem or weakness might be.

Here are things to check if you are having problems with posting:

- The combination of faster gait and new movement can cause lateral imbalance and result in thigh tension, which affects hip movement. So check lateral centering.
- Hands are too far back, not giving good support and affecting longitudinal centering.
- Weight is on the outside edges of the feet, making the joints tense and affecting your following the motion.
- Stirrup position might be set incorrectly relative to your proportions and saddle fit (refer to chapter 13).

If you have previously developed a good feeling for keeping your centering and grounding, posting should come quite easily. And if you should compete in English equitation classes, it's nice to know that the riders with the best posting trot are the most likely to be in the ribbons.

17

Cantering (Loping) and Galloping (Running)

Cantering, or loping if you are riding Western, is the point that every beginning rider looks forward to reaching. All the exciting stuff seems to happen at the canter, so the feeling is that once you can canter you've really arrived. And this is true as long as you realize that it means cantering well. Cantering badly is not fun at all for anyone.

Cantering is a comfortable gait to ride but a difficult gait to learn to ride well. Many of the disobediences and accidents that occur at the canter might be the result of poor riding, which unbalances the horse. An unbalanced horse is tense and thus more likely to spook or become resistant or dangerous.

The human body is hard-wired to canter, just as it is to walk and trot. In fact, toddlers use a two-legged version when they are in a hurry. But humans forget how to use the canter early in childhood. This makes it difficult to learn to ride the canter, as opposed to other gaits. One reason you don't use the canter is that, as a child, you copied the adults around you, who of course would only walk and run. But mostly it's because the gait has one phase in which all the weight is supported on one front foot. Since your "front feet" are not normally on the ground, you are unable to do this.

The one place where you can canter comfortably is in the water. Swimming sidestroke is cantering and is the easiest stroke after dog paddling (which is walking) to learn and to do for long periods. (Some people think that skipping is the same as cantering. It isn't.)

Luckily, as it happens, the horse's walk is very similar to the canter in the sequence and weight shifts. The sequence, or stride, of the walk is right hind, right front, left hind, left front (figure 17.1). Only one foot hits the ground at a time, which is what makes it so smooth. The canter sequence for the left lead—the stride during which the legs on the left side come farther forward than those on the right—is right hind, left hind and right front together, left front, then all four feet in the air (the moment of suspension). The right hind hits the ground first and the next stride begins (figure 17.2). We'll talk more about leads later on, but meanwhile, the canter sequence for the right lead is opposite: left hind, right hind and left front together, right front, all four in the air.

Not only is the foot sequence of the canter very similar to the walk, but, more important, so is the lateral weight shift, which is what makes the canter difficult for your body to learn to follow. (In the walk the thrusts are much less strong, so it is easy to follow.) In both cases the horse's weight starts over his right rear side, then shifts across the center to a diagonal support on his left hind and right front together, and finally to his left front.

Like the trot, the canter can be ridden in both full and half seat. But if at all possible, you should try to learn to sit the canter first. It is easier to canter in half seat, especially if the horse's canter is not very smooth. But because of the complicated nature of following the canter, it is easy to learn it incorrectly in half seat so that your body ends up doing a sort of posting movement that is not very comfortable for you or the horse. Later, when you try to sit, the posting becomes a bounce that is very difficult to change.

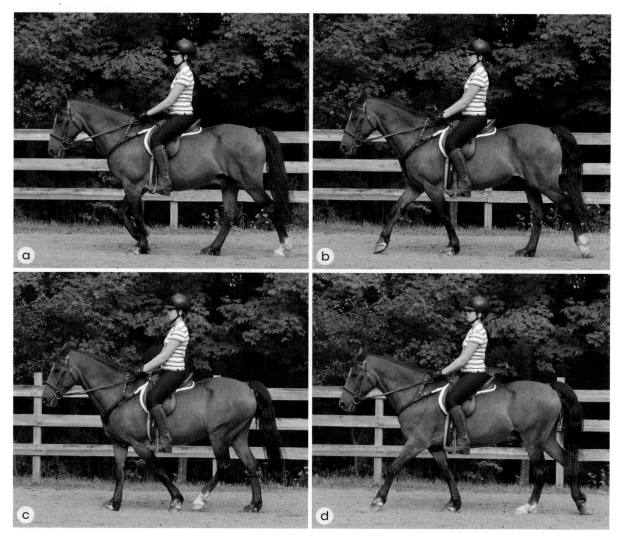

Figure 17.1 Sequence for the walk.

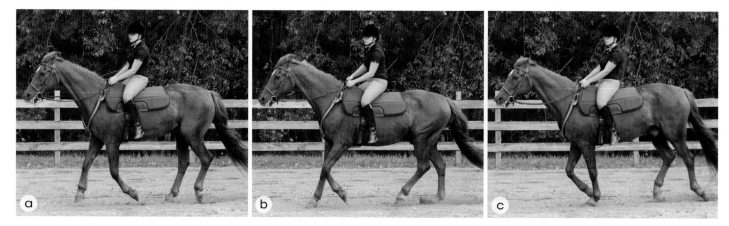

Figure 17.2 Sequence for the canter.

Other Similar Gaits

If you are very fortunate, you might have access to a horse that has one of the extra gaits beyond the usual walk–trot–canter, such as a single foot or a rack. These gaits are virtually identical to the walk but faster. Because only one foot hits the ground at a time, they are smoother than the canter but still enough like it to help your body through the learning curve. They also help your body adjust to the thrusts at a similar speed.

Preparing to Canter

The best way to start learning the sitting canter is on a bareback pad. The difficult part of the canter is staying centered laterally. If you start slipping to the side, you tense up in your upper leg and lower body, which makes it very difficult to sit. On the bareback pad, the rough surface of the pad and the horse's shape make it much easier to stay centered. The stirrups, on the other hand, are not much help if you lose your balance and your feet come up. And if you attempt to regain your balance by pushing on the stirrups, you lift your seat off the saddle and bounce.

The ideal horse for learning the canter is one that will pick up the canter directly out of the walk, do it smoothly and very slowly, and break directly back to the walk on a voice command. We had such a horse when I was a young teacher at my mother's farm. In addition to those skills, he was amenable to being ridden double, so we could put a small child behind an advanced adult. Chipper would pick up his little canter, and the child would be secure on a bareback pad with his arms around the adult's waist, cantering happily right from the start.

But the ideal isn't always available, so what are the most important requirements for the horse? First, the horse should be very nonthreatening both in his gait and in his behavior. He should not have a very flat back where you sit, or it will be difficult to stay centered. The small rise of the spine in the middle of his back makes it much easier—one cheek on one side, one on the other! His response, if you get disorganized, should be to stop rather than speed up. He should pick up the canter easily from the walk and, if possible when slowing down, reach the walk with a minimum of trot steps in between.

> To learn the canter, you will need to be able to post bareback because the horse often breaks from the canter to a trot that is too rough to sit.

So be sure your bareback posting skills are solid (see chapter 16).

You should also practice turns on bareback at the sitting trot until you can make the necessary adjustments to stay centered without having to think about it. Having someone lead you at the slow trot with your eyes closed, making unexpected fairly sharp turns in both directions, is an excellent training exercise. Being longed at the trot, both sitting and posting, is also helpful for developing your lateral centering skills.

Walking briskly down a moderate slope is another good exercise because the horse's movements are increased and the gait becomes a bit more like the canter. A good video of horses cantering with good riders aboard is an excellent way to train your brain, especially if you can view it in slow motion.

Finally, you can practice cantering on your own two legs. You have to practice very slowly at first, but since the moves are tucked away in your brain, they will come back to you. We used to have horseless horse shows at our stables, which included cantering, and students got really good at it.

Horseless Canter Exercise

The description is for the left lead, so in theory you would be standing on your right foot only at the start (phase 1 of stride).

1. Start from the standstill, holding your arms up in front of you as though you were holding a basketball.
2. Step forward with your left foot and simultaneously reach up and out with your right arm in a vertical circular movement (phase 2 of stride).
3. As your right arm starts down, let your weight begin to shift forward over your left leg and bring your left arm up and forward in the same circular movement (phase 3 of stride).
4. As your left arm starts down and you start to tip forward, give a little jump forward (moment of suspension) and land on your right foot.
5. Repeat.

When you're comfortable with the left lead, practice the right one as well. This sounds quite complicated, but most people learn it quite easily. The purpose of learning it, of course, is so that the canter will feel familiar to your body.

After you work with some or all of these preparatory skills, the time will come when you feel ready to try a canter on the bareback pad. Start with a fairly active walk, reviewing the seven steps. Try to exaggerate your following seat, using the muscles high up in your abdomen to roll your seat back and forth. At the same time, keep your buttocks muscles very wide and soft. Your lumbar spine (the small of your back) should go from slightly rounded to slightly hollow without locking in either position.

Now add some focus on your lateral following, making sure that even as your seat bones move, the pressure on both of them stays absolutely even, especially as you make turns. When you are thoroughly warmed up and secure, it's time to try the canter.

Earlier we talked about how, during each stride of the canter, the legs on one side come farther forward than—that is, they lead—the legs on the other (figure 17.2). And this has a purpose: Nature thinks of everything! When the horse canters on a curve, he can balance more easily if the legs that come farther underneath him are on the inside. Therefore, if he is cantering to the left, he should be on the left lead; when going to the right, he should be on the right lead.

We'll start with the left lead because most horses pick it up more easily and most riders find it easier to stay centered on left turns than right ones.

Bareback Cantering to the Left

Starting up is often the hardest part of the canter because it takes a fair amount of effort for the horse to lift himself into it. The instructor will guide you to get your horse into canter because different instructors and disciplines often train the horses to respond to different signals. Your early canters should all be left-hand around.

Begin by gathering your reins slightly, which is a signal to the horse that something is about to happen. Lift up a little on your grounding strap to help keep you sitting, just as you would if you were starting a sitting trot. Run through your seven steps again. Think about your gentle aids, especially intent.

The easiest command at this stage is a voice command such as "Rocky, canTER." If the horse is not voice trained, another easy method is to have a riding leader. Your horse follows and copies the lead horse. It is important for the canter to begin just as your horse starts down the long side of the arena so that your first strides are on the straight. When you're ready, you give the horse a light tap with the stick or a cluck to get his attention, if necessary. Then, as the lead horse starts, you give a light leading rein lift with your outside rein, cluck, and use your left abdominal muscles to roll your inside seat bone actively. Later on you will use a leg aid as well, but at this stage you want your legs to stay hanging loose.

If he should take more than a few steps of trot without cantering, especially if the trot is fast, post to the trot if necessary and bring him back to the walk using an active direct rein of opposition with your outside (right) hand. Then start again.

Some horses will pick up the canter more easily if you ask when you are about halfway around the corner to the long side that takes you toward the gate. However, if the horse tends to hurry toward the gate anyway, it's best not to use that method. In any case, the instructor, who is more familiar with the horse, will be able to help you find the best method of putting him into the canter.

As your horse picks up the canter (figure 17.3), lift up on the grounding strap and just think about the seven steps. By focusing on keeping your body correct, you won't be busy worrying about anything else—one of the major virtues of the steps! You should think principally about your following seat and lateral centering, but the other steps are important as well. *Your seat should not leave the horse's back at all*. If it does, focus on your lateral centering and growing.

You'll want to canter just a few strides at first, stopping before you reach the corner. If you are following a lead horse, he can be brought back gradually to the walk

Figure 17.3   Cantering bareback on the left lead.

as he gets to the corner. The instructor can also position herself to stop him at the same point. If you're on your own, use your voice in a quiet "Ho-o-o-o," take your right hand off the grounding strap, and use a soft active rein of opposition to ask him to break. As you feel him start to respond, prepare for a posting trot by lifting your toes into fixed-leg position, closing your hip angle and pressing your hands into his neck so that you can post comfortably for the couple of steps it will take him to reach a walk. Try to push your seat back as you close so that your center doesn't get ahead of his and cause him to lose his balance when he's trying to slow down. If he doesn't walk right away, use your right rein again to ask for it.

If this first try goes moderately well—you bounce a little, but not much, and the transitions both into and out of the canter are reasonably smooth—repeat the exercise a few more times as long as your skills stay the same or improve. Don't forget to use your grounding strap to help you stay grounded.

If you get worse as you repeat the exercise, stop and review some of the preparatory exercises before trying again. When you are learning a challenging physical task and you struggle at first, it is often helpful to stop actively trying to do the task for a time. When you come back to it, you will often find that your body has been working on it on some level, and you do much better.

Stick to short canters on straight lines for a while, although if you can go safely on the trail where there is a long, straight stretch, either level or very slightly uphill, and the horse won't try to race, the extra practice should make learning a little easier.

When you can stay centered and grounded with relaxed legs and arms and a light, steady feel on the grounding strap, you're ready for turns. Think about using the bounce of the gait, which is greater at the canter, to help you move your center inward rather than let it throw you outward. Soft eyes are also very important for this.

Plan on just going around one end of the arena the first time (that is, start at the beginning of a long side, go down and around the end, and finish at the end of the next long side). Think about how it went before you try again. Usually the lateral thrust on the turns is more than you expected. If necessary, do a walking or jogging and turning exercise a few more times.

Continue the pattern of two long sides and one short side a few more times. Again, don't get discouraged if it isn't perfect right away. If you've laid the ground work down well, it will get better every time. When you're fairly secure cantering around one end, you can canter the whole ring and keep going as long as you're relaxed and comfortable. You might notice an increased tendency on the part of the horse to cut in to the center. This just means that your center is still slipping a little to the outside and he is moving away from it. Don't try to steer him with the reins; just keep working on your centering and the cutting-in will diminish.

Bareback Cantering to the Right

When left cantering is going well, it's time to work the other direction. Before starting the right-lead canter, review your right centering to be sure that you are moving your center to the right and not just your shoulders, which is the common mistake (see the section called Staying Laterally Centered in chapter 6). Practice some short fast turns to the right at the walk. When you're comfortable with those, you're ready to canter to the right. You shouldn't have any trouble adjusting to the movement on the straight, but just in case, do one straight line without a turn before going on to the line–turn–line sequence. If you have little or no trouble adjusting to the right turns and your instructor says your position is correct, you can go ahead and canter as long as you're comfortable.

Cantering or Loping in the Saddle

When you can keep your centering with your legs relaxed and your seat staying on the horse's back so that you are moving as one on the bareback pad, you're ready to canter in the saddle. Because of the flatness and slipperiness of the saddle, lateral centering tends to be more difficult, but having the stirrups for lateral support should more than make up for that. You probably will find that holding the pommel or horn is easier than using the grounding strap

First review lateral centering with the stirrups in tight turns at the walk, and then sit the trot with stirrups on the straight and easy turns, finishing with some more difficult turns. Be very careful not to push yourself *up* but only to the side. If you find yourself bouncing more at the trot on turns, you're using too much stirrup and not enough upper-body centering. Remember that you want to maintain weight on your stirrups through gravity as much as possible, not by pushing on them.

When you're ready, repeat the same pattern of learning the canter that you did on bareback, starting with the left lead—straight line; straight line, curve, straight line; and finally continuous cantering. Repeat for the right lead (figure 17.4). Be sure you are secure at each step before moving on.

Figure 17.4 Cantering on the right lead in the saddle.

Changing Leads

Horses are quite capable of changing from one lead to the other while cantering or galloping. This is called a flying change and is not within the scope of this book. However, at the level that you will be riding, you might want to go from cantering around the arena in one direction to cantering the other way. The method used is called a simple change of lead. The easiest way to do it is to come around the short side of the arena and immediately turn to ride diagonally across to the opposite corner. As you approach the center, you ask the horse to slow down to either the trot or the walk. Then as you approach the opposite corner, ask for the canter on the new lead

A good way to start leaning this is to begin by trotting across the diagonals a few times, so you learn how to plan the turns. When you're comfortable with that, as you ride across the diagonal and approach the corner of the new direction, come to the walk, then ask for canter. You should be in the canter before you begin the corner.

Cantering in Half-Seat Position

While learning, avoid trotting in half seat just before cantering. The movements of your body in the two gaits are quite different, and trotting will confuse things. Start by walking first in full seat and then in three-quarter seat, and alternate between the two. Be particularly conscious of how your lower back and hips move. Your back hollows and rounds in each stride in the same way whether you are sitting or in three-quarter seat.

Take up the canter directly from the walk in full seat to the left, counting to yourself in each stride to keep the rhythm—*one* two three, *one* two three. As you approach a long side, close your hip angle slightly, take your grounding strap, and lift your seat off the saddle, staying centered and grounded. Your hips move in a small flat circle, forward and opening the hip, back and closing, but your seat stays at about the same level and never touches the saddle (figure 17.5).

Because you were successful in the sitting canter, the half seat should be very easy. If you find yourself bumping the saddle as though you were posting, go back to the walk and start again. When you are secure to the left, then try the right lead as well.

Figure 17.5 Cantering in half-seat position.

Galloping or Running

The difference between galloping (running) and cantering (loping) is partly the speed—the gallop (or run) is much faster. Because of the extension of the stride in the gallop, the footfall is also slightly different from the canter. Each foot in the gallop hits the ground separately; the left

Bringing a Bolting Horse Under Control

Research shows that a frightened horse will bolt—run out of control—only for the length of a lion's charge, or about 50 yards. After that, a calm rider who is using her aids correctly can gradually regain communication and bring the horse under control again though it may take time. It helps to remember in such a situation that nobody, horse or human, likes the feeling of being scared. If you can assist the horse in recovering his self-control, he will be more than happy to cooperate. These thoughts do not apply to a horse who is angry, and this is another reason that a good relationship is so important.

lead starts with the right hind, then the left hind, then the right front, and finally the left front, followed by the moment of suspension when all four legs are in the air. Because only one foot hits the ground at a time, the gallop is even smoother than the canter, so it is easier to follow.

Many novice riders associate riding at speed with being out of control. This is not necessarily true. *If the horse and rider are both calm and are in control of their bodies*, the horse is just as controllable at full speed as he is at the slower gaits. Naturally a stop takes longer and turns must be more gradual, but this is equally true of cars at higher speeds and is the result solely of the speed, not of unwillingness on the part of the horse to respond.

Learning to ride at the gallop is simply an extension of the canter. If your arena is large enough (100 by 200 feet or 30 by 60 m), you can canter around the end, then ask your horse to move on into a hand gallop, which is faster than a canter but not too fast for conditions. As you approach the next corner, ask him to slow down, then repeat on the next long side.

If your horse is good on trails, you have suitable trails with space and no hazards, and you ride with someone who can control her horse, galloping on trails is a lot of fun and comparatively easy. The only difficult part is if someone has a horse that insists on racing, because the other horses pick up on that and want to join in. A well-trained horse with a competent rider will let other horses gallop away while he continues to walk or trot calmly.

So the difficulty in galloping is not the gait itself but the tendency of both horses and riders to be insufficiently prepared to deal with the excitement. This is not within the scope of this book, but you should be aware that like driving your car on the highway, staying safe has a lot to do with using good judgment about your and the horse's knowledge and training. And if you plan ahead, you can always dismount.

Galloping is nearly always ridden in half seat because the horse needs the freedom of having the rider off his back. Also, although the movement is smooth, there is a lot of thrust. But the gallop is easy to follow. Generally the only danger is from a stumble or a sudden stop. That's where training your centering reflexes can often save you.

As with everything you have been learning so far, you need a certain amount of time and patience in order to feel really comfortable at the canter and gallop. And as always, consideration and understanding for your horse's problems as he deals with your mistakes will make the learning process safer and more fun for you both.

18

Leg Aids and Advanced Hand and Rein Effects

Well, finally, you're going to use your legs as something more than counterweights! But you had to practice that relaxed leg for a long time so that when you do start using your legs as aids, after each application you will automatically come back to the relaxed leg. And that's necessary in order for you to stay centered and grounded.

The purpose of the leg aid, as with any aid, is to communicate with the horse and to show him the best way to execute the desired action. The legs ask the horse for movement; the placement of the leg, the timing, and the other aids tell him the direction of and how much movement is wanted.

You might have read or heard that you need strong legs to make the horse do what you want. But you know by now that trying to use physical strength to *make* the horse do what you want is not the best way to work, especially if he is 10 times your size. The horse can feel a fly landing on any part of his body, so a light application of the leg is sufficient for communicating with him. This light touch is called a soft leg and is described in detail later in the chapter.

The application of the leg to the horse's muscles causes contraction of those muscles. It is similar to being tickled. Done in one way, it tells the horse to increase his speed. If the leg is used in a slightly different way, it helps the horse to gather himself, that is, to bring his hind legs more underneath his body to make it easier to push off. It's a little like a human racer on the blocks but not as extreme most of the time.

The release of the leg allows the horse to respond. If the rider's leg is applied too strongly and not released, it restricts the horse's ability to respond, especially with forward movement, and often results in resistance instead. Constant use of strong legs and failure to return to the relaxed leg (figure 18.1) after each application will make the horse unresponsive, requiring even more strength plus the use of whips and spurs, all of which are likely to result in even more resistance. Such horses need to be reintroduced to leg aids and soon learn to respond to softer aids.

Figure 18.1   Passive leg in ∩ position.

Classically, there are three positions on the horse's body where you apply your leg. They are in front of the girth, at the girth, and behind the girth. The terms refer not to the actual place where you apply the leg, but the position of the stirrup at the time. So the actual pressure on the horse may be several inches behind the stirrup itself. In theory there is only an inch or so difference between the positions, but often during training the positions are farther apart.

You can use leg aids on both sides at the same time, or on each side individually as the hind leg on that side comes off the ground. Some trainers prefer one method, some the other.

The Soft Leg

I was introduced to the soft leg by the late Nuño Oliveira, then coach of the Portuguese Olympic team. Along with the active hand and Centered Riding, I consider it among the great discoveries in my riding and teaching career.

The soft leg is exactly what the name implies. Rather than squeeze with the calf—and often the thighs and buttocks as well—or turn the toe out and bang the horse with the heel, the rider softly taps or rubs the horse's side with the inside of her calf. Once the horse understands that the rider is trying to communicate with him by way of the soft tap or rub, his response is relaxed and prompt, without the resistance that often accompanies a stronger aid. Besides creating a response that is more relaxed, the soft leg requires far less muscle strength from the rider than a squeeze.

Easy Does It

A student of mine was introduced to the soft leg aid soon after I learned it. Shortly thereafter she visited the college of her choice to try out for a place in their riding instructor program. Because she was a big woman, she was given a large and somewhat phlegmatic horse on which to demonstrate her skills.

In her nervousness, she forgot to carry a stick and was too embarrassed to ask for one. When she asked the horse to walk on, using the rather strong squeezing leg followed by a kick that she was accustomed to, she got no response from him at all. She tried several more times, getting more nervous and embarrassed as she continued to fail. Then she remembered about the soft leg she had been learning. She tried it, and the horse responded instantly. She went through her ride, and the observers told her later that they had never seen the horse go so willingly and so forward. (She was accepted into the program.)

The amount of pressure used with the soft leg, like that used when asking the horse to back up (chapter 7), is similar to what you would use when tapping someone in a crowded room to ask her to move and let you by.

There are two ways you might want the horse to respond to a leg aid with forward movement. One is to move at a faster gait; the other is to engage the horse's hind legs, bringing them more under his body. Besides the way in which you would apply other aids in addition to the leg aid, you would use the leg aid in a different way.

Applying the Soft Leg

With your leg in ∩ position, bring your toe in as though you were going to tap the girth with it until you feel your calf bump softly against the horse's side. Then immediately bring your toe up and out in a circular motion until the calf pressure releases and your leg returns to its original position (figure 18.2). The effect is for your calf to tap the horse's side lightly rather than squeeze or thump.

Your left toe will move in a counterclockwise direction and your right toe in a clockwise direction.

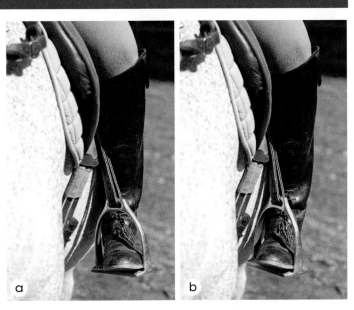

Figure 18.2 The soft leg (*a*) tap and (*b*) release.

Applying the Soft Leg Rub

To ask for more engagement, your leg rubs the horse's side instead of tapping. Your leg position remains the same, but your toe would come in and slide forward slightly and then up and out and back. Depending on your other aids, the horse will either lengthen his stride by taking longer steps or collect it, rounding his body and taking shorter, higher steps.

If the Horse Is Dead to the Leg

Since many horses are accustomed to the stronger aid or, worse, to a rider who grips with her legs to maintain position, the horse might have learned to ignore most leg pressure. A horse that has been ridden with an unnecessarily tight girth or cinch might also be unresponsive, or dead to the leg.

Horses that have become dead to leg aids will need some help figuring out how to respond. First be sure you are using the appropriate gentle aids—intent, eyes, and center. Then use the same approach that you used to teach the horse to respond to the stick. That is, you start with a very light tap and look for any sort of reaction from the horse. If he starts to move at all, you praise, wait, and repeat. If you get no response, try a voice aid, such as a cluck, or if the horse knows the command, "walk on," and again look for any sort of response and immediately praise. Finally, you would use the stick as described in chapter 10, or perhaps have someone on the ground lead him. Remember that your goal is not to force him to move but simply to teach him what the aid means.

Using these techniques, you can fairly quickly teach the horse to associate the soft leg with a request for movement.

Leg Aids for Lateral Work

As you begin to do more advanced work, you may use the leg to ask the horse to either step or bend his body to one side. Lateral leg aids are always used in conjunction with centering aids. If you are asking the horse to bend his body so that it follows a curve, you place your inner leg at the girth and your outer leg behind the girth, and use the rub effect.

If you want the horse to step sideways with his hind legs, you use the leg on the opposite side from the direction you want him to move. It is applied with a tapping action, behind the girth, while the reins are used to turn his head and restrict his reaction to move forward.

Like the ground work, lateral work while mounted takes practice to get the result without feeling the need to become aggressive.

You can try the two leg movements while sitting in a chair to feel how they differ. Just remember that all the movements are very small. While your foot and ankle rotate, only the inner side of your calf, not the back of it, should touch the horse. Turning the back of your calf against the horse creates unwanted tension in your thigh and buttocks, which among other things makes it more difficult for the horse to use the related areas in his body effectively. And you've worked very hard to avoid that.

As noted earlier, the leg aids work not on the pressure but on the release. That is, the pressure gathers the horse together and prepares him to move, and the release then allows him to do so. The same is true of the stick aids. In both cases you use a tap, which by definition includes a release. You need to allow time for the response, especially if he isn't sure what you want. So you would tap the side of the horse with your inner calf in the same way as you would tap someone on the shoulder with your hand. You would look for some sort of response. If the person looked around at you in a questioning way, showing that she heard you but didn't know what you wanted, you would not tap her any harder. Instead, you would do something—a look, a gesture, a word—to indicate that you needed her to move.

Assuming you have a horse that usually responds to a soft leg aid, if you apply the aid and don't get the expected response, it usually means that the horse is being blocked in some manner from responding.

Here are some of the common causes of blocking in response to the soft leg:

- Your center is off—that is, you lean forward so your center is in front of the horse's center.
- You rock your body back and forth, which unbalances the horse and blocks his center.
- You squeeze with your thighs or buttocks, which tenses the horse's back muscles, interfering with movement.
- The reins are too tight, which sends a mixed signal.

With a little practice, you will find the soft leg very easy to use and will be amazed at how little it disturbs your position and how well your horse responds.

The Passive Hand

As you move into more advanced work, you should be familiar with some hand and rein effects, even though you might not be ready or have no need to use them yet. As noted in chapter 15, hand effects relate to *how* you pull the rein, and rein effects relate to the *direction* in which you pull. I use the term *bit* in most of the text, but the principles apply to any device whether it works on the horse's mouth or not. Much of the information in this section is quite advanced and somewhat complex. You should not expect to figure it all out in one reading, so it would be best, after glancing through it, to read small sections, think them over and try them out over an extended period.

The active hand that you have been using (described in chapter 15) asks the horse to yield to a soft pull on the rein by using careful timing and by releasing as soon as the horse indicates discomfort by pulling. However, especially in English riding, there are times when you *don't* want the horse to yield to the rein but rather to use the rein.

The horse, who balances with his head and neck, can learn to use the reins to help balance and ground.

When done correctly, riding the horse in contact or on the bit, using a passive or following hand, helps both rider and horse to ground in much the same way that pairs figure skaters balance and ground each other through the use of their hands and arms. This is considered an advanced concept, but it doesn't have to be. The passive hand involves being able to follow the movements of the horse's head in such a way that the contact is steady and even all the time, through every little change the horse makes, and does not *interfere* with the horse's balance. This sounds very difficult but, as you already know, your body moves in the same way as the horse's body. That means that as your pelvis is being moved in direct relation to the movement of the horse's hind legs, that movement causes a response in your upper body and arms that is in direct relation to the horse's front legs and thus to his neck and head. If you walk on the horse without reins, use your following seat, and allow your arms to hang passively at your sides, they will begin to move with the horse's front legs. The movement is smaller but easily observable from the ground, especially if the horse has an energetic walk. So the passive hand is really quite natural.

In addition, all the work you have been doing with the grounding strap, working with your balance so that you can maintain a light, steady contact on the strap, has been teaching your body about following the reins. *As the horse moves, the grounding strap follows the motion of his front legs in exactly the same way the reins follow the movement of his head.*

But following with the reins does feel different at first, mostly because your arms don't swing in the same way as when you walk on foot and the horse's head movements are more subtle than those of his shoulders. So you need to practice some exercises at the walk until you can follow the horse's movements easily. First, your following seat must be very smooth and correct without tension, and you should be able to hold the grounding strap in light contact with both hands and maintain the same pressure constantly and evenly with both hands.

So that you don't hurt the horse accidentally while you're learning, for this work the horse should wear either a padded halter or a padded side-pull hackamore (with no shanks). The halter and side pull are about the same, but a side pull is usually easier to get a snug but not overly tight fit (figure 18.3*a*). A longeing caveson is also a good choice, since the better ones are designed not to twist around the horse's face to a one-sided pull (figure 18.3*b*). You'll see why this is important when you start the exercise.

In whatever discipline you ride, *the reins must be long enough so that the horse can put his nose all the way to the ground without pulling you out of position* (review the sections on lengthening and shortening the reins in chapter 11). You also might find it easier to do the introductory walking work on a bareback pad so that you can feel the movement of your following seat more clearly.

Riding in Contact for Curb Bits (Western)

Riding in contact is not used a great deal with the curb bit because the nature of such bits is that it takes a very skillful hand not to cause the horse any discomfort. However, there are times when it is a very useful skill to have, so learning it using a milder device might come in handy later on in your career.

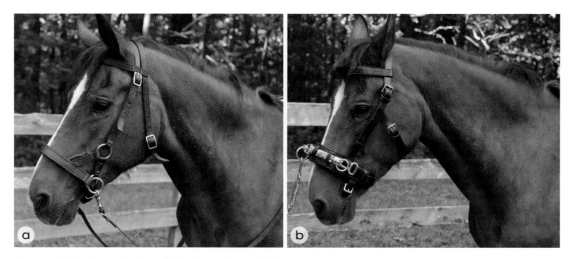

Figure 18.3 Properly fitted (*a*) side-pull and (*b*) longeing caveson.

Walking With the Passive Hand

If possible, the horse you start learning on should have a free, swinging walk and should accept a feel on the rein without pulling or snatching. You probably will work in the arena, although walking home from a trail ride is a very good way to practice because of the free forward walk most horses offer in that situation.

Every horse has one side that he is softer on than the other. For most horses this is the right side. In the arena, after you are both warmed up, take the rail in the direction that places the horse's soft side toward the rail, which will probably be left-hand around. Check your centering and grounding, then focus on your following seat for a minute. Also, without taking any contact, hold the reins and check your hand and wrist position to make sure they are correct (see Picking Up the Reins in chapter 11).

When you are ready, drop your inside (left) rein or hold it very loosely along with the grounding strap and shorten your right rein until you can feel the same contact with the horse's head that you had with the grounding strap. Your elbow should be slightly in front of your rib cage. Because you will have a slight pull on the rein, you should keep your low back a little firmer so that your center tells the horse to keep going. Your eyes, voice, and intent will also help.

Now just ask the horse to keep walking. If he starts to pull heavily against the rein, let some rein slide through your hand so that he can extend his head and neck as far as he needs to in order to lengthen and loosen his body while you maintain the light contact. If he starts to turn in off the rail, use your lateral centering aid to encourage him to stay out, or at least not to make too cramped a circle. As long as no snatching of the rein is involved, turning away from a single following rein is perfectly correct. (See the section titled Holding Hand later in this chapter.) If necessary, you can change to a leading active hand, starting with a release, to lead him back to the track again and then return to the passive hand. If he continues to cut in, he might be getting tired, so you could stop or change direction and let him work on the other rein.

Holding the Reins Western Style

You might find it easier at first to hold the rein like a Western rein, entering your hand between your thumb and forefinger rather than around your ring or little finger. This way of holding the rein makes it easier to keep your wrist in the correct position. However, it is not as sensitive a way to feel the contact, so you should return to the normal way of holding English reins as soon as you feel ready.

Think about your following seat and keeping your arm and shoulder totally passive. Imagine that the rein is elastic and that you want to keep it lightly stretched. Go through your seven steps in your mind. This is a good time to ride to music if it's available because you want to engage your right brain as much as possible, and music (classical, not rock) helps you to do so. You are looking for a steady, soft feel that does not cause the horse to resist (figure 18.4). Don't keep going too long at a time because it can be tiring for the horse to work on only one rein.

When you and the horse are comfortable in the first direction, reverse and work with the other

Figure 18.4   Using the passive hand during the walk.

rein. If you started with his soft side first, he will be more willing to take the new rein, but he might also tend to take the rein too much and cut in or circle more. As long as the contact is elastic and doesn't create tension or serious resistance, working on the circle is all right. Or, as previously, you can change to the active leading rein to encourage him to go back on the rail, but don't make an issue out of it.

Finally, take up both reins and try to keep an even contact on both of them. You might not be ready to do this in the first session, so be patient with yourself. The following hand is really a natural skill because you are using your hands to help yourself ground while holding something that is supportive but not rigid. Holding someone's hands while you learn to balance on ice skates comes to mind. Don't attempt to use your reins to guide the horse. You can let him go wherever he wants at first and then use your gentle aids to guide him as your contact becomes more even.

When you are riding with both reins in passive contact, you will nearly always find that the horse wants to take more contact on one rein than the other, which will tend to make him turn. To keep straight, you have to keep the rein pressure even by loosening the tighter rein and taking up on the looser one. Use your other aids and perhaps some active hand on the heavier side to help him to stay straight. By keeping the rein pressure even yourself, you encourage him to push off evenly with both hind legs, which helps him to stay straight.

Trotting With the Passive Hand

When the horse is walking (or cantering), his head is moving relative to the rest of his body, and your body (particularly your shoulders) is staying comparatively still. Therefore, your *hands have to move* independently of your body to follow the horse's head. However, during the trot, especially the posting trot, the horse's head stays comparatively still while your body moves up and down. Therefore, *your hands have to stay relatively still* to follow the horse's head while your elbows open and close to follow the rise and fall of your body (figure 18.5).

This could be a fairly difficult skill to learn, except for one thing: your old friend, the grounding strap. Or in the case of posting, it might be the pressure on your horse's neck, depending on whether you post in a more closed or more open position. In any case, by now you should be very accustomed to trying to keep a steady feel on the neck or grounding strap to keep you in longitudinal balance. If you have never posted in a slightly open position, that is, balancing with a light pull on the grounding strap, you should work on that for a while before trying to post in contact with the horse's mouth.

Your stirrup leathers should also stay vertical so that your feet stay underneath your center with no longitudinal swing. If you can post correctly with the grounding strap, you should be able to learn to post and maintain contact with the reins while keeping your hands quiet (figure 18.5).

As with the walk, you probably want to start with the reins attached to a very mild hackamore or a halter. For the sitting trot, the bareback pad will probably be easier. Your grounding strap should be a little loose so that you can adjust your hands on it to get the position you want, that is, in the correct position relative to the horse's head at the trot (straight line from elbow to bit when seated).

For the sitting trot work, you should use a horse with a fairly smooth gait. You should also be able to sit the trot without any loss of contact between your seat and the saddle or pad and stay centered both laterally and longitudinally while maintaining a light steady contact on the grounding strap.

When you begin the trot, start by hold-ing the grounding strap and reins with

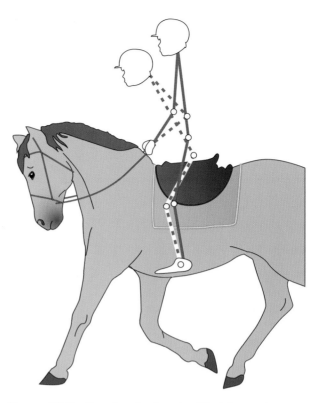

Figure 18.5 Keeping the hands still while posting.

the reins slightly loose, as you have been doing (figure 18.6a). Trot for a short period to make sure you can keep a light steady feel on the strap, then try holding one rein in passive contact while keeping the other hand on the grounding strap (figure 18.6b). Then switch hands. You should probably work this way for at least several lessons before you try riding without using the grounding strap at all. The result should be that you can stay comfortable and grounded using the reins in such a way that the horse is also comfortable and grounded.

If you have serious difficulty sitting the trot or keeping your hands quiet during either the sitting or posting trot, it's possible that your lumbar spine is not as flexible—and shock absorb-ing—as it should be. See a competent health care professional to address this.

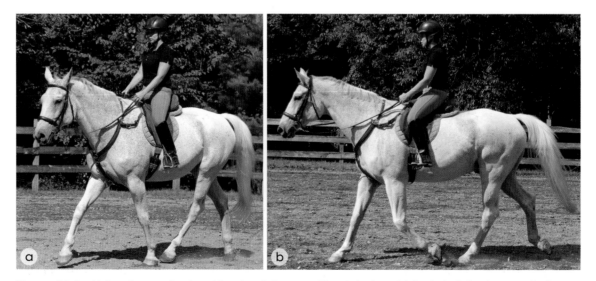

Figure 18.6 Using the passive hand for the sitting trot. The right (outside) rein is following passively.

The passive hand is the hand effect you usually use when you are working on a skill with the horse in English riding. You might consider it part of the seven steps. You want to keep his attention and keep a connection with him but not change what he is doing. To ask for something different, you would use your other aids or one of the other hand effects. Of course, you shouldn't ride the horse in contact for extended periods because he will tire. If he shows signs of discomfort such as constantly asking for more rein or shaking or tossing his head, he's telling you he needs a break.

The Holding Hand

The holding hand is an extension of the concept of passive hand. It involves taking a firmer hold with the rein or reins while still following the movement. As with the passive hand, the pressure will not necessarily be equal on both reins; that is, the horse might want to take more support from one rein. You have to adjust the pressure if you want him to stay straight. The horse should never feel heavy or dead in your hands or lean on the reins, either of which would indicate loss of balance. If he feels heavy, allow him to take more rein and try to help him balance by moving your center back and adding some soft leg.

In either English riding or in Western using two hands, if you use the holding hand with both reins while asking the horse to move forward against the additional pressure, the horse must use more impulsion, that is, more energy to push against the pressure of the rein. At the same time you are giving him more support. This is the way you ask for extension in the gaits.

Since you *don't* want the horse to give to the pressure of the rein, your hand can be slightly below the line of the elbow to bridle. Be careful not to lose the wrist position. Your thumb will point toward the ground rather than toward the horse's muzzle (figure 18.7).

Figure 18.7 The holding hand.

If you are riding downhill so that gravity is creating more forward pressure from the horse, using the holding hand helps to support and ground him, especially at the faster gaits. Using the holding hand on one rein might initially cause the horse to turn his head in that direction in order to avoid taking pressure on that side. As explained in chapter 15, this floppiness is known as going behind the bit or bridle. It causes the horse to lose his grounding and causes you to lose your connection to his feet. This is the equivalent of a person picking up something moderately heavy in one hand, such as a bucket of water. If she bends sideways toward the bucket, she soon finds that she can neither balance nor ground in that position. However, if she bends her body to the opposite side, pulling against the pressure only as much as is necessary to balance it, carrying the bucket becomes much easier.

From this concept arises the advanced way of initiating a turn. If you use a holding hand on the outside rein of the intended turn—that is, hold on the left rein to begin a right turn—the horse should take hold on the rein and start turning his head to the right. To take that extra hold on the rein, he must push against it with his hind leg. Since it is the left rein, he must engage his right hind leg, which is also necessary to help him balance on the right turn. So beginning the turn by asking the horse to take the outside rein first makes the execution of the turn more balanced.

Exploring the Rein and Opposite Hind Leg Connection

To understand how the rein works with the opposite hind leg rather than with the one on the same side, stand in front of a heavy table, counter, or window sill with your feet a couple of feet away. Lean forward and place your hands on the table so that you are using them to balance. Check to make sure the pressure is even on both sides. Without hurrying, pick up one hand and hold it off the table while you lift up the opposite foot. You should find that quite easy to do and still feel secure. Try it with both diagonal pairs of hands and feet.

With both hands on the table and both feet on the floor, check to make sure you are square. Now, still without hurrying, pick up one hand and then the foot on the same side. You will probably find that you have to hesitate before you can pick up the foot and shift all your weight to the opposite side, and you still don't feel as secure with this lateral support as you did with the diagonal support. Try going back and forth from diagonal to lateral support on both sides.

If you are making a more extended turn, such as a circle, once the horse's body is in correct turning position he will have to take a longer step with his outside legs, because they have a longer distance to travel. Therefore you would take a slightly heavier feel on the inside rein to enable this. This is quite an advanced concept, and requires an acute awareness of how the horse is reacting to your aids.

The Fixed Hand

The fixed hand is one of the two most advanced of the hand effects and requires both a skillful rider and an advanced horse. The rider sets her hand a little bit so that it doesn't quite follow the horse's movement, creating a release-and-take effect like a very small active hand action. In conjunction with the other aids, the advanced horse interprets this and responds by softening and giving slightly on the appropriate rein or reins. It is part of the invisible aids that riders aspire to.

Combing the Rein

Combing the rein is most useful with a horse that has had the reins hung on by a rider, interfering with his balance to the point that as soon as he feels any contact he resists, usually by snatching the reins. When you comb the reins, you slide your hand on the reins so that the contact stays very soft and elastic; thus the horse never really feels the restriction of a steady pull. The action is similar to combing the lead rope, outlined in chapter 7.

For combing, the reins must be long enough for the horse to put his head all the way down without either of you feeling any pull. To comb both reins, hold the reins near the end with one hand up near your chest and the reins slightly loose. Place the other hand palm down across the reins (figure 18.8a). Be sure to keep your wrist soft and high. Squeeze the reins very gently with your fingers and slide your hand up the reins, creating a slight pressure on the horse's head (figure 18.8b). When you reach the other hand, change hands and comb with the other hand. Once the horse discovers that rein pressure does not mean that you will restrict his head, he will relax and be more willing to accept the rein aids.

If he resists mostly on one side, you can comb just one rein, using the same hand with each stroke. Combing the rein is also a good exercise if you tend to grip the reins or otherwise restrict the horse's head movement.

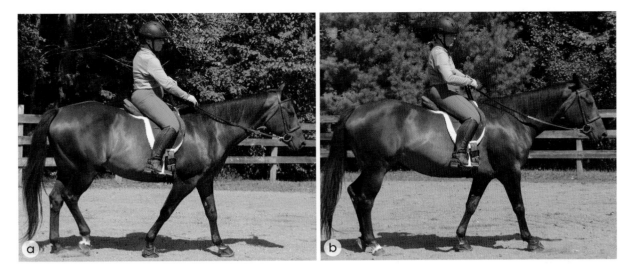

Figure 18.8 Combing the rein.

The Taking Hand

This is the other very advanced hand effect. It is, unfortunately, the most often taught to inexperienced riders, and the easiest to abuse. It is applied in the same way as the holding hand (that is, taking a steady, firm pressure on the rein). But instead of releasing or easing if the horse gets heavy on the rein, you give the release only if the horse *gives* to the pull with his head and neck. At first glance, this might seem like a desirable result. But if you remember, it's his feet you need to affect. When the horse gives to a steady pull with his head alone, he loses his grounding, so responding with his feet is more difficult. Therefore it is essential that the training is carried on to the point where the horse maintains his grounding and gives with his feet as well. It's similar to when you were teaching the horse to back up on the ground. First he was rewarded for yielding with his head alone, but as soon as possible you asked him to reconnect so that he moved his feet as well.

Remember what we said earlier about how you carry something heavy in one hand and still stay grounded and balanced. To do so, you must lean *away* from the steady pull, not give to it. However, if you developed your strength and balance, and understood the goal, you could learn to carry something heavy in one hand, stay upright and still maintain your grounding. Horses who are correctly trained in the taking hand learn to do this kind of thing and to perform very advanced work using very light rein contact.

Types and Applications of Leading Reins and Reins of Opposition

In chapter 15, the terms *leading rein* and *direct reins of opposition* were introduced and used for accomplishing some basic tasks. Here we look at the variety of movements each of these general terms encompass and how they are typically applied.

When differentiating these types of effects, I use *direct*, *opening*, and *indirect* because they are easy to understand and make the relationship between leading reins and reins of opposition clear. Other terms and definitions of rein effects are used, and I also use those common names in this section so that they will be familiar to you.

Leading reins act in the same way that the lead rope acts when you lead the horse on the ground (as described in chapter 7). The operative word here is *lead*.

On the ground, the direction of pull on the rope must be forward—ahead of a line extending out the sides of the horse's mouth. This causes the least interference with the horse's natural movement; therefore, it is the easiest for him to respond to correctly.

On the horse, what makes a rein leading, rather than in opposition, is the upward angle of the rein as it leaves the bit. As described previously, in order for the rein to be leading, it must be used at an angle of at least 45 degrees upward from the horizontal (see figure 15.8).

Leading-Rein Effects:

- Direct rein, is on a line parallel with the horse's neck—that is, no lateral (sideways) effect (figure 18.9*a*).

- Opening rein is on a line away from the horse's neck (laterally) (figure 18.9*b*).

- Indirect (also called bearing or neck) rein is on a line across the horse's neck (laterally). The rein itself should not actually cross the horse's neck (figure 18.9*c*).

Figure 18.9 Leading-rein effects.

Reins of opposition all involve a certain amount of pressure in opposition to the horse's forward movement. Used with the correct hand effects, this should not interfere with the horse.

Reins of Opposition:

- In the direct rein of opposition, the pull is straight back *along* the line of the horse's path (figure 18.10*a*).

- In the opening rein of opposition, the pull is back and somewhat *outside* the line of the horse's path, away from the withers (figure 18.10*b*).

- In the indirect rein of opposition, the pull is back and inside the line of the horse's path, toward the withers (figure 18.10*c*). (Indirect reins of opposition have some variation in angle, but should not cross the horse's neck.)

Figure 18.10 Reins of opposition.

The names of these effects are quite similar, but each has a distinct impact and use. What differentiates the rein effects is the way they affect the horse's feet. In the descriptions that follow you will learn how the effect is applied and the desired result.

Leading Reins

The direct leading rein is generally used with one rein and a snaffle bit to initiate a simple turn (as described in chapter 15), especially if either rider or horse is inexperienced, as it is the least restrictive (figure 18.11). As the horse's head turns he steps over with the front foot on the same side to balance himself, thus initiating the turn. Since there is no opposition, his front leg can move freely. The other legs follow naturally.

The direct leading rein can also be used with one or both reins to help the horse rebalance.

The opening leading rein asks more directly for the horse to lead his head to the side, initiating or continuing the turn as above. It also tends to lead his front leg more to the side, because of the lateral pull (figure 18.12).

The indirect leading rein, or neck rein, initiates a turn by bringing the horse's head in the desired direction via pressure against the upper neck on the opposite side. It is more commonly used in Western riding with a curb bit, however, especially during training, it is often used in both disciplines to help the horse to understand the turning aid by using the opening and neck reins together (Figure 18.13).

A very common mistake in neck reining is to use too much force, so that instead of just a light pressure on the horse's neck, there is strong pressure on the neck and also on the bit, which is painful and causes tension and resistance. There is also a tendency— especially in left hand turns if the rider carries the reins in her right hand—for the rider to move her center to the left thus blocking, and confusing, the horse.

Figure 18.11   Direct leading rein.   **Figure 18.12**   Opening leading rein.

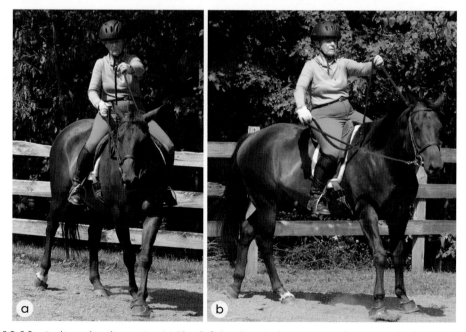

Figure 18.13   Indirect leading rein. *(a)* The left leading indirect rein is bringing the horse's head and front foot to the right, and the right rein is direct but passive. *(b)* The left leading indirect rein with the right opening rein of opposition is bringing the horse's right front foot across.

Reins of Opposition

The direct rein of opposition is the most commonly used rein effect. The direction of pull is straight back on a line parallel to the horse's path and on an angle to form a straight line between the rider's elbow and the bit.

Used with an active hand and on an angle slightly above the line of the elbow to the bit, the direct rein of opposition asks the horse to bring his feet more underneath himself (collect himself) to slow down either his tempo or his speed or both, or to transition to a different, slower gait or halt. Used with a passive hand on the line of the elbow to the bit, it offers support to the horse, allowing and aiding him to ground and helping the rider to ground as well

Used with a holding hand slightly lower than the line of elbow to bit, the direct rein of opposition allows the horse to take more support for the bit. When used with one rein, it helps the horse to balance and ground while initiating a turn in the opposite direction (figure 18.14a).Used with both reins, it supports the horse during extension or when riding downhill (figure 18.14b).

The opening rein of opposition can be used with an active hand to initiate a turn in the same direction (figure 18.15). However, if too much opposition is applied, it restricts the horse's shoulder and front leg on the same side, making it hard for him to turn. Since the hind leg is also restricted, it interferes with his balance. If a direct holding hand is used first so that the horse turns his head

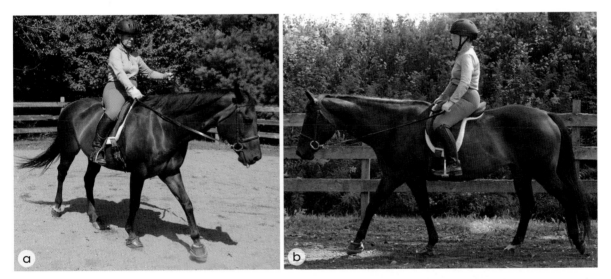

Figure 18.14 Direct rein of opposition. *(a)* The right direct rein of opposition used with left opening rein for a left turn. *(b)* The horse has lengthened both stride and frame.

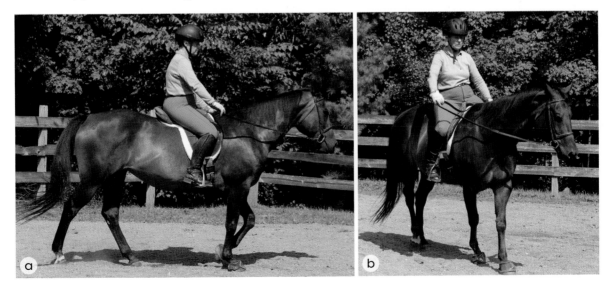

Figure 18.15 Opening rein of opposition.

Correcting a Common Problem

One common cause of abuse of the indirect reins of opposition is a rider who constantly rides with her right rein in indirect position. No matter how often she is corrected, as soon as she is distracted, the hand goes back to its old habit. This is actually quite easy to correct, once you understand the cause.

Way back when you first sat on the horse and thought about position, we talked about sitting evenly on both seat bones and that it was common to sit unevenly unless you were careful. If you sit on your seat bone on the left side and back on your buttock on the right, the top of your right hip will be back. This makes a twist in your upper body and results in your right arm coming across your body instead of straight back. To correct this, you must push your right hip forward as described in chapter 5 in the section titled Mounting: Getting It Right From the Start.

If you have trouble maintaining this, it is likely that the cartilage in your hip joint is shortened and needs to be stretched. This will take some time, but you can do it. My chiropractor discovered the problem in my body, and I was able to overcome it in my 50s. The exercise consists of walking with your hand on your right iliac crest and pushing forward against your hand just before you lift your right foot to take a step.

slightly in the opposite direction, it opens up the shoulder. The opening rein then asks the horse to move that shoulder and front leg toward the rein. The horse is then said to be in a counterbend.

The indirect rein of opposition is usually described as either in front of the withers or behind the withers. These names refer to the angle at which the rein is applied. As the names imply, the indirect rein of opposition in front of the withers goes from the bit along a line that would pass across the horse's neck just in front of the withers, while the other passes just behind the withers. In actual practice, the rider's hand should never cross to the opposite side of the horse's spine.

The action of the indirect rein of opposition is to shift the horse's weight onto the opposite front leg if used in front of the withers or the hind leg if behind the withers. However, in practice, the weight shift needed is rarely as precise as that, so there can be quite a bit of variation in the actual direction of the pull.

The indirect reins of opposition are very easy to abuse because they are very restricting. The most common damage is to the horse's hocks because the hind leg cannot step forward as much as nature intended, so the impact is too sharp. It's like stepping off a step that isn't there. My trainer, who taught me about such things, called the indirect reins of opposition hock breakers and would never allow me to use them for more than a couple steps before opening the rein and allowing the horse to step forward again!

Developing Good Legs and Hands

It might be some time before you have a need for some of the hand and rein effects described in this chapter. For the moment, think of them as tools you can try out with due regard to your horse's responses. Depending on the direction your riding career takes, you might never use more than a few of them, or you might become highly skilled with all of them. Either way, a little more knowledge never hurts.

When people talk about riding aids, they usually mean hand and leg aids. But the gentle aids are equally important. With regard to your legs, understanding the soft leg will mean that your leg aids will give the best results possible for your horse, since strength is not a factor.

During your riding career, you will hear a lot about the importance of good hands and the difficulty in achieving them. I have read that it takes 25 years to develop good hands. Using the methods described in this book, I have taught many riders who developed good hands in about 5 years. The combination of building a centered, grounded foundation and thus a secure seat, and understanding that your task is to work with the horse, not master him, will result in good skills in all areas, including your hands, and therefore your ability to communicate with your horse in the most sympathetic and consequently the most effective way.

19

Handling Hills With Confidence

Many riders who are perfectly comfortable on level ground are very uncomfortable on hills, especially the downhill stretches. Instead of having that nice expanse of head and neck up in front of you, it is now level or even below you. If the horse is at all insecure about downhill riding, it can be quite scary.

As with everything else, to maintain your own confidence you must be centered over your base. Hills (and we're talking about anything that is steep enough or long enough to get your attention) are somewhat stressful for the horse because he has to walk up and down the hill carrying a rider, so they should be ridden with your weight, and therefore your base, on the stirrups rather than on your seat. This gives the horse's back more freedom, which allows him to engage his hind legs more effectively for either pushing uphill or braking downhill.

Standing Body Balancing Exercise

To find out what your body does to stay balanced on hills, you should try it out on foot first. Find a hill steep enough so that the top of the hill is above eye level when you stand at the bottom and long enough for you walk up at least three steps.

Stand up straight on the level ground first, go through the seven steps to make sure you are centered and grounded, and look around you (figure 19.1a). See where your ankles are relative to your shoulders and how far it is to the ground directly in front of you. Go stand near the bottom of your hill so that you are on the slope but the hill is in front of you. Check your centering again and look again at your ankles and at the ground in front of you. Your ankles and shoulders will be in the same position relative to each other, but the ground in front of you is much closer (figure 19.1b). Now go up and stand on the slope near the top, facing down. Your ankles and shoulders will still be lined up, but the ground will appear to be much farther away (figure 19.1c). This makes your body feel that you have much farther to fall and is one of the reasons that downhill is scary.

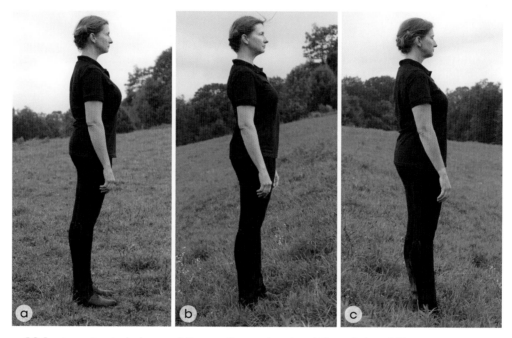

Figure 19.1 Learning to balance while standing on level, uphill, and downhill terrain.

Look at the three photos and notice how the person's body is always perpendicular to an imaginary horizontal. The angle of the ground might be upward, level, or downward, but the person's body remains the same. Only her feet adapt to the angle of the hill so that she can remain grounded.

Half-Seat Body Balancing Exercise

Go back to your hill, but now take a half-seat position (see chapter 14) so that your knees are moderately bent and you are leaning somewhat forward from the hip but still feel centered and grounded. Try this on the level, uphill, and downhill, keeping your knees bent about the same amount (figure 19.2). Be sure to keep your knees directly over your toes in all three positions. Notice how your upper-body angle has to change slightly to keep you in balance, that is, to keep your center over your feet.

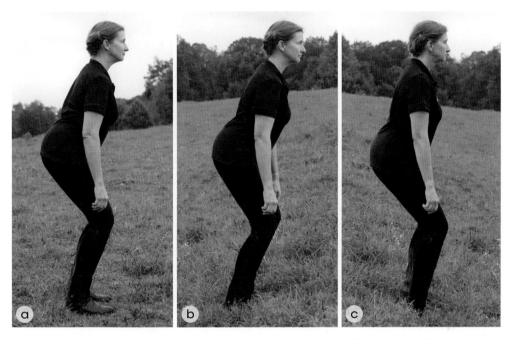

Figure 19.2   Learning to balance in half-seat position on level, uphill, and downhill terrain.

Also try going from half-seat position to standing upright, and sway forward and back a little bit. You'll find that if your center starts to move downhill, having your knees bent gives you much more security. Riding in a saddle that allows a shorter stirrup, and thus more bent knee, makes downhills a little easier.

You didn't have to think much about staying centered when you were standing on the hill because your body naturally found a position of comfortable balance. The difference when you're on the horse is that the stirrups swing forward and back. You can use this to your advantage to help you balance, but it requires an adjustment in your thinking about stirrups.

The tendency is to think that, since your feet aren't supposed to move around, the stirrups should always hang in the same place. Some saddles even have wedges on the back so your foot and the stirrup can't go back. However, when you are going uphill or downhill, in order for your stirrup leather to stay vertical, which is the only position in which they can safely support you, your stirrups must move forward or back from their normal position (figure 19.3).

Figure 19.3 Correct downhill leg position. The vertical stirrup leather and center are slightly behind the base.

To prepare your body for this while you are still on the ground, stand in half seat facing downhill, but let your body come back so that your knees are behind your toes. This is a very common error in riding downhill. It is the result of *pushing* on the stirrups, making them go out in front of you ahead of the vertical. You then have to lean farther forward in order to stand, and the result is a very insecure feeling. To avoid this, think to push your knees forward a bit, as though you were going to kneel.

Downhill Practice With a Partner

Most horses need some balancing support on the reins on the downhill if the hill is steep. To practice working with the horse to stay balanced, work with a partner and take turns using ropes or reins held in your hands, walking down the hill with one person being the horse and the other the rider. The "horse" should lean a little forward to mimic the balance of having a rider on her back, keeping her arms a little more in front of her and using the reins to balance herself. She should allow her arms to move moderately with the movement while the "rider" follows the movement and tries to help her. The "horse" can also rotate her upper body to one side for a few steps and then the other, as a horse will sometimes do on a long hill to give each side a little rest.

Working with a real horse in this way takes considerable skill by the rider, so you should avoid riding steep hills, except slowly on an experienced horse, until you have quite a few rides under your belt. If you are riding in an open area, and can do so without damaging crops, riding a zigzag pattern both up and down hill is easier for both horse and rider.

Let's go now to the horse and try the same exercises.

Riding Uphill in an English Saddle

As you begin riding hills, work on a hill that has a fairly steep part and then a less steep area so that you can learn more gradually. It should be long enough so that the horse can walk three or four strides up or down the hill but not much longer than that, especially where it is steep. If you're a little unsure of your control, have someone capable on the ground lead the horse so he can be stopped wherever you need him to be.

Riding Hills Bareback

You have to be careful if you're riding bareback up a steep hill, especially without a pad. It is quite easy to find yourself sliding off over the horse's tail! Try to avoid such situations. But if you have to try it, use the mane or grounding strap. If it becomes too difficult to stay on, slide off, walk up on foot, and remount at the top, using the hill to help you. This is a good reason not to ride alone!

On the uphill, your hands will be farther up the horse's neck than usual, so your grounding strap should be fixed so it will slide up his neck, or you can hold his mane instead. After you and the horse are warmed up, take up a half-seat position. If you're accustomed to riding with fairly long stirrups, try shortening them a hole or two to allow more bend in your knees.

Start on the level in half seat, standing still facing the hill at whatever degree of steepness you feel comfortable with. When you are ready, ride over to the hill and walk up it just far enough so that all four of the horse's feet are on the hill. Keeping your hands on the grounding strap or mane, find your balance such that your whole body, especially your legs and feet, feels secure and relaxed.

Relative to the saddle, your center will be farther forward and your feet farther back than they would be on the level, but a line dropped from your center to your bubbling spring will fall slightly behind the horse's center, as it should.

Now you're ready to walk up the hill. Go to a closed position with your hands pressing lightly on the horse's neck, but keep hold of the grounding strap as well. As the horse starts upward, depending on how steep the hill is, there might be quite a lot of thrust pushing you back—down the hill—even at the walk. When you feel this thrust, allow your hip joint to close so that your buttocks, rather than your shoulders, slide back. Your feet might go back as well so that you keep the alignment between center and base and the stirrup leather vertical (figure 19.4).

Figure 19.4   While riding uphill, the Western rider cannot lean as far forward and must use the cantle for some support. The English rider can lean forward and maintain her center over her stirrups.

Riding Downhill in an English Saddle

When you are learning to ride downhill, the hill should be very moderate in both length and steepness. A caution: If the hill seems long and steep to you, and especially if the horse shows any reluctance to go down it, dismount and lead him down to the bottom, then remount and ride him partway up—only as far as seems comfortable, and err on the side of caution—then turn right so you're facing across the hill. Go through your seven steps and get thoroughly comfortable before you turn to face downhill. If you still don't feel comfortable, ask for a hand leader to help the horse balance. If one is not available, dismount and find another hill or another horse, or try again another day.

When you feel ready, turn and face down the hill.

It is especially important when riding downhill to keep your eyes level and soft.

You must look straight out and let your soft eyes see where the hill is. Hold the grounding strap and do your centering and grounding. Make sure that your feet don't sneak out in front of your knees; that is, your knees should not feel as though they could lock, and your upper body should be nearly vertical (figure 19.5).

Now you're ready to walk down the hill. Because the horse is using his legs as brakes, downhill gaits tend to be more exaggerated or rougher, so your leg joints need to be very flexible. You should be particularly careful to keep your toes open and relaxed because curling your toes will make your ankles and thus the other joints much stiffer. You must also lean slightly forward to keep from getting thrown back by the horse's forward motion.

Figure 19.5 Correct position for riding downhill.

Polishing Your Skills

Work on both uphill and downhill in this step-by-step manner until you feel that you and the horse are fairly secure. Then you can work a large circle starting on the level, walking up the hill, then in a big turn on the level at the top, and finally back down the hill. If you have a perfect hill, you can use the moderately steep face for the uphill, the wide area at the top and bottom to rebalance and turn, and the gentle and longer slope on the side for the downhill. When you feel really secure, you can ride downhill across the steep face at an angle a few times. Then when you're ready, go straight down.

In some parts of the world it is necessary to get down slopes so steep that the horse, instead of moving at a normal gait, sits back on his haunches and slides until he reaches level ground at the bottom. These call for a different technique and training, and a horse that is accustomed to the work.

Handling Hills in a Western or Other Deep-Seated Saddle

Review the previous sections on riding hills in an English saddle so that you understand the underlying theory. For most hill work you will be able to follow the same procedures. However, if the hills are very steep you may have to adapt your position to keep both yourself and the horse in balance.

Although getting your weight off your seat when riding on steep hills is desirable from the point of view of saving the horse, depending on the style of the saddle it sometimes isn't practical in a Western saddle. This is one reason that Western saddles use much thicker padding than English saddles. Staying seated is necessary partly because the shape of the Western saddle seat is intended to keep you in one place, with your upper body vertical over your seat bones. In addition, the fenders of a Western saddle should, but again, depending on the individual saddle, might not, allow for the forward-and-back movement of the stirrups necessary for using your feet for support on the hill as you would in an English saddle. Instead, you remain in full seat or a light three-quarter seat, with your weight distributed between your feet and your seat bones. With your leg soft and relaxed, your leg weight rests on the stirrup, keeping you from losing it without requiring any muscular effort. Having a relaxed leg also allows your leg to find a naturally correct position as much under your center as possible. Avoid using muscular effort to push on the stirrup because it tends to lift you off the saddle—and possibly off the horse!

Because you are in something closer to full seat, some of your shock absorption must be taken up in your lumbar spine, which should be kept as long and loose as possible. For this reason, growing is a very important part of your warm-up for hill work. Your spine is most flexible when it is neither arched nor rounded; either position tends to lock it. Remember that as the horse moves your body, your lumbar area moves forward and back to absorb the movement, and it does that best when it is allowed to take the position that is the natural result of the growing exercise.

Riding Uphill in the Western Saddle

You can follow the same procedure described earlier in the chapter, both on the ground and starting the hill work. If your saddle restricts your leg movement, modify your position. Start with an easy uphill, keeping your seat bones lightly on the saddle and closing your hip angle as much as necessary or as much as is possible with the horn. As the uphills get steeper, if you feel that your abdomen is getting uncomfortably close to the horn, draw your navel back toward your spine and allow your back to round as much as is comfortable and necessary. Since uphill riding has very little jolt to it, the slight loss of flexibility in your lumbar spine shouldn't be noticeable.

Keep your hands, especially your rein hand, well out in front of you to allow your horse full use of his head and neck. This also prevents you from accidentally catching the horse on the mouth. Drawing your hand back will make you curl up more. You can use your other hand on the horn or swell or even the mane for support if needed.

Riding Downhill in the Western Saddle

On a steep downhill, you can stay in an almost full seat, letting your legs hang naturally with just a light pressure on the stirrup. Keep your eyes soft and looking outward rather than down, especially if you have any fear of height. If that is the case, use the seven steps both before and during the descent. Use your hand on the horn to help keep your body upright; stay very tall, and allow your seat to follow as freely as possible. If the bit or hackamore you are using is very mild, and if you have sufficient skills, offering some light following hand support will help the horse to balance and ground.

Putting Your Skills to Good Use

When you go out trail riding in unfamiliar country, never ride at speed where you can't see what's ahead of you. Unless both you and the horse are very skillful, it can be dangerous if you find yourself at the top of a steep hill while galloping without room to stop or turn away.

In most areas, hill-riding skills are necessary in order for you and your horse to get the greatest possible enjoyment out of trail riding. The benefits are worth the time it takes to learn to do it well.

20

Jumping Made Easy

Jumping is in many ways much less complicated than most people think. To begin with, you have to know how to *tell* the horse to do all the other basic things— walk, trot, canter, turn, and stop—on command. But, except in very advanced dressage, it's not possible to teach him to *jump* on command. For all practical purposes, what makes a horse jump is the jump itself, and the jump and the horse must be in a position such that it is easier for him to jump it than go around it.

If there is no jump, he won't leave the ground, so getting him to leave the ground is not your problem. Your goal is simply to keep the horse balanced and going down the line that includes the jump. If you do so, by the time you get to the other end, the horse will have jumped the jump because the jump is there. If he stumbles just in front of it, he might crash through it, and there is nothing you can do about it. You sometimes read about the rider "lifting" the horse over the fence. This simply can't be done.

What you want to learn about jumping, then, is not how to make the horse do it but how to stay out of his way so he can jump as effectively as possible. The first rule of riding is to avoid doing anything that interferes with the horse's balance. This applies double to jumping. The two elements that most affect the horse's balance are your center—including your weight—and the reins.

The reason that we covered riding hills in the previous chapter, before explaining jumping, is that jumping involves the same forces as does going up and down a hill. The horse's body goes up, levels out, and goes down. However, it all happens quite quickly, and if the jump is high the forces are quite strong.

Phases of the Jump

The jump is made up of five phases: approach, liftoff, flight, landing, and departure.

Approach
The horse ideally goes toward the jump at a steady pace. The forces on your body are just the normal thrusts of the gait, which you have learned to adjust to and stay centered during. The speed is dependent on the height of the jump and the horse's power and skill. A slower approach is better for most purposes because it allows more time for adjusting the takeoff distance, which should be approximately equal to the height of the jump.

Liftoff
This phase begins when the horse brings his forehand up. He must bring it up high enough so that his front legs will clear the jump. This is the most crucial moment; if he is too close during liftoff or too far away or not high enough, he will catch his front legs on the jump. If it doesn't give way, he will take a scary and perhaps dangerous fall. When it's done right, his front feet hit

the ground, and then he uses the power of his front legs, shoulders, and back muscles to lift his forehand into the air. Only after his front legs are off the ground do his hind legs come down ahead of where the front legs left the ground.

Flight

The horse uses his hindquarters to thrust his entire body forward. Since his body is tilted upward, when it goes forward it also goes up and over the jump.

Landing

Gravity brings the horse's body down on the other side of the jump. His front legs hit the ground and then quickly come off the ground and start to move forward as the hind legs come down somewhat farther forward than where the front legs hit.

Departure

The horse usually takes a stride or two after landing to recover his balance completely, then continues as before.

To stay centered over the horse, you need to understand the thrusts that occur during the jump. During the liftoff, the horse changes direction; rather than go straight forward, he turns to go upward. Because of the laws of inertia, your body tends to continue forward, so *the thrust during liftoff is forward*. When he pushes off into flight, he starts suddenly in the new direction (upward), so *the thrust pushes your body back*. Finally, when he lands, going from downward to forward again, it stops him briefly, but your body again tends to continue the way it was going, so *relative to the horse you are being thrust forward*. Forward, back, forward: These are the thrusts you have to deal with to keep from interfering with the horse's balance as he jumps.

Staying Centered During the Jump

When I was teaching jumping initially, the usual method was to teach riders to go forward at the moment when the horse took off into the flight. This was supposed to keep the rider from being left behind, that is, falling back with her upper body and landing heavily on the horse's back. Needless to say, this degree of timing is very difficult to teach and results in many mistakes and refusals—stopping suddenly in front of the jump—as the horse loses his balance when the rider goes forward too soon.

Over time, and through many sources, I found other and better ways to teach jumping, finally putting together a system that makes jumping moderate-sized fences an easy skill to learn. We're not talking about jumping in advanced competitions or over very high fences, because those require specialized horses and more complex skills. We're just talking about jumping moderate-sized fences such as you might meet on the trail—fences that any sound horse can handle easily.

> In order for the horse to jump successfully, *you must ride him in such a way that you don't interfere with his ability to balance with either your center and weight or the reins.*

In spite of what you might have read about jumping, you do not go forward (ahead of the horse's center) when the horse jumps. In fact, it is the most dangerous thing that you can do. As emphasized throughout this book, because of the support provided by the horse's hind legs, getting *behind* his center almost never will get you in serious trouble as long as you stay more or less in the saddle, because it doesn't unbalance him. Getting *ahead* of his center will always cause him problems with his balance, which will certainly affect his ability to jump and might cause him to fall.

What you will learn to do when you jump is amazingly simple: You stay back the entire time! Yes, that's what I said: You stay back the entire time. And no, that is not the same as getting left behind and hurting the horse.

Here's what happens: When you approach the jump, you take a slightly closed position (see Half-Seat Closed Position in chapter 14) with your knuckles resting on the horse's neck (figure

20.1*a*). You use your hands, holding the grounding strap and pressing forward on his neck, to keep you from going forward during the liftoff (figure 20.1*b*). When he goes into flight, your body is pushed back, *and you allow it to go back just the way it did when you rode uphill!* That is, your hip angle closes and your hips slide back (figure 20.1*c*). When he starts down at the end of the flight, your body will instinctively rebalance itself by opening your hip angle as your legs find the downhill position relative to the horse (figure 20.1*d*). When he lands, your hands, still on his neck and aided by your downhill leg and body position, will keep you from falling forward until he moves off and the thrusts become the normal thrusts of the gait (figure 20.1*e*).

Figure 20.1 The phases of the jump are (*a*) approach, (*b*) liftoff, (*c*) flight, (*d*) landing, and (*e*) departure.

Just as when you were riding downhill, it is important when the horse's motion is throwing you forward that you don't push your feet forward. This would cause your upper body to have to *lean* forward too much in order to stay centered over your feet. If this occurs during the takeoff, since your hip angle is already closed, it leaves you no place to go when he begins the flight. If it occurs as he begins the landing, being too far forward could be dangerous if the horse should land badly. If you think to push your knees forward as though you were going to kneel, it will keep your feet where they belong.

Teaching Your Body to Ride the Jump

Learning and practicing your position over jumps begin with cavaletti: poles placed on the ground or just above it, spaced so that as the horse trots over them he takes one step in between (about 4 feet or 1.2 m). He doesn't jump them, but you begin to feel the basics of the thrusts of liftoff, flight, and landing as he takes a high step over each pole. In the beginning the poles should be placed in a jump lane so that steering is not an issue (figure 20.2).

Figure 20.2 Cavaletti and jump lane.

Begin the exercise by working for a few minutes in a lightly closed position at the trot. If your horse responds to voice commands or you can hold your position comfortably while you use a rein aid, do some upward and downward transitions. Focus on not allowing your center to move forward as the horse slows down and allowing your hips to close and slide back as he speeds up. You will use your legs and feet as well, pushing your knees forward on the downward transitions to prevent your feet from sliding forward. The goal is to develop your awareness of the slightest change forward in your centering and instantly correct it. With practice, your body will do this without any conscious thought on your part.

Jump Lane Exercises

When you are ready, review the seven steps, continue your trot in the same position, and direct your horse into the jump lane. Use soft eyes and intent, focusing on riding at a steady pace to the far end and keeping your center behind the horse's throughout. You'll feel a little bounce at each pole, but otherwise it should feel smooth and steady. After a few lessons, when you're ready, you can add a wide, low—about 8 inches (20 cm)— crossbar after the last

Figure 20.3 Cavaletti and crossbar.

pole, leaving a distance in between equal to that between two poles (figure 20.3). The horse should just give a little hop over it and continue to trot.

When you are thoroughly comfortable at the trot and over the cavaletti and small crossbar, which may take a bit of time, the next step is to start working in closed position at the canter, focusing especially on staying centered longitudinally as you did at the trot. Since the jump stride is very similar to the canter stride except for the height, getting comfortable at the canter will make following the jump easier. Again, work on transitions, keeping centered with your eyes and knees soft through the changes.

Now you're ready for something a little more like a jump. Use a jump lane with a series of cavaletti but with a slightly higher crossbar, about 18 inches (45 cm). Begin at the trot. Then as you approach the crossbar, think about asking for a canter on the landing. Just being a little stronger with your center and perhaps using a cluck or voice command just before takeoff should be enough because the jump stride is so similar to the canter stride. Allow the horse to continue in the canter for a few strides or until you feel balanced.

When this step is easy and smooth, add a second obstacle (figure 20.4). It should follow the first crossbar by a space large enough to allow the horse to take two comfortable cantering strides. For the average horse, 28 feet (8.5 m) works well, but somebody experienced should set it up and perhaps try it with your horse to make sure it will be easy for him and smooth for you. The second obstacle should be a more substantial crossbar around 2 feet (0.6 m) high.

Figure 20.4 Cavaletti and two crossbars.

You should practice this exercise for some time until you can literally do it with your eyes closed—a very good exercise. Move the jump lane around regularly so that it is in different places in the arena to keep the ground from getting too dug up around the jumps and so that you and the horse practice jumping in both directions. When jumping small fences feels as smooth and easy as galloping, you're ready to move ahead.

Trusting the Horse

The thing that makes jumping tricky is if the horse approaches the jump badly so that he jumps awkwardly. The goal is finding the right spot, the place at which the horse must leave the ground to jump easily and smoothly. And he has to get to that spot with the right impulsion, which is a combination of speed and power in good balance at the end of a stride, when his front feet hit the ground. So, how do you help the horse do all that? The answer is, unless you're very advanced, you don't! You let the horse figure it out.

Next question: How does the horse learn to find the spot for himself? He learns from the same exercise that you've been using: by placing a series of jumps in such a way that he gets to each jump at the proper spot. The cavaletti bring the horse to the first crossbar at the right spot, which places him for the second one. You can then add one more, perhaps a small oxer at perhaps 30 feet (9 m), but again, ask for help to get the correct distance.

An oxer is made of two obstacles very close together so that the horse jumps them as one. The first part of the obstacle can be something as simple as the cross bar shown here, a set of poles placed vertically, or a more solid obstacle such as a box painted to resemble a stone wall. The second part of the obstacle is always a single pole, either the same height or higher than the first part (figure 20.5). By making the fence wider, the horse makes more of an effort without having to jump higher. Notice in the photos that all the fences have a ground line, that is, a pole or other objects on the ground directly in front of the fence. The horse uses the ground line to judge his takeoff distance.

As long as the horse jumps smoothly, once you've had quite a bit of practice so that your body knows what to do, you can gradually increase the size of the jumps, increasing the distance between them as well. Correct distances are crucial for this learning experience, so be sure you get them right. You must take into account your horse's skill and experience, but it's useful to know that any sound horse can easily jump a simple four-foot (1.2 m) fence.

After plenty of practice, the horse develops an eye for distance, and you develop confidence in him. At that point you move away from the jump lane and set up small single fences around the arena with plenty of room for him in each approach to adjust his stride. The hard thing for *you* is learning to mind your own business, which is to ride the horse and not try to second-guess his knowledge about the takeoff spot. Looking beyond the jump to the end of the line you are riding keeps you focusing on that instead of the jump itself, which, as you now know, is the horse's problem. If you just think about using the seven steps to keep yourself steady and

Figure 20.5 Cavaletti, two crossbars, and an oxer.

Take Care of the Canter

Some time ago I was riding in a clinic with a local show-jumping professional. The horse I was riding seemed to have a lot of trouble finding good spots to jump from. I began to realize that the problem might be that he was quite awkward at the canter in the rather small arena. I started to focus on just helping him with his canter and trying to keep him balanced and not worrying about the takeoff spots. He got to some of the jumps a bit close and some a bit far away, so it didn't seem like a very consistent round to me. But when we finished, the instructor was very enthusiastic and said it was the best round she had seen the horse do. By keeping the canter consistent, the jumps also appeared consistent. I have since used that technique with great success on other horses.

balanced, he can do the same. The only things you should say to the horse are to keep going (that's intent and center) and where to go (eyes and intent and turning aids if needed). It is important to plan so that you don't have to do any steering for the last two or three strides, when the horse needs to be undisturbed. Singing or counting in rhythm with his gait as you canter along helps you to focus on his movement instead of on the jump.

At this stage, you are jumping several jumps that are spread out. Instead of staying in a slightly closed position the whole time, with your hands pressing on the horse's neck, after each jump you straighten up to a more open position (figure 20.6), which allows you to use your rein aids more easily. Then when you get the next jump lined up, you quietly close your position and just think about keeping going.

Figure 20.6 Proper position when riding between individual fences.

Giving the Horse His Head

When the jumps are fairly low, an experienced horse doesn't need to stretch his head and neck very much. Just moving your hands forward to where they function as a comfortable support for your closed position will make the reins loose enough. However, when the jumps get larger or more difficult in terms of either shape or location—such as up or downhill—the horse might need more freedom to extend his neck and head. Very experienced riders can follow the horse's head movement throughout the jump, but for most people it's enough to learn how to release the reins without losing position.

This movement is called a crest release because you slide your hands up the horse's crest. Many riders misunderstand this release: Instead of moving just the hands forward, they go forward with the whole body, which of course brings the rider's center ahead of the horse's. This makes it far more difficult for the horse to jump well and can easily lead to a fall for either rider or horse.

The correct way to perform the crest release is to *use the forward thrust of your hands to help you push your center back.* That is, as you push forward with your hands, you push back with your hips at the same time, using your lower leg as well to assist the backward movement (don't forget about your knees!). You used this move when you learned closed position (see Closed-Hip Exercise in chapter 14). Allow your hands to *slide up* the horse's neck, *not push down* on it.

Even if you don't expect to jump bigger fences, the crest release is a useful skill to have in case your horse takes an awkward fence, which can happen to the best of them. If you practice a small crest release over the jumps you are comfortable with, your body will be able to adapt nicely if the need arises.

Jumping Courses

A jump course is a series of jumps placed to form a pattern. The simplest one is twice around, which consists of two fences on each long side of the arena, with about four strides in between the two. The rider starts at one end. After performing a warm-up circle at the trot, rider and horse continue around the arena, usually at the canter, over all four fences and then continue a second time, finishing by returning to the trot and perhaps circling again before leaving the arena.

More difficult courses have jumps in various locations around the arena, in the center as well as on the rail, with turns of varying degrees of difficulty, and combinations of jumps requiring greater athletic ability of the horse.

The way to think about courses is the same way you have learned to think about individual fences. That is, the horse does the jumping. Your job is to make it easy for him. That means you have to plan where you are going to go so that the horse has the best chance to do each jump well. Obviously the more difficult courses require a very experienced team of horse and rider to be successful. But if you have learned to jump single jumps well, simple courses are not out of reach.

The best way to learn about courses is to lay out a "jumpless" course. That is, you place jump standards or other markers to represent fences. You can put a rail on the ground for each jump if you like, but it isn't necessary. You can add cones at what I like to call the go point—the point, usually about two strides away, at which you have to turn over control to the horse. You ride around first at the walk or trot between the jump standards or markers, treating them as though they were jumps. You try to get a good approach to each one, which means figuring out how to plan your turns toward each line of jumps so that you can become almost passive at the go point. When you and the horse are comfortable at the practice gaits, you can go the canter, then set up small crossbars and other obstacles in between your markers.

Refusals and Runouts

When the horse doesn't take the jump he is headed at, it is known as a refusal or runout. A refusal occurs when the horse stops dead in front of the fence; a runout is when he runs by the fence on one side or the other.

What should you do about these behaviors? First rule: *Do not ever punish him.* It is always easier for a half-ton horse traveling at 15 miles per hour or more to keep going straight ahead than to swerve or stop suddenly (remember the four-foot rule). You have to figure out what went wrong to make him decide that he would rather make the extreme effort to refuse than to keep going.

> Olympic Grand Prix gold-medal winner William Steinkraus told me that he never asked a horse to jump a fence that he wasn't absolutely sure the horse could jump safely and well. As a result, his horse trusted his judgement completely and approached every obstacle with confidence in their ability to succeed.

Causes of Refusals

The most common cause is rider error, which means doing something that disturbs the horse's balance or grounding when it's too late to recover, which makes him feel he can't get over the fence. The most frequent error is jumping ahead of the horse, that is, allowing your weight to go forward just before takeoff in anticipation of the jump. But since you have learned to stay back at all times, this should not be a problem. However, if the horse has been ridden by someone who frequently made that mistake, the horse might anticipate it and require some retraining in confidence building.

If you learned to jump incorrectly so that your body has developed a go-forward reflex that you can't get past, the section titled Jumping for Western Riders later in this chapter should help you through the difficulty.

The second common error is called dropping the horse. This usually occurs with horses that tend to approach the jump too fast for a variety of reasons. The rider, in an attempt to slow the horse down, takes a heavy hold on the reins (hangs on his mouth). When she feels him starting to lift off, she quickly loosens the reins. Since the horse was leaning on the reins, he loses his balance and stops.

Other common causes include the following:

- Facing an inexperienced horse at a jump that is unusual either in shape or in the material used, such as flower baskets as a ground line. The horse is so busy trying to figure out what the object is that he isn't prepared to jump it. For this reason an inexperienced horse should be allowed plenty of time to inspect new obstacles. He should also be introduced to many types and shapes of obstacles at low heights.

- Getting to the jump at a very awkward spot. If this happens, start your next approach from a different place, or plan your turn differently.

- Slipping or stumbling badly just before liftoff. Use judgment to determine whether or not it is safe to try again.

Causes of Runouts

The same conditions that cause refusals can also cause run-outs. This is particularly true with horses that have difficulty stopping. However, there is nearly always a lateral imbalance of some kind as well.

Either the rider is not laterally centered, making the horse feel awkward, or, more commonly, the rider hangs on one rein so the horse pulls the other way to get his balance. The horse might also use the rein pull to help turn away because he feels the lateral imbalance and does not want to jump (see the section titled the Holding Hand in chapter 18).

Frequently you get a cause and effect wherein the rider expects the horse to run out to one side and hangs on the opposite rein, unwittingly making it both necessary and easy for the horse to run out. Working on your lateral centering and the uses of the active and holding reins helps in these cases. However, you should keep in mind that if you feel the need to steer the horse in the last two strides in order to get him to jump, there is some other problem that you need to address. For example, a horse that is unsure of his jumping skills might tense up in front of the fence, shortening stride and cramping his body into a crooked position, which leads him into a runout. The solution is to work on both your and the horse's lateral balance, including the rein balance. Work first on the flat and then over small fences until the horse gains confidence.

Jumping for Western Riders

Jumping is not something normally done in a Western saddle, but if you trail ride, there are occasions when a small obstacle blocks the trail. If you compete in trail classes, there are often one or more jumps in the pattern. In either case it's useful to be able to ride over the jump safely and competently.

If the fences are low, and depending on the conformation of both rider and saddle, the techniques used above can be adapted for jumping in a western or other deep seated saddle. You still use a closed position, but it is modified to allow for the length of your stirrups and the height of the pommel, just as you did on the hills.

However there is a second technique which can be used for almost any situation. You might, for example, be faced with a largish ditch which the horse will certainly jump, but which might be difficult to handle in the more open position required by the saddle. It is also a good exercise for anyone who has a preexisting tendency to jump ahead of the horse (throw the body forward).

Jumping in a Western saddle is based on the same principle we have been talking about: When you jump, you stay back the whole time. The difference is that in an English saddle you can go back in closed position, and this is somewhat limited in a Western saddle because of the horn.

Up until the early 20th century, there was no such thing as the forward position over jumps. Everybody rode to the fence in full seat, sitting up straight or even leaning a little back. When the horse jumped and threw you back as he began the flight, you swayed back with your shoulders instead of your hips. This is now called the backward seat as opposed to the forward seat. Correct backward seat is still used in some countries in steeplechases (a race over large solid obstacles).

Backward seat is not the same as getting left behind, where the rider's body comes crashing back onto the horse, causing him severe discomfort and even causing his hindquarters to land on the fence. Getting left behind occurs when the rider, approaching the jump in half seat, *allows her body to fall forward—that is, allows her hip joint to close—when the horse starts the liftoff*. Then when the backward thrust comes along a second later, her body is out of control and gets thrown violently back. In normal correct jumping, the force that throws you back is not severe. It's the getting ahead followed by getting thrown back that creates the violent result. If you are riding in a Western saddle in full seat, resisting the forward thrust (that is, not getting ahead of the horse's center) is quite easy because you can use your hands on the horn in the same way as the English rider in closed position uses her hands on the horse's neck. If you are trying to correct a tendency to jump ahead of the horse, you can ride to the fence in open three-quarter seat, leaning back a little and holding your grounding strap firmly. Working with only small fences, you can change your body's reflex from jumping ahead to staying back. Having your seat securely in the saddle makes a strong position, and your stirrups are of some help as well.

It is essential to make sure that your reins are quite loose. With your hands on the horn, if the horse should take an awkward jump or stumble, he could receive a severe jab on the mouth, which would hurt him at the time and possibly affect any future attempts at jumping. If your approach to the go point is correct, your gentle aids should be enough to take him over the jump.

You can use all the same practice techniques for learning to jump in an English saddle that are described earlier in this chapter to practice jumping in the Western saddle. Begin by working on transitions between the walk and jog, allowing your body to sway back when the horse increases pace, but *not* allowing it to sway forward when he decreases pace.

The next step is the cavaletti and jump lane (see the Jump Lane Exercises section earlier in this chapter). When you set up the cavaletti, they should be spaced at a distance that is comfortable for the horse to take one step between them in his natural jog stride. Begin with the walk so the horse gets accustomed to stepping over the poles. At the jog, your lower back needs to be firm to prevent your hip joint from closing but still flexible so that you can stay seated, not bounce up off the saddle. If you should do so, and your feet are under your center, your body should recover just as it does when you post.

Continue the jumping exercises as described for the English saddle and progress through the practice jumps. How high you decide to jump depends on how softly you can sit as the effort becomes greater. Just remember that the horse feels in his back every bump that you feel in your seat.

Whatever your discipline, jumping within your skill range is fun for both horse and rider. If you learn it correctly, it's not at all frightening for either you or your horse. As with other aspects of riding, you'll be glad you put in the time and effort to learn to do it well.

Conclusion

The previous chapters have given you most of the tools you need in order to ride a trained horse and get the results you want. As you continue to practice and improve, you will face situations in which you can apply the lessons you learned here. You will also learn more as you continue to ride. I have been riding and teaching for many, many years, and I still learn something every time I teach or work with a horse.

Let's talk a little more about the learning process and how to think about it.

You begin by *learning about* a new task or skill. It is explained to you or demonstrated so you get the idea. But you still have a lot of questions about the procedure.

When you can perform the task without having to ask any more questions about the steps, you have *learned* it. When you can perform the task without having to think about the steps at all (that is, your right brain has worked it out so that the task is now a reflex), you *know* it. And finally, when you have performed the task or used the skill with many horses and situations so that you know its uses and benefits and how it works, you *understand* it.

In this book, you have *learned about* a number of things to do with horseback riding. With time and practice I hope you will *learn* and eventually *know* most if not all of them and *understand* many of them. And if you continue to ride, you will constantly learn about much, much more—which is the way it should be. Just try to remember that learning about is only the first step.

There's a saying that goes right along with this: "The only stupid question is the one you should have asked but didn't."

The Horse Already Knows What to Do

That is, he was born knowing how to walk, trot, canter, turn, stop, and jump. Your goal is learning not how to *make* him do these things but how to make what you want him to do both obvious and easy. Of course, as you practice something—correctly, of course—the horse begins to know what you want, and that in itself makes the task easier. Conversely, if you ask him in ways that make it hard for him, he will anticipate that and be more resistant.

Break It Down

Break down each new lesson into as many steps as necessary. For example, if you want to learn to make voltes (small circles 6 meters in diameter), you would begin with large, simple turns of 90 degrees or less in the horse's easy direction. Once those are smooth and correct, you would start making more extended turns and sharper turns and work in both directions, but not all at the same time. If you ran into difficulties, then you would try to analyze the problem. Did you try to progress too quickly? Were your aids not quite correct? Does the horse perhaps have a soundness problem that shows up only under this particular stress?

One of the most basic rules is "If it isn't easy for both of you, it isn't right." If you keep that thought at the front of your mind whenever you are trying something with your horse, whether it's new or old work, you will never go very far wrong.

Use Punishment Sparingly and Correctly

Up to now we have never mentioned punishing the horse, except to say don't do it. Most of the time, you can deal with undesirable behavior by following the cardinal rule of horse training: If you want the horse to do something, you make it the easiest, most desirable thing to do. That's why, throughout this book, we describe techniques that make the correct performance easy for the horse. In addition, you have to study all situations of misbehavior in some depth to make sure that the behavior is not in *expectation* of punishment or the result of clumsy handling or riding. You don't want to punish him for something he doesn't understand or can't help doing.

But occasionally you run across a horse that either has learned that he can do something that he knows he isn't supposed to do and does it without provocation, or is trying something out to see how you respond. It's usually something that no one has ever told him he shouldn't do—something that is just naughty. This sort of behavior is usually found in very young horses that haven't learned the boundaries yet. Sometimes it is found in slightly older horses that were brought up more or less alone, so there were no mature horses around to teach them social graces.

When we speak of punishment, it should *never* cause the horse any real pain. At the most, it should cause some discomfort. You must also apply it in such a way that he can instantly relate to the behavior you are trying to correct.

The problem with disciplining a horse is that you can't tell him that he has to give up watching TV for a week; nor can you put him in a time-out. So how can you make him realize that you won't accept his behavior without frightening him or perhaps making him angry?

If you watch horses in a herd, you can see that occasionally one horse lets another horse know in no uncertain terms that his behavior is unacceptable. For example, geldings like to play a lot of rather rough games, which involve grabbing of halters, striking, and making playful noises. It can go on for some time with mutual enjoyment. But sometimes, one of the horses will play a little too rough and hurt the other horse. Horse 1, who has been hurt, will express his displeasure with a loud, angry squeal, followed by wheeling and perhaps kicking, but not with the intention of making serious contact. He will then walk away in a huff: "I'm going to take my ball and go home. So there!" Horse 2 gets out of the way quickly and looks a little unsure and wistful, and they both start to graze. Then after a few minutes, they go back to their game.

So what do we learn from the way horses interact with other horses that they like and trust? The intention of horse 1 is to make his feelings about horse 2's *behavior* absolutely clear, but he doesn't want to actually hurt him or lose the friendship and trust. Your intent should be the same. Not "I'm really mad at you and I'm going to punish you so it hurts and you remember." Rather, "What you're doing makes me uncomfortable, and I want you to know that and not do it anymore."

The best kind of discipline is the kind that occurs in such a way that the horse associates it with what he did and doesn't associate you with it at all. For example, a friend was showing me a horse she was looking at, and we decided to take him out to the arena and watch him move. As I led him down the aisle toward the arena, I was carrying a little crop in my other hand, which I had been waving up and down in front of his face to act as a barrier because I was aware of his desire to speed up. For most horses, that is sufficient for keeping them from trying to pass. However, he suddenly sped up and started to charge past me in anticipation of being turned loose. There was no room in the aisle to quickly circle him—the move of choice in this situation—so I bopped him on nose with the butt end of the crop, right in the middle of his nose where it isn't very sensitive. Not very hard, just hard enough to surprise him. He was looking at the arena and never saw the stick at all, but it made him think he had run into something. It

Mares Don't Want to Have Fun

It's worth knowing that geldings in the same herd who know each other well nearly all play harmless games with each other. They pretend to bite, strike, and kick, but always in fun. Mares, on the other hand, while they have friendly relationships with one another, do not play fighting games. When a mare is unhappy with another horse and wants to warn her, she will usually make a face or turn her tail, but she will not approach another horse in the playfully aggressive way that geldings will. You have to be thoughtful and observant when putting horses of both genders out in groups. Like people, not everyone gets along with everyone else, and new horses especially have to be introduced to the group very gradually.

surprised him just enough so he didn't want to do it again. Not knowing where the force came from, he decided to play it safe and let me lead.

Sometimes, however, you want the horse to know that he must respect you and your space, usually for safety reasons. As your handling skills improve, the times when the horse can take over will become very few. In addition, there are lots of ways to create and earn his respect, which involve a solid knowledge of horses' body language and communication methods. As you get deeper into riding, you should look into these (see the appendix at http://tinyurl.com/d8pv7nz for resources).

There are very few circumstances in which you need to punish the horse. Here is the only one I can think of offhand: I was working with a young horse I knew quite well, and we had become good buddies. I was grooming him and talking with his owner about his work, standing just in front of his shoulder. He picked up the front foot nearest me and put it down, and I didn't pay much attention. A minute or so later, as we continued talking, he picked up his foot and reached out with it a little before putting it down, which caught my attention, but I continued to ignore him. Another pause, and he picked up the foot again. This time he reached out with it more, so it was very close to a strike—a blow with the front foot, which geldings often use when playing together. I instantly slapped him on the neck hard enough to make a noise but not hard enough to hurt my hand, much less his neck, and said, "No!" very firmly. He gave me this very sheepish "I guess you don't want me to do that" look. I then patted him, gave him a little scratch on his withers, and told him I was sorry. He never tried it again.

Just to clarify, one of the things that horses, especially geldings, have to learn is that humans are much slower and more fragile than horses are, so the horse has to treat humans accordingly. A horse that strikes at a human, even in play, can cause serious injury. That was the only reason for the punishment. While the horse didn't understand that, he did understand that it wasn't acceptable. And we remained friends.

Love, Trust, and Respect Your Horse

The bond between you and the horse is really what it is all about. The people who get the most enjoyment out of riding, and whose horses are usually the happiest, are the people who have a good relationship with their horses. In a relationship based on love, trust, and respect, neither one wants the other ever to be hurt.

Glossary

active hand—A hand effect that asks the horse to yield to a soft pull on the rein by using careful timing and releasing as soon as the horse indicates discomfort by pulling. The soft pull and release may be repeated until the desired response is achieved.

aids—The various ways in which a rider communicates with a horse while riding. Listed alphabetically, they are the center, eyes, intent, legs, reins, seat, stick, voice, and weight.

backward seat—A jumping exercise to prevent a rider from going forward with her center. It is based on a 19th-century jumping technique.

bad hands—Using the reins in a way that interfers with the horse and causes him to resist.

bareback pad—A thick pad used without a saddle or stirrups, to enable the rider to find balance and relaxation using her center. It is fastened to the horse using a surcingle or attached girth and a breastplate.

bight—The extra rein at the buckle or knot end that hangs loose from the hands when the reins are being held for riding.

bit—A device, usually of metal, placed in the horse's mouth. The bit enables the rider, via the reins, to help the horse to balance and ground. It is also a means of communication.

box stall—A large rectangular stall, usually 10 by 10 feet (3 by 3 m), entered through a door or gate.

breastplate—A device that fits in front of the horse's shoulders, fastens to the saddle or pad, and prevents it from sliding back.

bridging the reins—Holding the bight ends of one (half bridge) or both (full bridge) reins in the opposite hand. This allows the rider to remove one hand and ride with both reins in the other.

bridle—A harness, usually leather, that fits over the horse's head and holds the bit in the horse's mouth.

bubbling spring—The point on the underside of the ball of the foot that must be in contact with the stirrup when riding in order for the rider to be grounded.

canter—See gaits.

cavaletti (singular, cavaletto)—Poles placed on the ground or just above it and spaced so that as the horse trots over them he takes one step in between.

centering—Maintaining balance by moving the physical center of the body, located in the pelvis, as necessary to keep it over the base, which would be the seat bones when sitting or the bubbling spring when standing. It also keeps the rider's center over the horse's center as he moves.

cinch—The strap used to hold a Western saddle on the horse that fastens under the horse's belly. It is made of thick string and has a large loop or buckle that fastens with a strap and a special knot.

cinchy—A state of discomfort and resistance in a horse when the cinch or girth is too tight.

collection (gaits)— A shorter, higher step in the gait without a decrease in tempo.

combing the rein or lead rope—A hand effect used on a horse that is afraid of rein pressure. It involves sliding one hand at a time up the reins or rope so that the contact stays very soft and elastic and the horse does not feel the restriction of a steady pull.

counterbend—Having the horse's body bent in the opposite direction to the turn he is making, or, in the arena, the direction in which he is traveling, for example, bending his body to the right when moving left hand around.

crest release—Moving the hands forward while pressing the body backward to keep the rider centered during the jump and giving additional freedom to the horse's head for balance.

crossbar—An obstacle consisting of two poles each with one end raised on a support to form an x shape. Often it is used as a small obstacle for training

crossties—Ropes or straps fastened to a post on each side of the place where a horse stands to be groomed or otherwise worked with on the ground. Each crosstie has a snap on the end which is fastened to the ring on the side of the horse's halter. Crossties discourage the horse from moving around unnecessarily.

croup—The highest part of the horse's hindquarters.

crowding—Occurs when a horse pushes against a person who is trying to walk past him into the stall, trapping the person against the wall.

curb bit—More commonly used in Western riding, but also used in English riding with a snaffle to form a double or full bridle. The curb has a single rein ring on either side that is attached at the end of a shank fastened to the mouthpiece. It has a chain or strap under the horse's chin. It acts on the horse's bars, chin, and poll to create lowering of the head and flexion.

dead to the leg—Unresponsive to leg aids.

diagonals—In the posting trot, refers to the diagonal pair of legs (one front and the opposite hind) that move up and down in synchrony with the post. Diagonals are named by the front leg, i.e. the right diagonal would be right front and left hind. Generally when riding in an arena, the rider posts on the outside diagonal.

direct rein of opposition—A rein effect in which the pull is straight back along the line of the horse's path as opposed to out to either side.

dropping the horse—Describes a situation, usually in jumping, where the rider is using a heavy contact on the reins, causing the horse to be leaning against them. The rider drops the horse by suddenly releasing the rein pressure as the horse is preparing to take off, causing him to lose his balance and either to stop or to jump dangerously.

English riding—Using an English saddle, tack, and attire; so named because the sport was brought to the east coast of the United States by English settlers. An English saddle has a smoothly curved seat, long wide flaps down the sides and thick padded panels under the seat. The stirrups are made of metal and hang from long narrow straps. Many different and diverse disciplines use an English saddle.

extension (gaits)—A flatter, longer stride in the gait, without an increase in tempo.

fender—On a Western saddle, the wide leather strap that holds up the stirrup and protects the rider's leg from chafing.

fixed hand—The most advanced hand effect. The rider sets her hand so that it doesn't quite follow the horse's movement, creating a release-and-take effect like a very small active hand action.

fixed leg—When riding without stirrups, positioning the lower leg as though the feet were in the stirrups, as opposed to the loose leg.

following seat—Allowing the seat bones to follow the movement of the horse's back with a constant, even pressure.

forehand—The part of the horse from the back of the shoulder area forward.

full bridge—See bridging the reins.

full seat—Sitting with all the upper body weight on the saddle seat, as opposed to half seat.

gaits—There are three common ones: The walk and trot are functionally identical to humans' walking and running. The third gait is the canter, or lope in Western, which since it has a phase where all the weight is carried on one front leg, is found in humans primarily in the swimming side stroke. The gallop, a faster form of the cantor, is called the run in Western. Some breeds have extra gaits, most of which are variations of the walk, or combinations of two gaits—one with the front and one with the hind legs. The other true variation is the 'pace,' in which the legs on the same side work together, rather than diagonal pairs as in the trot.

gallop—See gaits.

gelding—A castrated male horse.

girth—The wide strap, usually leather or nylon, that holds an English saddle in place; it passes under the horse's belly and fastens to straps on either side of the saddle.

going behind the bit—When a horse is not willing to use the bit to ground against, usually either because the rider's hands are too strong or not steady, or because the bit is too severe to be comfortable.

going on the forehand—When the horse allows his balance to be ahead of his center, thus increasing the likelihood of his falling, especially if the rider allows her center to get ahead as well.

grounding—A state of being in which mind and body are centered, relaxed, and confident and thus prepared to respond instantly and correctly to whatever may occur.

grounding strap—A device that fits around the horse's neck just in front of his shoulders. It is fastened in place to the saddle and girth and has a long strap at the top that the rider uses for security and to help her balance and ground. It also assists the rider in learning how to follow the horse's movements with her hands.

ground tie—Used in Western riding to keep a horse stationary who has been trained to stand still if the reins are dropped on the ground.

hackamore—A communication and grounding device used on the horse's head instead of a bit. It works by pressure on his nose and lower jaw.

half bridge—See bridging the reins.

half seat—Riding while standing with all body weight on the stirrups, as opposed to full seat.

halter—A device that the horse wears on his head to which a rope is fastened when needed to work with the horse on the ground. The two basic types of halters are rope and leather or nylon.

hand effect—Any one of several different ways to use the reins to communicate with the horse. See also rein effect.

hand gallop—A controlled, extended form of canter.

hand leader—A trained person walking on the ground and leading a ridden horse so that the rider is free to work on other skills without worrying about controlling the horse.

hindquarters—The area on the horse from the flanks and back.

holding hand—An extension of the passive hand. This is a hand effect where the rider takes a firmer, steadier hold with the rein or reins while still following the movement.

horn—A raised handlelike object on the front of a Western saddle, intended to hold a lasso.

impulsion—A combination of the horse's energy, strength, and willingness.

indirect rein—See neck rein.

indirect rein of opposition—A rein effect in which the pull is back and inside the line of the horse's path, further defined as on a line either in front of or behind the horse's withers.

intent—Mental focus on a goal or plan of action. This is usually the first step in preparing to ask the horse to perform the action.

jog—Slow trot.

jumping ahead of the horse—The rider moves or allows her weight to go forward just before takeoff in anticipation of a jump, unbalancing the horse.

keepers—Small fixed leather loops next to the buckles on bridles or other strap equipment. These are used to control the excess strap.

lead (v)—Walking or jogging on the ground while holding the horse by the bridle reins or a lead rope.

lead (n)—*(a)* Short for lead rope. *(b)* Term designating which lateral set of legs come farther forward during the canter stride. Generally the horse should be on the inside lead when turning. A horse turning left would be on the left lead.

leading rein—A rein effect in which the direction of pull is 45 degrees upward, creating a minimum of opposition, thus making it easier for the horse to use his front legs.

left-hand around—Riding in the arena so that the horse's left side is toward the center.

leg aid—The use of pressure of the leg or legs to ask the horse to move his body.

longe—A long line attached to the horse's halter or other device and held by the instructor or trainer. The horse then moves in a circle around the handler. Longeing is used for training both horses and riders.

loose leg—When riding without stirrups, allowing the lower leg to hang free and move naturally with the horse's movement, as opposed to the fixed leg.

lope—Western term for canter.

mare—A female horse.

neck rein—A rein effect used primarily in Western riding in which the rein is carried up to a 45 degree angle or above, then pressed against the side of the horse's neck. It may be used in conjunction with a leading rein on the other side.

neck strap—See grounding strap.

opening rein—A rein effect in which the direction of pull is upward at 45 degrees and away from the horse's neck.

opening rein of opposition—A rein effect in which the pull is back and somewhat outside the line of the horse's path, away from the horse's withers.

passive hand—A hand effect in which the rider follows the movements of the horse's head in such a way that the contact is steady and even all the time through every change the horse makes. The horse and rider benefit from this effect since it allows them to help each other to balance and ground.

oxer—A type of fence for jumping. It consists of two obstacles placed close together and jumped as one. The first can be a simple pole or cross bar, or a more solid structure, the second one is always a single pole placed beyond, either at the same height or higher.

poll—The topmost point of the horse's head, between the ears. It holds back the crownpiece of the bridle or halter, lessening the pressure against the horse's ears.

posting—Rising in the stirrups and sitting again during each stride of the trot. It is less tiring than standing and smoother than sitting the gait.

quiet aid—An aid other than the rein and leg aids. A quiet aid is less obvious to the observer and less likely to cause discomfort to the horse.

refusal—When the horse stops unexpectedly in front of a jump.

rein aid—The use of the reins to communicate with the horse.

rein effect—The direction of the pull on the rein when applying an aid.

right-hand around—Riding in the arena so that the horse's right side is toward the center.

run—Western term for gallop.

runners—Small sliding leather loops on bridles or harness to hold down the tip ends of straps.

runout—When a horse runs by the fence on one side or the other, rather than jumping over it.

saddle—A device that the horse wears on his back, on which the rider sits. Its primary purpose is to hold the stirrups on the horse in such a way that the saddle stays centered on the horse even if most of the rider's weight is on one stirrup.

seven steps—Yoga-based movements and positions that help the body to ground, especially in periods of fear or tension.

snaffle—A type of bit with a single rein ring on either side that attaches directly to the mouthpiece. It acts on the corners of the horse's mouth and is the easiest for the horse to ground against.

stirrup—A device attached to the saddle by a long adjustable strap. The rider's feet rest on the stirrups, which give her lateral stability at all times. By standing in the stirrups at the faster gaits the rider is able to use her ankle, knee, and hip joints to take up the shock of the movement more effectively than when sitting.

soft leg—A method of applying the leg aids without causing tension in the rider's lower body.

split reins—Two separate unconnected reins. Used in Western riding.

stirrup gather strap—The part of a Western saddle used to prevent the stirrup leather from bunching up under the ankle and prevent the stirrup from flipping up through the fender.

stick—A device used to make contact with the horse, usually on the hindquarters, for the purpose of communication. The types of sticks include the whip, crop, bat, and quirt.

straight (standing) stall—A stall that is long and fairly narrow, with no door, about 4 by 8 feet (1.2 by 2.4 m).

surcingle—A strap to hold pads or blankets on the horse; it passes around the horse's barrel and fastens back to itself.

tack up (v)—To get a horse dressed for riding.

taking hand—A hand effect in which the rider uses a steady, firm pressure on the rein; release is given only if the horse gives to the pull with his head and neck.

transition—A change from one gait to another or a change in pace in the gait itself.

three-quarter seat—A semi-standing position in the saddle. The rider's weight is on her feet, but her seat is touching the saddle.

tree—The rigid skeleton of the saddle which gives it shape. When the saddle is properly fitted and placed over the horse's withers the tree prevents it from turning sideways.

trot—See gaits.

twice around—The simplest jump course used in competition. It generally consists of two fences placed on each long side of the arena. The rider circles the arena two times, jumping each fence twice.

volte—A circle 6 meters in diameter.

Western riding—Using a Western saddle, tack, and attire; so named because it was developed in the western part of the United States, settled originally by Spain. A Western saddle has a high pommel with a horn and a high cantle. The stirrups are made of wood or plastic and may have a leather protective cover over the front of the foot, and they are suspended from a wide heavy strap. Western riding includes many different disciplines.

withers—The projecting spine of the horse behind the base of the neck and the point at which the horse's height is measured.

Index

Note: The italicized *f* and *t* following page numbers refer to figures and tables, respectively.

purpose of 151
term 125
three-quarter position 157-159, 158*f*
halt, starting from 66. *See also* refusals;
        stopping
halters
    fit of 62, 62*f*
    leather or nylon 58-61, 60*f*, 61*f*
    rope 56-58, 56*f*, 57*f*
hand and wrist positions
    on grounding strap 46-48, 47*f*
    half-seat closed position 161, 161*f*
    on reins 111, 201, 201*f*
    while posting 200, 200*f*
hand effects
    active hand 83, 168-170, 169*f*
    fixed hand 202
    good hand development 208
    holding hand 201-202, 201*f*
    passive hand 196-201, 199*f*, 200*f*
    taking hand 203
hand grooming 28-31
hard eyes 16-17
Hartel, Lis 1
heels down 156
helmets 6
herd animal characteristics 24
Hillebrand, William 63
hills
    balancing exercises 210-211, 210*f*, 211*f*
    bareback 213
    in English saddles 212-215, 213*f*, 214*f*
    leg position for 211-212, 212*f*
    in Western saddles 213*f*, 214*f*, 215-216
hindquarters
    defined 71
    moving 72-73, 72*f*
    walking around 30-32, 31*f*
hip joint
    in half seat 151-155, 152*f*, 153*f*, 154*f*
    in incorrect hand position 208
holding hand 201-202, 201*f*
hoof picks 90-91, 91*f*
hoofs
    cleaning 90-94, 93*f*
    parts of 91, 91*f*, 92*f*
    protection instinct 27
horses
    characteristics of 24-25
    conformation of 139, 139*f*, 160
    gaited 64
    moving around 29-32, 31*f*
    parts of 29*f*, 58*f*, 91*f*, 92*f*
    teeth and bars 164, 164*f*

I

inertia exercise 105
inertia law 104
instructors, finding 3-6

intent 11, 99
introductions
    closed space 25-26, 26*f*
    open space 26-28, 27*f*

J

jackets 7
jog 118-120, 119*f*, 120*f*. *See also* trot
jump courses 224
jumps
    canter effects on 223
    centering during 218-220, 219*f*
    crest release in 223-224
    learning and practicing 220-222, 220*f*,
        221*f*, 222*f*
    phases of 217-218, 219*f*
    position between fences 223, 223*f*
    refusals and runouts 224-225
    trusting horse 222-223
    in Western saddle 225-226

K

kicking 30-32, 30*f*
Klimke, Werner 101

L

lateral centering
    in canter 187, 190
    exercise for 63, 63*f*
    on ground 21, 21*f*
    on horse 49-52, 50*f*, 51*f*
    left vs. right turns 62
    spine flexibility in 62, 62*f*
lateral leg aids 196
leading-rein effects
    introduction and practice 170-172, 171*f*
    types of 204, 204*f*
    uses for 205-206, 206*f*
leading techniques
    combing lead rope 72
    dealing with resistance 79
    holding extra rope 78, 78*f*
    ineffective 70, 77, 79
    leadership position 78, 78*f*
    line of pull 170, 170*f*, 204
    starting 79-80, 80*f*
    stopping 81, 81*f*
    turning 81-83, 82*f*
    for uncooperative horses 83-86
leads, in canter 185, 191
learning process 87, 227-228
leather or nylon halters
    fit of 62, 62*f*
    putting on horse 59, 60*f*
    removing 61, 61*f*
left brain 17
leg aids 194-196, 194*f*, 195*f*, 208
leg-on mounting 37-38, 38*f*

About the Author

Gincy Self Bucklin has been teaching riding for more than 60 years. Her students have included recreational riders of all ages and levels, many of whom have also shown successfully and some of whom have become professionals themselves. While many experienced instructors teach only advanced riders, Gincy has also worked extensively with beginners and intermediates, believing that in order to be successful at the advanced level, riders must know and perfect the fundamentals from the start. She now works with instructors to share the teaching methods presented in her books.

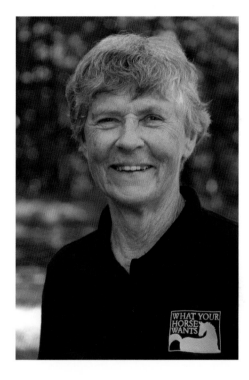

Gincy's mother was well-known equestrian author Margaret Cabell Self. Gincy was also fortunate to grow up in an area that had many world-class instructors and clinicians, including Sally Swift, George Morris, and Nuño Oliveira. Some of her early instructors trained with European trainers during the 1920s and '30s while the cavalry, where much of the equine knowledge was developed, was still in existence. Gincy is a retired Centered Riding instructor and is an American Riding Instructors Association level IV instructor.

Gincy has been writing about horses and riding since 1987. She is the author of *What Your Horse Wants You to Know, How Your Horse Wants You to Ride,* and *More How Your Horse Wants You to Ride.* She has been a contributor to national horse magazines, including *Equus* and *Horse Illustrated.* Currently she writes a regular column for *Riding Instructor,* the quarterly publication of the American Riding Instructors Association (ARIA), and maintains her own website, http:// whatyourhorsewants.com. Gincy lives in East Dummerston, Vermont.